Generative Modeling for Computer Graphics and CAD:
Symbolic Shape Design Using Interval Analysis

GENERATIVE MODELING FOR COMPUTER GRAPHICS AND CAD

Symbolic Shape Design Using Interval Analysis

John M. Snyder

with a foreword by James T. Kajiya

ACADEMIC PRESS, INC.

Harcourt Brace Jovanovich, Publishers

Boston   San Diego   New York
London   Sydney   Tokyo   Toronto

ACADEMIC PRESS, INC.
1250 Sixth Avenue, San Diego, CA 92101-4311

United Kingdom Edition published by
ACADEMIC PRESS LIMITED
24–28 Oval Road, London NW1 7DX

ISBN 0-12-654040-3

Contents

Foreword

The inquiry into representation, manipulation, and analysis of shape with computers is one of the central themes of computer graphics. In fact, one could say that computer graphics was born when Ivan Sutherland had the idea that Geometry is Structured Data. Before that, people merely used computers as automated graph paper; after that, geometry could be manipulated by computer.

Modeling is an area where, every once in a while, a dazzling new idea will have implications that are explored in years of hard research work, system building, and eventually commercial products. The list of such ideas is short: certainly included are homogeneous coordinates, Coons surfaces, constructive solid geometry, and NURBS.

This book is about an idea that may be a candidate for that short list. During the time that I've watched John Snyder develop these ideas, my understanding of shape has taken a profound transformation. John's work has taught me that every shape has an inner logic—a way it should be thought about. That logic is captured in a meta-shape.

Before this work, I thought about a shape as a collection of polygons, or a sculpted surface. But that view is very limited. With a sculpted surface there's really no difference between a spoon shape and a chair shape; it's all a matter of positioning the control points in the right places. But a spoon shape has an inner logic, shared by all spoons—and that logic is completely different from that of a chair.

John and I have spent many hours trying the discover the logic of different everyday shapes. It's an intellectually challenging and exciting endeavor, one that is quite pleasurable when one hits on the right logic of a shape. Because of this, shapes are no longer just inscrutable lumps, but a series of puzzles—sometimes easy and sometimes difficult.

Do you want to read this book? If you have a serious interest in computer graphics, it's for you. You should also have some experience in the trade. If you've completed an introductory course, made some pictures, and attempted to produce an ambitious picture or animation, you're experienced. Even if your primary interest is in image synthesis or animation, modeling should be important to you.

There's an old saying at Caltech that has proved true many times: "Good modeling can save bad rendering, but good rendering can't save bad modeling."

James T. Kajiya
Pasadena, California
April 1992

Preface

The purpose of this book is to present a new, symbolic approach to shape representation that I believe is useful to the CAD/CAM and computer graphics communi-
ties. This book primarily addresses two audiences. First, it is intended for people
who want to know how human beings can specify and manipulate shape. I believe
the representational abstraction described in this book to be elegant, powerful, and
suitable for a new generation of commercial CAD programs. The specific implementation I describe is just a first step toward the realization of a truly capable and
easy to use geometric modeling system. It is my hope that this first step nevertheless demonstrates the merits of the representational abstraction, and will encourage
its incorporation in future CAD and animation programs.

Second, it is intended for people working in the area of computational geometry who are interested in a new, robust class of algorithms for manipulating shapes.
This class of algorithms employs interval analysis, and includes algorithms for ray
tracing, interference detection, polygonal decomposition of parametric surfaces,
CSG on solids bounded by parametric surfaces, and offset operations on parametric curves and surfaces. These algorithms can be implemented separately from
the modeling system described in this book. However, the inclusion functions on
which these algorithms depend are naturally implemented in the system described
here, with each symbolic operator having an inclusion function method, thus allowing inclusion functions for the arbitrary composition of the operators. (This
kind of inclusion function is termed a "natural interval extension" in Chapter 5.)
The result is that the algorithms can be applied to a great variety of shapes, while
the implementation remains simple.

What exactly is generative modeling and what good is it? Because of the nov-
elty of the generative modeling approach to geometric modeling, I believe some
answer to this question should be given in the Preface, although it is answered
much more completely in Chapters 1 and 2.

Shapes in the generative modeling approach are represented as multidimensional, continuous, piecewise-differentiable parametric functions. A set of symbolic operators on such functions is used to build complicated shapes by simple
composition of the symbolic operators. The book describes a language that allows

the procedural specification of shapes represented with these symbolic operators. Many shape examples are presented to show how conveniently shapes can be specified using this language. My intent here is not to extol the particular syntax of the modeling language presented, but instead to show the usefulness of modeling by composing high-level, symbolic operators. The language described here was chosen because it makes these ideas concrete, and because it is part of a working system.

This book also discusses the kinds of operators useful in a geometric modeling system, including arithmetic operators, vector and matrix operators, integration, differentiation, constraint solution, and constrained minimization. Associated with each operator are several methods that compute properties about the parametric functions represented with the operators. This book shows how numerous rendering and analytical operations can be supported with only three methods: evaluation of the parametric function at a point, symbolic differentiation of the parametric function, and evaluation of an inclusion function for the parametric function (inclusion functions are defined in Chapter 5).

One advantage of the generative modeling approach is that it allows specification, rendering, and analysis of many kinds of shapes, including the standard 3D curves, surfaces, and solids, as well as higher-dimensional shapes such as surfaces deforming in time, and volumes with a spatially varying mass density. The approach also supports powerful, high-level operations on shapes such as "reparameterize this curve by arclength," "compute the volume, center of mass, and moments of inertia of the solid bounded by these surfaces," or "solve this constraint or ODE system." An implementation of the approach, called GENMOD, has been used in our computer graphics research lab at the California Institute of Technology for a wide variety of applications, including creating surfaces for computer graphics animations, modeling the body shape and fur of a teddy bear, constructing 3D solid models of elastic bodies, and extracting models from MRI data. In fact, almost all the figures in this book were made using GENMOD.

Unlike most other geometric modeling approaches, a further advantage of this approach is that it is closed, meaning that modeling operations can be applied to any results of earlier modeling operations, yielding valid models. Because of this closure property, the symbolic operators can be composed very flexibly, allowing the construction of higher-level operators without changing the underlying implementation of the system. Because the modeling operations are described symbolically, specified models can capture the designer's intent without approximation error.

The book is organized as follows: Chapter 1 examines how geometric modeling approaches may be compared, discusses some approaches used in the past and their problems, and introduces the generative modeling approach. Chapter 2 answers the question, "What is a generative model?" and traces the development of the generative modeling approach. Chapter 3 presents a series of shape specification examples. Rendering of generative models is treated in Chapter 4. Chapters 5 and 6 discuss how robust tools for the analysis of generative models can be developed using the technique of interval analysis. Inclusion functions, and their use in creating algorithms to solve systems of constraints and constrained minimization problems, are treated in Chapter 5. These algorithms, in turn, are applied to higher-level problems in geometric modeling, such as CSG, in Chapter 6. Appendix A provides an overview of the GENMOD language. Appendix B presents more elaborate examples of GENMOD specifications that do not fit conveniently in the text. Proofs of the interval analysis theorems used in Chapters 5 and 6 can be found in Appendix C.

As the reader will undoubtedly realize, much of the work presented here is research in progress. I therefore have tried to point out areas for future improvement, as well as describe what has already been implemented. Although much remains to be done, what has been done gives me confidence that this approach may lead to the solution of many nagging problems in geometric modeling. It is my hope that the ideas are described adequately enough to stimulate continuing, fruitful work in this area of symbolic, interval-based geometric modeling.

John M. Snyder
Pasadena, California
April 1992

Acknowledgments

Jim Kajiya first presented the idea of generative models to me at the end of 1987. It was an intriguing approach that encompassed many of the shape representation schemes I had often pondered and even implemented. Jim and I began work on a SIGGRAPH paper, setting out to test the effectiveness of the idea by modeling some complicated shapes, including the steering arm in Plate 7. Since then, the initial program we worked on has grown into what we believe is a useful and interesting environment for geometric modeling.

I am very grateful to Jim for all his help and guidance. As my thesis advisor, Jim never failed to recognize my research progress, however small. Nor did he fail to point out areas for further study or improvement, always in a spirit of encouragement. Not only is Jim a fountain of technical information, but working with him is an enjoyable experience. I also thank Jim for his enthusiasm for the project, even when it took unexpected turns.

Many thanks are due to Al Barr, with whom I have done postdoctoral work for the last year. Al has had great enthusiasm for the project and has provided advice on many interesting applications. He has also given me the freedom to spend a great deal of time working on this book. I also thank Al for his constant encouragement in this often tedious endeavor of writing, and for his many thoughtful suggestions for making the book better.

I am grateful to Alan Norton and IBM for their generous grants to Jim Kajiya's lab while I was a student there, and for their support of many trips to IBM T. J. Watson Research Center to port my system and make it available as a tool in the computer graphics research lab. I am also grateful to the NSF Science and Technology Center for Computer Graphics and Scientific Visualization for its support in producing this manuscript.

My colleagues at Caltech have also contributed much to this work, and deserve mention: Brian Von Herzen, John Platt, Tim Kay, Ronen Barzel, Devendra Kalra, Rajiv Gupta, Kurt Fleischer, Jed Lengyel, Dave Kirk, David Laidlaw, Jeff Goldsmith, Clark Brooks, Bena Curin, Adam Woodbury, Mike Meckler, and Allen Corcoran. I owe Tim Kay thanks for his help to make the hidden-line-eliminated figures and for backing up the electronic source of this book. Ronen Barzel has provided extensive help with typesetting. David Laidlaw, Adam Woodbury, Clark Brooks and Allen Corcoran have pointed out errors and made many helpful suggestions. I am especially grateful to David Laidlaw and Adam Woodbury for their careful reading. Jed Lengyel, Devendra Kalra, and others in the Caltech graphics group headed by Al Barr, worked with me on the SIGGRAPH '88 film "Going Bananas," from which the images in Plate 1 were taken.

I would also like to thank my software guinea pigs — those who have used some version of my modeling program: Jed Lengyel, Devendra Kalra, Paula Sweeney, Cavi Arya, and David Laidlaw. Nothing brings a software designer so down to earth as users. Jed Lengyel deserves special thanks for many thoughtful suggestions during the formative phase of this project.

Thanks also go to Jim Blinn, Steve Taylor, and Joel Burdick, for their helpful suggestions. Special thanks go to Jim Blinn for finding a long list of typographical errors; he has also pointed out many imprecise or confusing sections, which I hope I have corrected.

Finally, my greatest thanks is reserved for my wife, Julia, and my parents. This book is dedicated to them.

Index of Figures

App. B. GENMOD Code Examples

Chapter 1

Introduction

The computer is emerging as a powerful tool in the design and analysis of 3D shape, an important concern in fields such as computer-aided design and manufacture (CAD/CAM), computer graphics, art, animation, mathematics, computer simulation, computer vision, and robotics. As the computational speed of computers continues to increase, so does their potential to model shapes with greater interactivity and sophistication. Recognizing this potential, researchers in both academia and industry have devoted much attention in the last 20 years to the area of geometric modeling, the study of the representation and analysis of shape.

Perhaps the greatest strides in geometric modeling have been made in the use of computers to make fast, high-quality images of geometric models. At the same time, many techniques have been developed to allow human designers to specify and manipulate geometric models inside the computer. Yet, as anyone who has used a mechanical CAD program knows, entering 3D shape into the computer remains a difficult, time-consuming task. Why is the specification of 3D shape so difficult for human beings? What constitutes a good geometric modeling system? What, if anything, is wrong with current approaches to geometric modeling, and how can they be improved?

To answer these questions, it is helpful to decompose a geometric modeling system into three parts: a shape representation, a user interface, and a set of tools for manipulating that shape representation. The representation defines what a shape is. The interface allows shapes to be specified. The tools determine what can be done with the shapes. To give an extremely simple example, surfaces can be represented by a set of 3D control points, and a set of polygons whose vertices are in this set. A user interface appropriate for this representation might be an interactive program that allows the addition, deletion, and modification of these points, and the linking together of the points to form polygons. Alternatively, the interface might consist of a simple language allowing the user to specify points and polygons procedurally. Finally, the tools appropriate for this representation might consist solely of a program to render the polygons, or might include tools to compute geometric properties of the resulting polyhedra, such as the volume they enclose, or the locations where they intersect.

While it is true that no useful design can be completed without an appropriate representation, user interface, and set of shape manipulation tools, I believe the representation to be the part of a geometric modeling system which most determines its quality. The representation guides shape designers, structures their thinking, and limits the kinds of shapes they will even consider modeling. The representation also structures the thinking of the implementor of the geometric modeling system, affecting the kinds of shape manipulation tools that will be supplied, how well they work, and how fast.

This book is about a new representation for a geometric model, called a *generative model*. What a generative model is will be summarized later in this chapter, and completely defined in Chapter 2. Before that, we will look at shape representations used in the past and some criteria for evaluating these shape representations.

1.1 User vs. Machine Shape Representations

In this discussion, it is important to distinguish between a *user representation* of shape, a representation manipulated by a human designer which serves as an interface between man and computer, and a *machine representation*, manipulated solely by the computer. For example, a geometric modeling program may allow the user to specify objects such as spheres, cones, and cylinders, but will render these shapes as collections of polygons. In this case, the user representation consists of spheres, cones, and cylinders, while the machine representation is a collection of polygons.

This distinction is important because the overall efficiency of shape design is more directly related to the quality of the user representation than the machine representation. Through the user interface, designers see the user representation of a geometric modeling program; they may be completely unaware of the existence of a machine representation. The machine representation affects design efficiency only insofar as it affects the speed and robustness of shape manipulations. For example, if the machine representation is only an approximation to the user representation, then conversion from user to machine representation introduces approximation errors. The following criteria for evaluation of a shape representation are intended to apply to user representations.

1.2 Criteria for Evaluation of a Shape Representation

Three criteria may be used to evaluate the quality of a user shape representation:

1. Ease of specification — how easy is it for a designer to enter shapes into the computer?

2. Renderability — how quickly and realistically can images of the shapes be generated?

3. Analyzability — what analytical operations are allowed on shapes? How fast and robust are these operations?

Ease of Specification

The first criterion, ease of specification, assesses how efficiently designers can enter and change their designs. The ease of specification thus relates to the cost of design. Moreover, the shape specification structures the designer's thinking, making some types of shapes easy to reason about and specify, some more difficult, and some entirely out of the domain of consideration. It is possible then that some potentially better designs are excluded by the nature of the shape specification.

Ease of specification may be further broken down into the following categories:

- Naturalness — does the representation correspond to the way designers think about the shape?

- Compactness — how much information is required to specify the shape?

- Completeness — how large is the class of shapes that can be represented?

- Controllability — can the designer predict what shape will result from a given input?

- Editability — can the designer modify shapes easily?

- Validity — is it impossible for designers to specify invalid shapes?

- Accuracy — is the representation only an approximation of the designer's intention? If so, how faithful is the approximation?

- Closure — if shapes are specified by composing operators on lower-level shapes, is the result of the operations always a valid shape that can be used as input in further operations?

These categories are adapted from [REQU80], with some modifications to shift the emphasis from machine representation to user. For example, [REQU80] also includes as a criterion the concept of *uniqueness*; that is, whether or not a given shape has a single representation. A designer is not likely to be too concerned with uniqueness, and in fact, would probably prefer that a rich set of representations exist from which to pick the most convenient. Uniqueness, however, is an important consideration for a machine representation, which may need to test two representations for equality, at considerable computational cost.

Renderability

The second criterion, renderability, measures the quality of visual feedback given to the designer. Visual feedback is extremely important in the design process, for both commercial computer graphics and mechanical design. Ideally, rendering should be fast and provide a good idea of the shape. In practice, a rendering method is a compromise between computational speed and quality of visualization. Different shape representations admit different forms of rendering, which lie on a spectrum of speed/quality tradeoffs.

Current technology for shape rendering comes in a variety of forms. Wireframe (line drawing) and z-buffered, solid shaded images are common and useful forms of visual feedback. These forms of rendering are fast enough on many of today's engineering workstations to allow real-time or near real-time rendering of quite complex shapes. More photorealistic forms of rendering, such as ray tracing and radiosity, are currently too slow for interactive feedback, but provide additional cues such as shadows, transparency, and more sophisticated lighting models which may aid in visualizing the shape. We expect that these higher-quality, slower rendering techniques will soon become fast enough for interactive use.

Analyzability

The last criterion, analyzability, evaluates how suitable the shape representation is for analyzing and simulating collections of shapes. Shape operations that are important in this context include

- compute physical quantities about the shape — moments of inertia, center of mass, surface area, volume

- compute geometric queries about the shape or shapes — proximity with other shapes and collision detection, finding curves of intersection between surfaces, determining whether a given surface is a valid solid boundary

- compute feasible/optimal parameters for parameterized shapes — find a parameter for a parameterized family of shapes that solves some set of constraints and/or optimizes some objective function

In assessing the analyzability of a shape representation, it is important to consider the generality of operations that are allowed, the accuracy of these operations, and their computational speed. Often, there is a natural relationship between a shape representation and its analytical properties [TIMM80, LEE82a]. For example, the volume of a solid specified as an extrusion of a 2D closed curve is simply the product of the area enclosed by the curve and the height of the extrusion. On the other hand, the natural forms of analysis admitted by a shape representation are not the only ones that need be used. A representation can be converted to one more amenable to analysis. Of course, the conversion required may involve substantial computational cost and/or introduce approximation error.

1.3   Previous Work in Shape Representation

Not surprisingly, the major emphasis in shape representation research has been on curves, surfaces, and solids. Since the beginnings of the field of computer graphics, curve and surface representation research has largely focused on piecewise parametric polynomials, such as the Coons patch [COON67], Bezier curves and surfaces [BEZI74], and B-spline curves and surfaces [RIES73, GORD74]. Algebraic curves and surfaces (shapes specified as a solution to a polynomial equation) are another widely used form [BLIN82, HANR83, SEDE85, SEDE89]. New shape representations are also being studied, including deformations and more general implicit and parametric shapes.

For many applications, such as for computer-aided manufacture, shapes must be modeled as solids. The area of *solid modeling* is concerned with the design and analysis of 3D solids. Solid model representations involve two main representational themes: boundary representations and CSG. *Boundary representation*, or *b-rep* models represent solids by their surface, curve, and point boundaries. *Constructive solid geometry*, or *CSG* models represent objects as a composition of Boolean set operations on points contained within the solids [REQU77c, REQU78]. These two techniques are not mutually exclusive. The Alpha_1 modeler developed at the University of Utah allows CSG operations on b-rep shapes [COHE83].

The following sections analyze current shape representation schemes according to the criteria established in Section 1.2.

1.3.1   Polyhedra

Polyhedra are solids bounded by a set of polygons. Because they are defined by
the polygons that form their surface, polyhedra are a simple boundary representation. Polyhedra were investigated as a computer shape modeling representation by
Baumgart [BAUM72, BAUM74] in a system for computer vision research called
GEOMED. In the work, he introduced the idea of *Euler operations*, which transform objects by adding or removing faces, edges, or vertices. Baumgart's work
has formed the basis for many systems that allow users to interactively create and
edit polyhedral shapes.

Research into polyhedral representations remains active.   Chiyakura and
Kimura [CHIY83] combined polyhedra with polynomial parametric patches to
round corners of solids and represent curved faces. Many researchers have investigated computation of Boolean set operations on polyhedra: Turner [TURN84],
Requicha and Voelcker [REQU85], Putnam and Subrahmanyam [PUTN86], Laidlaw, Trumbore, and Hughes [LAID86], and Naylor, Amanatides, and Thibault
[NAYL90]. Segal [SEGA90] has studied error control and validity maintenance
for toleranced polyhedral shapes.

Polyhedral representations are clearly natural in representing a useful class of
objects — objects that are bounded by planar facets. They are not appropriate as
a user representation for general, curved solids but can be used as an approximate
machine representation. Such an approximation has many drawbacks, which will
be discussed later. Perhaps the greatest advantage of polyhedral representations is
their renderability. Polygons are easy to render, especially with graphics hardware
available today. The analyzability of polyhedra may also be attractive. Lien and
Kajiya [LIEN84] have presented algorithms for the direct computation of integral
properties for polyhedra.

1.3.2   Piecewise Parametric Polynomial Shapes

Piecewise parametric polynomials are the main shape representation of computer graphics and CAD/CAM. The research literature contains numerous spe-
cializations, extensions, surveys, and applications of the piecewise polynomial
form [DEBO72, DEBO78, COHE80, TILL83, KOCH84, BOHM84, BARN85,
BART87, BARS88]. Parametric polynomial shapes are typically specified through
a series of control points, which the curve or surface interpolates. The resulting
shapes tend to be easy to control and edit for free-form specification and allow
designers control over simple aspects of the shape, such as its continuity.

A very general form, called NURBS, for nonuniform, rational, B-splines, is
being used in many new geometric modeling systems. The advantage of NURBS
over traditional (nonrational) representations is their ability to represent simple
quadrics like spheres, cones, and cylinders exactly.

Piecewise parametric polynomials are a complete representation. Given enough patches to interpolate the desired shape, any smooth shape, however complicated, can be specified to any degree of accuracy. Despite its generality, specifying a multitude of control points over a shape is often an undesirable method of modeling. Specification tends not to be compact. Editing is difficult because of the number of control points and because they are only distantly related to high-level properties of the shape the designer may wish to control.

The rendering of piecewise parametric polynomial surface has received much attention. Conversion of parametric polynomials into polygonal meshes can be done by very efficient algorithms. New hardware is also being developed to directly rasterize these shapes [SHAN87, SHAN89]. Rendering using ray tracing is an ongoing area of research [KAJI82, SEDE84].

Analyzability of parametric polynomials is quite good. Global properties, such as volume and moments of inertia of solids bounded by nonrational polynomial patches, can be computed analytically. However, proximity and intersection testing involves solving polynomial equations of high degree, making parametric polynomial shapes less attractive than algebraic or more general implicit shapes.

1.3.3   Algebraic Shapes

An algebraic shape is a shape formed by the zeroes of a polynomial equation, typically of low degree. For example, algebraic cubic curves (the solution of a third-degree polynomial in two variables) and quadric surfaces (the solution of a second-degree polynomial in three variables) have been used many times in geometric modeling.

Algebraic shapes have been used in some very early modeling/rendering systems [WEIS66, WOON71]. These early systems used quadric surfaces as the basic modeling tool and were therefore not general in the types of specifiable shapes. Sederberg [SEDE85] has proposed the idea of piecewise algebraic shapes. Like the parametric polynomial shapes discussed previously, these shapes form a complete representation, but a very low-level one.

Several algorithms exist for direct, scan-line rasterization of quadric surfaces [WEIS66, WOON71, SARR83]. Algebraic shapes may also be rendered by ray tracing. Quadric surfaces are especially simple, since ray/surface intersections can be computed by solving a quadratic equation. Ray intersection for more general algebraic shapes is investigated in [HANR83, HANR89]. Although rendering is possible with direct rasterization or ray tracing, neither method takes advantage of fast graphics hardware geared towards the rendering of polygons, making piecewise parametric shapes more attractive for real-time rendering.

The analyzability of algebraic shapes is attractive for several reasons. Point classification (determining whether a point is inside or outside the shape) can be done with a simple polynomial evaluation. Computing intersections between algebraic shapes also require solution of polynomial systems with fewer variables than with parametric polynomials. Computation of the intersections between quadric surfaces, for example, is described in [SARR83] and [MILL87]. Both characteristics of algebraic shapes are useful in solid modeling systems. Quadric surfaces and polyhedra have also been combined in a geometric modeling system [CROC87].

1.3.4   Sweeps

A *sweep* represents a shape by moving an object (called a *generator*) along a trajectory through space. The simplest sweep is an *extrusion* which translates a 2D curve along a linear path normal to the plane of the curve. Surfaces of revolution are also sweeps of 2D curves around an axis. Sweeps need not use only 2D curves; for example, sweeps of surfaces or solids are useful operations. Sweeps whose generator can change size, orientation, or shape are called *general sweeps*. General sweeps that use 2D curve generators are *generalized cylinders* [BINF71].

Several researchers have studied sweeps [GOLD83, CARL82b, DONA85, WANG86, COQU87]. Barr's *spherical product* [BARR81], is an example of a sweep that translates and scales a constant 2D-curve generator. Carlson [CARL82b] introduced the idea of varying the sweep generator. Wang and Wang [WANG86] have explored sweeps of surfaces for use in manipulating numerically controlled milling machine cutter paths.

Sweeps have been used in solid modeling systems for many years (e.g., GM-Solid, ROMULUS). Lossing and Eshleman [LOSS74] developed a system using sweeps of constant 2D curves. Alpha_1, a modeling system developed at the University of Utah, has a much more sophisticated sweeping facility [COHE83].

One of the advantages of sweeps is their naturalness, compactness, and controllability in representing a large class of man-made objects. For example, objects that are surfaces of revolution or extrusions are best represented as sweeps. Sweeps are not complete however. Verification of the validity of sweeps also causes problems. For example, it is easy to generate degenerate closed sweeps that do not enclose a solid area by translating a generator curve in the plane of the curve.

Direct rendering of general sweeps is difficult. Rendering using ray tracing has been studied for various limited forms of sweeps [KAJI83, VANW84a, VANW84b, BRON85]. Kajiya [KAJI83] has studied ray tracing of extrusions. Van Wijk has studied ray tracing of conical sweeps that translate and scale a 2D cubic spline curve [VANW84a], and ray tracing of tubes formed by sweeping a sphere [VANW84b]. Bronsvoort and Klok [BRON85] give an algorithm for ray tracing curves swept along arbitrary 3D trajectories.

Rendering may also be achieved through conversion of the sweep to another form, such as a polygonal mesh. Since sweeps are naturally converted to general parametric functions, this method is fast and easy, as will be discussed in Section 1.3.6.

Analyzability of sweeps is good. Calculation of volume integrals over the region enclosed by a sweep can be simplified using Gauss's theorem from vector calculus. Under certain conditions, integrals can further be simplified into products of line integrals over appropriate sweep curves. As in the case of renderability, the discussion of analyzability of general parametric functions in Section 1.3.6 applies.

1.3.5 Deformations

Deformations are operations that transform simple shapes to more complex shapes by deforming the space in which the simple shape is embedded. For example, given a sphere in $\mathbf{R}^3$, a more complicated shape can be designed by deforming the sphere via a function $D: \mathbf{R}^3 \rightarrow \mathbf{R}^3$. Each point on the sphere is transformed through the function D, yielding a deformed sphere. The concept of deformations has received some attention in geometric modeling. Barr [BARR84] has examined a set of primitive deformations (bending, tapering, and twisting) that are useful in modeling, as well as differentially specified deformations. This work demonstrated the usefulness of deformations as a geometric modeling tool, but left open many problems of how to represent and specify a general set of deformation primitives.

Several researchers have also examined 3D deformations that are represented using polynomials specified with 3D control points [SEDE86]. Such deformations tend to become unwieldy for complicated shapes since many control points must be specified, but may be useful for free-form sculpting of shape.

The rendering or analysis of shapes formed with deformations varies with the types of primitive shapes that can be deformed and the types of allowable deformations. A deformation of a parametric surface, for example, yields another parametric surface and so can be treated in the same way (see Section 1.3.6). Deformations of implicit surfaces can also be treated as implicit surfaces if the deformation is invertible.

1.3.6 Non-Polynomial Parametric Shapes

It is reasonable to expect that parametric shapes based on a more general representation than piecewise polynomials could provide a more compact and powerful basis for modeling than piecewise polynomials, while still retaining their generality. However, parametric surfaces more general than piecewise polynomials have not received much attention in the fields of computer graphics and computer-aided geometric modeling. Specific types of nonpolynomial parametric shapes have been used, such as Barr's superquadric surface [BARR81].

Parametric shapes are amenable to fast rendering with polygon-based graphics hardware. The parametric functions representing the shapes are evaluated over a series of points in parameter space to form polygons. Rendering using ray tracing is more difficult, but has been studied by several researchers [TOTH85, JOY86, BARR86].

The analyzability of parametric shapes is mixed. Computation of physical properties of parametric shapes is often simple, especially when the parametric domain is suitably restricted (e.g., to a rectangle for parametric surfaces). Calculation of the proximity or intersection between general parametric shapes has been a difficult problem (although it has been solved for some particular examples, such as Bezier curves), which has traditionally been solved with ad hoc and non-robust numerical methods.

1.3.7   Non-Polynomial Implicit Shapes

Implicit shapes of more generality than the algebraic shapes discussed previously have been used to a limited extent in geometric modeling. The TIPS solid modeler [OKIN73] represented solids as Boolean operations on implicitly represented half-spaces. Blobby models, models formed by the isosurfaces of decaying fields of point sources, are another example of implicit shapes [BLIN82, NISH83, WYVI86]. While not more general than algebraic shapes, they are a useful representation for modeling smooth surfaces surrounding a collection of points.

Rendering of implicit shapes is most easily accomplished using ray intersection algorithms. For this type of rendering, implicit shapes are computationally superior to parametric shapes, since the required numerical iteration takes place over a lower-dimensional space. Kalra and Barr [KALR89] have presented a robust algorithm for intersecting rays with general implicit surfaces. Alternatively, implicit shapes can be polygonalized and rendered using polygon-based graphics hardware. Polygonalization of implicit shapes is a difficult problem; a heuristic approach is described in [BLOO88].

Analyzability of implicit shapes is mixed. Geometric queries such as point classification (i.e., is the point inside or outside the shape?) are simple for implicitly described shapes. On the other hand, sampling of points over an implicit shape is difficult, often requiring elaborate, non-robust, and slow numerical algorithms.

1.4   Areas for Improvement in Shape Representation

The current techniques for shape representation are lacking in the following fundamental ways.

High-Level Operations

Geometric modeling is made easier when the human designer can use high-level operators that directly control important aspects of the shape. The following are examples of such high-level operations:

- reparameterize a curve by arclength

- compute the volume of the solid enclosed by a set of surfaces

- compute the closest point of a shape to some other shape

- compute the flow lines of a vector field

The results of such operations should be allowable input to the modeling system, allowing further high-level operations. As an example, the designer might want to solve for a particular parameter of a shape such that its volume equals a given constant.

Existing geometric modeling systems do not allow such high-level operations, or suffer from problems of closure and approximation error. Without a direct representation of such operations, approximation errors can accumulate in an uncontrollable way (see the Control of Error section). For example, a geometric modeling system may represent a sphere as a set of polygons, discarding the original intent of the designer. Without knowing that this collection of polygons approximates a sphere, the modeling system cannot determine how many polygons should be used in order to achieve a specified accuracy in some operation, such as determining the surface area of the sphere. Clearly, a single set of polygons will not work for any degree of accuracy in any modeling operation.

Generality of Synthetic Techniques

Synthetic techniques for shape representation establish a set of primitive shapes and a set of primitive operations. Complicated shapes are then built from simpler ones by composition of the primitive operations. Synthetic techniques are useful because they provide a simple way of managing shape complexity: although each operation is simple and easily comprehended, a series of such operations can produce very complicated shapes.

CSG, the most common example of a synthetic technique, is an extremely useful and natural means of specifying complicated shapes. Yet, in existing implementations, its usefulness is hampered by restrictions on the set of allowable primitives. Sets of primitives which current CSG implementations support include: polyhedra; sets of specific primitives such as blocks, spheres, and cylinders; general quadric surfaces; and b-reps bounded by NURBS. Each of these sets of primitives is useful but either incomplete or too low-level.

Designers also face a lack of synthetic operations other than CSG. Researchers are currently studying operations such as filleting, blending, and offsetting. Blending, for example, allows two solids to be joined such that the interface between the two is smooth rather than sharp as in CSG. These newer synthetic operations show promise as a higher-level specification tool but are much more difficult to manipulate and analyze.

Combinations of Techniques

It is probable that each of the various methods of shape representation has some realm of applicability. One representation may not be the best for every shape a designer wishes to specify. For example, blobby models (Section 1.3.7) can fit a smooth surface to an unstructured collection of points. Polynomial deformations, such as the free-form deformation (FFD), may be useful in 3D sculpting systems [SEDE86]. Sweeps are good for certain mechanical parts, such as an airplane wing or the steering arm of Plate 7. Yet there have been only limited attempts to combine the various representations into a single system. Especially significant is the inability of modeling systems to handle both parametric and implicit shape representations because of the difficulty of conversion.

Multidimensionality

Current geometric modeling work has mostly avoided multidimensional representation schemes and concentrated on modeling rigid surfaces and solids in three dimensions. Modeling of important systems, such as shapes that deform in time, or shapes that contain nonhomogeneous distributions of mass, temperature, and stress, are mostly beyond the capabilities of current technology. Systems that do include some multidimensional modeling do so in a post-processing simulation phase that separates specification of the "extra" dimensions from the 3D geometric information and makes more difficult the feedback of information from simulation phase to design phase.

Parameterizability

Related to the lack of multidimensionality of shape representations is the lack of parameterizability. Many solid modeling programs supply predefined generic primitives that let the designer vary a few simple parameters to create instances of the shape. For example, families of gear or bracket shapes are commonly parameterized. Unfortunately, current shape representations do not allow designers to create parameterized shapes themselves. For example, a designer might like to design a shape where positions of drill holes can vary according to their position on another part, or design a connecting part that can bend around another part whose size is presently unknown. Once a shape is parameterized, it then becomes useful to allow the designer to specify constraints for the parameters, or functions that the parameters should optimize. Results of such parameter selection should then be allowable input to the continuing design process. Such parameterizability is currently beyond the state of the art.

Control of Error

Control of approximation error is a problem area for shape design systems. This is especially true for systems that are not *exact*; that is, systems in which the machine representation of shape is only an approximation for the user representation. For example, a polyhedral approximation to a curved solid will give incorrect results for geometric queries such as intersection. These errors are typically difficult to control. As a result, approximation error may be limited in an ad hoc manner (e.g., increase the number of polygons in a polyhedral approximation until the result "looks" right). Even if the errors can be controllably limited, an unacceptably high computational cost may be required.

Approximation error becomes an even greater problem when approximate intermediate results are fed back to the design. For example, consider approximating a general parametric surface by a piecewise polynomial parametric surface. The surface is deformed, a solid is subtracted from it using Boolean set operations, and the result is deformed again. It is then tested for intersection with another surface. At each stage, the original approximation error is magnified, possibly causing the last intersection test to yield incorrect results.

1.5   The Generative Modeling Approach

Specification

The generative modeling approach developed in this book has its roots in the sweep method of representing shape. The approach specifies sweeps procedurally, in a fashion similar to other procedural methods in computer graphics: shade trees [COOK84], Perlin's texturing language [PERL85], and the POSTSCRIPT graphics language [ADOB85].

Shape specification in the approach involves combining low-dimensional entities, especially 2D curves, into higher-dimensional shapes. This combination is specified through a powerful shape description language that builds multidimensional parametric functions. The language is based on a set of symbolic operators on parametric functions which includes arithmetic operators, vector and matrix operators, integration and differentiation, inversion, constraint solution, constrained optimization, and ODE solution. Associated with each operator are several methods that compute properties of the parametric function represented with the operators. For example, one method computes the value of the function at a particular point. Although each primitive operator is fairly simple, high-level shapes and shape-building operators can be defined using recursive combination of the primitive operators. Chapter 2 discusses the kinds of operators and methods useful in a geometric modeling system.

Like CSG, and unlike most other geometric modeling approaches, this modeling approach is closed, meaning that further modeling operations can be applied to any results of modeling operations, yielding valid models. This closure property means that the symbolic operators can be composed very flexibly. Higher-level operators can easily be constructed from the primitive ones, as we will see in many examples in Chapter 3.

The approach encourages the modeler to build parameterized families of shapes rather than single instances. Shapes can be parameterized by scalar parameters (e.g., time or joint angle) or higher-dimensional parameters (e.g., a curve controlling how the scale of a cross section varies as it is translated). Such parameterized shapes, called *meta-shapes*, allow easy modification of the design, since the modeler can interact with parameters that relate to high-level properties of the shape. Multidimensional shapes are also easily specified using parametric functions of high input or output dimension.

Although the generative modeling approach is based on sweeps and general parametric shapes, it supports combinations of representational styles, including deformations, CSG, and implicit shapes. Very general deformations are easily expressed within the same generative modeling language and can be applied to any parametric shape. Algorithms for approximating CSG operations on solids whose boundaries are defined using generative surfaces are described in Chapter 6. Implicit shapes can also be represented in the approach by solving equations represented in the modeling language. Algorithms for approximating implicit shapes are also described in Chapter 6. In general, shapes specified using CSG operations or described implicitly require much more computation to render and analyze than those represented as parametric functions, within the generative modeling framework.

We have found the generative modeling approach a natural, compact, controllable, and editable shape representation for a large class of shapes. For example, an airplane wing is naturally viewed as an airfoil cross section that is translated from the root to the tip of the wing. At the same time its thickness is modified, it is twisted, swept back, and translated vertically according to other curves. Many other types of objects are naturally described in this way: propellers, turbine blades, even bananas. Those that are not may have parts that are describable in this way. The use of Boolean operations, deformations, and other synthetic techniques can then complete the specification. Chapter 3 demonstrates the convenience of the generative modeling specification with many examples.

Renderability

Although direct rendering of generative models is difficult, interactive rendering speed is achieved through conversion to a more suitable form such as a polygonal mesh. This conversion can be done quickly, with only ad hoc error control, or more slowly with direct control over approximation error. Sampling and rendering techniques for generative models are described in Chapter 4. Techniques to approximate parametric shapes that limit a user-defined approximation error metric are treated in Section 6.3.

Slower, higher-quality rendering is also possible with ray tracing. Techniques to intersect rays with parametric surfaces can be robustly implemented using constrained minimization, as described in Section 4.1.2.

Rendering of multidimensional shapes can also be supported by animating or superimposing instances of the shape at various parameter values. Ways in which an interactive modeling system can handle such shapes is described in Sections 4.1.4 and 4.3.

Analyzability

The generative modeling representation admits a diverse set of operations, including many unavailable in other modeling systems. These operations can be used to compute physical quantities like arclength, surface area, and volume of objects. They can be used to compute how close two objects are to each other, to find curves of intersection of surfaces, and to choose parameters for parameterized objects that solve a given system of constraints and/or optimize a given function. To compute these operations, shapes are not approximated by a less general form such as a collection of polygons or polynomial patches. Instead, operations are done directly on the shapes as specified so that errors can be controlled, even when intermediate results of operations are fed back to produce more complicated shapes.

Computation of physical quantities like surface area or volume is accomplished using the integration and differentiation operators described in Chapter 2. Section A.5.3 presents an example of a library that computes such physical quantities. The rest of the operations are computed using the technique of interval analysis. The main benefit of interval analysis is that it can solve problems so that the results are guaranteed to be correct, even when computed with finitely precise floating point operations. This is accomplished by using inclusion functions that compute bounds on functions relevant to the problem, thus controlling approximation errors. Chapters 5 and 6 describe the technique of interval analysis and how it can be applied to problems of analysis on generative models.

1.6   Generative Modeling: The State of the Art

This section describes the research context of generative modeling — what previous work contributed to it, what is new about the approach, and what problems still remain for the future.

1.6.1   Previous Work Related to Generative Modeling

Generative modeling is based on existing work in the area of geometric modeling. In particular, the idea of sweeps (Section 1.3.4) forms the conceptual basis of the generative modeling shape representation. Little research, however, has focused on the following questions:

- How can sweeps be specified by the modeler in a general and powerful way?

- What tools are appropriate to allow swept shapes to be rendered and simulated?

Generative modeling expands the power of the sweeping technique and provides robust tools for rendering and analysis of swept shapes.

The generative modeling approach includes constraint solution as a primitve, symbolic operator. The idea of geometric modeling with constraints is not new. Researchers have studied several modeling systems that employ automatic, numerical constraint solvers. Sutherland's Sketchpad system [SUTH63] solved linear constraints involving line segments and arcs of circles, a technique still employed in many of today's interactive CAD systems. Nelson's JUNO system [NELS85] solves more complicated constraints using Newton–Raphson iteration, still in two dimensions. Borning's THINGLAB [BORN81] supports solution of 3D constraints. While the use of constraints in geometric modeling is frequently convenient, it is only one possible design style. A procedural approach, in which the shape is directly transformed via an explicit formula, is also a useful design style. The generative modeling approach combines both design styles by making constraint solution a primitive operator, which can be combined procedurally with other operators. Further, unlike these other approaches, the generative modeling approach uses interval analysis as a solution method for constraint problems. Interval analysis is a more robust technique than local iteration methods like Newton–Raphson, which typically require a good starting point to converge.

Conventional CAD systems interpret the modeler's specification to produce a list of low-level operations on the model. The original specification is then discarded or stored independently of the resulting model. However, the idea of using a high-level representation that can parameterize shapes in terms meaningful to designers is not new. Rossignac, Borrel, and Nackman [ROSS88] have advocated such a system. They propose a CAD system which captures the high-level intent of the designer using an interpreted language. They describe a 2D prototype system, called MAMOUR, that implements these ideas. The generative modeling approach extends this work to three-dimensional (and higher-dimensional) shapes.

This work also borrows from the work of researchers in sampling and approximating general parametric surfaces. Von Herzen [VONH89] has investigated the approximation of general parametric surfaces using Lipschitz bounds, a special case of an interval method. In this work, a single Lipschitz constant was specified for the entire parametric shape. The generative modeling approach extends this work by generalizing the kind of inclusion functions used and providing for automatic generation of the inclusion function. The bounds thus obtained are much tighter and are automatically computed from the shape representation.

Although it has received little attention, the use of interval methods in computer graphics and geometric modeling is not new. Mudur and Koparkar [MUDU84] have presented an algorithm for rasterizing parametric surfaces using interval arithmetic. They also have suggested the utility of such methods for other operations in geometric modeling. Toth [TOTH85] has demonstrated the usefulness of interval-based methods for the direct ray tracing of general parametric surfaces. Most recently, interval methods have been used for error bounding in computing topological properties of toleranced polyhedra [SEGA90], for contouring functions and rendering implicit surfaces [SUFF90], and for ray tracing implicit surfaces [MITC90].

Finally, the generative modeling approach can be compared to mathematical symbolic manipulation programs, such as Mathematica [WOLF91]. The system described here is similar to such programs, but is tailored to the geometric modeling task in many ways. Significant differences between generic symbolic mathematics programs and the approach described here are:

1. The generative modeling approach gives the user access to higher quality, interactive graphics to aid in visualization. In particular, users having z-buffer graphics hardware can define shapes and quickly visualize them, even when they define a parameterized shape family. The interpreted language also allows much more flexible use of graphics.

2. The generative modeling approach advocates a smaller and different set of operators. These include, for example, a curve operator that allows curves to be imported into the system from an interactive curve editor, and constraint solution and constrained minimization operators based on a robust interval analysis approach rather than local numerical methods.

3. The generative modeling approach allows the tying together of various interactive programs as a front end to the symbolic representation. Embedding the modeling language in a standard programming language facilitates inclusion of such programs. For example, in our research we have tied the curve editor program to the interactive shape visualization tool to allow the user to see a shape change as he modifies its input curves.

4. The generative modeling system includes many operator libraries built from primitive operators and designed especially for the design and analysis of geometric models.

5. The generative modeling approach includes sampling and approximation algorithms useful for the geometric modeling task. These include the table lookup sampling algorithm of Section 4.2.1, and the implicit curve and surface polygonalization algorithms of Chapter 6.

In a real sense however, the work described in this book can be thought of as the application of symbolic mathematics tools to the geometric modeling problem.

1.6.2   New Work Described in this Book

The geometric modeling approach advocated in this book is new in many respects:

- It handles multidimensional and parameterized objects, and objects of different dimensionality simultaneously.

- It is based on a shape description language of greater generality than used in previous work. In particular, it makes available operators such as integration, differentiation, constraint solution, and global minimization as modeling primitives.

- It uses a high-level representation. The results of operators are not discretized or approximated with polynomials, nor is the high-level description discarded. Instead, a continuous, symbolic representation of the shape is always maintained, which can be queried in various ways using operator "methods," such as evaluation of points on the shape.

- It controls errors through a consistent use of interval-based methods.

- It supports many robust algorithms for shape manipulation, using only two basic algorithms: one which computes solutions to a system of constraints, and another which computes the global minimum of a function, subject to a system of constraints.

- It is extensible and modular. The representation is based on a set of primitive operators on parametric functions, each having a few methods.

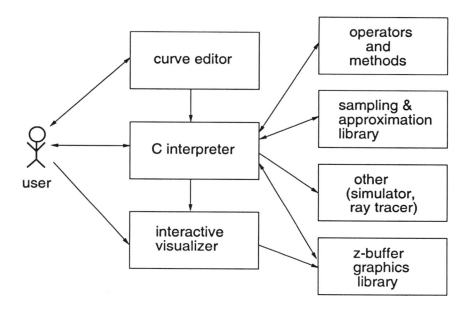

Figure 1.1: The GENMOD system. □

Some new algorithms for shape manipulation are also presented in this book, including algorithms to approximate (more specifically, polygonalize)

- implicitly defined curves to user-defined tolerances

- implicitly defined surfaces to user-defined tolerances

- parametric surfaces according to user-defined sampling criteria

- the results of CSG operations on solids bounded by parametric surfaces

New applications of interval-based algorithms to geometric modeling are also described to solve problems such as proximity computation, point enclosure, ray intersection, and approximation of curve and surface offsets without self-intersection. Chapter 6 presents these new algorithms.

The GENMOD System

GENMOD, a prototype geometric modeling environment implementing the approach described here, is pictured in Figure 1.1. Like the Alpha_1 system, GEN-MOD is based on an interpreted general purpose language (ANSI C) to allow flexible and interactive shape design. The language allows calls to a substrate of compiled code, which does the bulk of the computation. Typically, only the interface routines, which create GENMOD shapes and initiate rendering and simulation, need be interpreted. Nevertheless, the full power of an interpreted language is often useful, especially in a research environment. Appendix A documents the GENMOD language, which is used in the examples of Chapter 3.

A curve editor is used to produce curve files used by GENMOD for free-form design of shapes. Currently it supports several types of piecewise cubic curves. The curve editor can be run as a separate task, or run under the direction of GENMOD, allowing the user to see shapes change as the curves they depend on are edited. This mode of operation has proved to be an extremely convenient means of creating models for our computer graphics animations.

The sampling and approximation library provides modules to adaptively approximate parametric shapes according to user-specified criteria, and includes the kd-tree algorithms described in Chapter 6. The library also includes algorithms to approximate implicitly defined curves and surfaces and compute trimming operations on parametric surfaces.

1.6.3   Future Work

Much work remains to be done to improve the generative modeling approach. First, the user interface described in this book is not suitable for many potential users. Although the programmable aspect of the prototype system GENMOD is powerful and useful in a research environment, it requires a fairly sophisticated mathematical background and a substantial training investment. I believe a user interface for less sophisticated users could be designed by assembling an appropriate set of meta-shapes for which users could supply the necessary curves and other parameters. In any case, more research is needed to investigate good user interfaces for the symbolic representation presented here.

Many technical aspects of the approach are also in need of more study, including:

1. Addition of symbolic integration to enhance the speed of the integration operator

2. Addition of new symbolic operators including a boundary value ODE solution operator, and a PDE solution operator

3. Design of faster algorithms for constraint solution and constrained minimization. This probably requires algorithms to enhance the convergence of these algorithms using more optimal combinations of interval Newton methods and local enhancements.

4. Improvement of algorithms for solution of the linear interval equation (see Section 5.3.5)

5. Further investigation of synthetic methods for representing shapes, such as shape blending

6. Design of algorithms to compute a meta-shape using data from a real object, such as magnetic resonance or laser range-finding data, to allow capture and modification of existing shapes

7. Design of fast realistic rendering algorithms, especially algorithms that will allow real time rendering of shapes with diffuse shadows. More study is also required to design an interface that provides the user with convenient access to a whole collection of rendering methods including z-buffer, ray tracing, and volume rendering techniques.

8. Investigation of the implementation and uses of powerful, new methods like the degree method of Section 2.2.4

9. Investigation of new interfaces to the generative modeling representation, such as a 3D free-form sculpturing tool

10. Improvement of the implicit curve and surface approximation algorithms to handle non-manifolds (e.g., self-intersections and boundaries) and other prohibited behaviors of the solution. The discussion in this book outlines how such improvements may be achieved, but further development and testing are required.

Chapter 2

Shape Representation

In Chapter 1, a set of shape representations was examined and a new approach, called generative modeling, was summarized. This chapter defines generative models and discusses their utility in shape modeling. It examines how generative models may be represented in a way that is easy to specify, render, and analyze. Specifically, it answers the following questions:

- Why represent generative models as parametric functions specified by symbolic operators?

- What set of symbolic operators should be used?

- What computations should be performed on generative models? How should these computations be performed?

Finally, this chapter looks at the history of generative modeling representations that have been implemented as part of our research.

2.1 Generative Models: A Domain of Shapes

A general modeling system should be capable of representing any physically meaningful shape (mechanical parts, faces, trees, clouds) so that it can be specified, rendered, and analyzed easily. This is impossible with current technology. Even if we restrict ourselves to man-made, mechanical parts, the representation problem is still very difficult. Modeling systems "solve" this problem by restricting the shapes they deal with to a narrow domain. Polyhedra, parametric polynomials, and Boolean operations on simple solids are the most common shape domains. The goal of this work is to extend the domain of shapes in modeling systems through the use of generative models.

A *generative model* is a shape generated by the continuous transformation of a shape called the generator. Typically, a generative model is formed by transformation of a lower-dimensional generator. As an example, consider a curve $\gamma(u): \mathbf{R}^1 \to \mathbf{R}^3$, and a parameterized transformation, $\delta(p, v): \mathbf{R}^3 \times \mathbf{R} \to \mathbf{R}^3$, that acts on points in $p \in \mathbf{R}^3$ given a parameter v. A generative surface, $S(u, v)$, may be formed consisting of all the points generated by the transformation δ acting on the curve γ,

$$S(u, v) = \delta(\gamma(u), v).$$

More specifically, a cylinder is an example of a generative model, as shown in Figure 2.1. The generator, a circle in the xy plane, is translated along the z axis. The set of points generated as the circle is translated yield a cylinder. Mathematically, the generator and transformation for a cylinder are

$$\gamma(u) = \begin{pmatrix} \cos(2\pi u) \\ \sin(2\pi u) \\ 0 \end{pmatrix} \qquad \delta(p, v) = \begin{pmatrix} p_1 \\ p_2 \\ p_3 + v \end{pmatrix},$$

yielding the surface

$$S(u, v) = \delta(\gamma(u), v) = \begin{pmatrix} \cos(2\pi u) \\ \sin(2\pi u) \\ v \end{pmatrix}.$$

Generative models are a general form of sweeps. Sweeps in the CAD and computer graphics literature are limited to the movement of the generator along a trajectory through space, accompanied by simple (usually linear) transformations of the generator. Generators are typically curves in 2D or 3D space. A generative model allows arbitrary transformations of generators. Generators and transformations may be embedded in space of any dimension. They may be functions of any number of parameters. This book focuses on generative models that are continuous and piecewise smooth.

2.1.1   Why Generative Models?

Generative models are natural for specifying many man-made shapes. Manufacturing processes are often conveniently expressed as transformations on generators. For example, the shape of an extruded solid can be represented by a transformation of a planar area. A milled shape can be represented by Boolean subtraction of a generative model from a block (or appropriate initial shape of the work piece). The generative model appropriate in this case is formed by a transformation of the

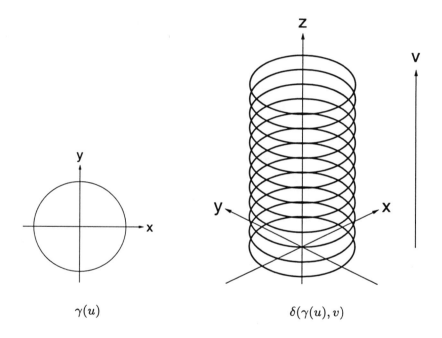

Figure 2.1: Generative model example. A cylinder is an example of a generative model. Its generator, $\gamma(u)$, is a circle in the xy plane. Its transformation, $\delta(p, v)$, simply adds v to the z coordinate of p. The application of δ to γ translates the generator along the z axis as a function of v, forming a set of circles comprising a cylinder. □

cutter tool shape that simulates its movement through space as it removes material from the work piece.

The usefulness of the generative modeling approach is not limited to the mimicking of manufacturing processes. Totally synthetic generators and transformations can be used. Generative modeling can be seen as a device for human modelers to conceptualize shape. Very complicated shapes can be built with a series of transformations that act on simpler generator shapes. Chapter 3 will discuss many examples of generative models not directly tied to simulation of manufacturing processes.

Generative models are easy to control and edit, since they encourage building high-dimensional shapes from low-dimensional components. For example, it is easier for a designer to specify a few 2D curves controlling the cross section, trajectory, and scaling of a shape than to specify hundreds or thousands of 3D points on the shape.

Generative models are not limited to rigid 3D shapes. They can represent shapes deforming in time, shapes that are functions of manufacturing variables, or shapes composed of nonuniform materials. Such shapes can be represented using generators and transformations that are functions of desired parameters (e.g., parameterized by time) or that are embedded in a space of dimension greater than three (e.g., a 4D space (x, y, z, d) where d is the component representing density). Generative models allow meta-shapes through parameterized generators and transformations. Chapter 3 presents many examples of meta-shapes.

Renderability of generative models is good through approximation by polygons or patches, or by ray tracing (rendering will be treated in Chapter 4). Analyzability is good for computing integral properties. Further algorithms for analysis using interval methods are presented in Chapter 6.

2.2 Specifying Generative Models

To make the idea of generative models useful, we need a method of specifying generators and the transformations that act on them. In doing this, we must necessarily restrict the domain of all mathematically conceivable generators and transformations to a set that can be specified in a computer-implementable system. Choosing a method of specification involves a trade-off between power of expression and speed of computation.

We propose specifying generative models through symbolic operators that build parametric functions. The following sections motivate and discuss this specification scheme.

2.2.1   Parametric Functions and the Closure Property

As we have seen from the cylinder example, a generative model can be expressed as a parametric function, as shown in Figure 2.2. If a generator is represented as a parametric function, a generative model that transforms this generator is also a parametric function. To see this, let a generator be represented by the parametric function

$$F(x)\colon \mathbf{R}^l \to \mathbf{R}^m.$$

A continuous set of transformations can be represented as a parameterized transformation

$$T(p;q)\colon \mathbf{R}^m \times \mathbf{R}^k \to \mathbf{R}^n$$

where $p \in \mathbf{R}^m$ is a point to be transformed, and $q \in \mathbf{R}^k$ is an additional parameter that defines a continuous set of transformations. The generative model is the parametric function[1]

$$T(F(x);q)\colon \mathbf{R}^{l+k} \to \mathbf{R}^n.$$

The ability to use a generative model as a generator in another generative model will be called the *closure property* of the generative modeling representation. The use of parametric generators and transformations yields closure because transformation of a generator can be expressed as a simple composition of parametric functions, resulting in another parametric function. In fact, the use of parametric generators and transformations blurs the distinction between generator and transformation. Both are parametric functions; the domain of a generator must be completely specified, while the domain of a transformation is partly specified and partly determined as the image of a generator.

Parametric functions that are evaluated on *rectilinear domains*, domains that are composed of cartesian products of intervals of $\mathbf{R}$, are especially convenient for rendering and computation of global properties. The simple form of the domain makes sampling and integration easy in a computer implementation. As will be shown in the section on non-Cartesian topology on page 30, restriction of the domain of parametric functions to rectilinear subsets of $\mathbf{R}^n$ does not result in a practical loss of generality.

Parametric functions are not the only basis for representing generative models one could choose. Generators and transformations can also be determined by implicit functions. An implicit function describes a shape as the set of points that solve a system of equations rather than as the set of points that are the image of a mapping. We first consider implicitly defined generators. Given a transformation

$$T(p;q)\colon \mathbf{R}^n \times \mathbf{R}^k \to \mathbf{R}^n,$$

---

[1]More precisely, the generative model is the set of points in the image of $T(F(x);q)$ over a domain $U \subset \mathbf{R}^{l+k}$.

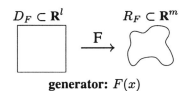

generator: $F(x)$

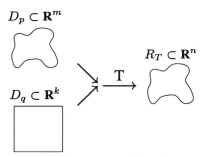

transformation: $T(p;q)$

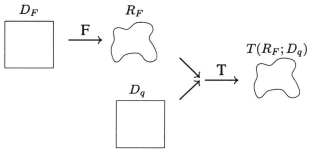

generative model: $T(F(x);q)$

Figure 2.2: General generative model. In this figure, square regions represent rectilinear domains of parametric functions; squiggly regions represent the images of parametric functions. The generator of a generative model is represented as the image of the parametric function $F \colon \mathbf{R}^l \to \mathbf{R}^m$ over a rectilinear domain D_F. The transformation of a generative model is represented as the parameterized transformation $T(p;q)$, where $p \in D_p$ is a point to be transformed and $q \in D_q$ is its parameter. The resulting generative model applies the parameterized transformation to the generator. That is, the generative model $T(F(D_F);D_q)$, is the image of a parametric function evaluated over the rectilinear region $D_F \times D_q$. $\square$

and a function that determines an implicit generator,

$$F(x)\colon \mathbf{R}^n \to \mathbf{R}^m,$$

a generative model can be expressed as the set

$$\left\{ T(x; q) \mid F(x) = 0,\, q \in \mathbf{R}^k \right\}.$$

Such a generative model representation is partly parametric and partly implicit; that is, a generative model is represented as a parametric function, part of whose domain is specified implicitly.

The set of transformations can also be determined implicitly. Under certain conditions, a function

$$T(p; q)\colon \mathbf{R}^n \times \mathbf{R}^k \to \mathbf{R}^k$$

can be seen as a transformation of p by determining a q for each p that solves $T(p; q) = 0$. Such a formulation has problems in that T may determine more than one or no q for a given p.

Although an implicit representation is valuable in many circumstances, rendering of general implicit shapes is a costly computation. Interactive rendering methods currently available require computation of the boundary of a shape, which must be approximated as a mesh of polygons or polynomial patches. Finding points on an implicitly represented shape requires numerical solution of systems of equations. In contrast, a parametric representation can often be rendered by repeated evaluation of simple analytic formulae.

Terminology

A parametric function, F, is a function from $\mathbf{R}^n$ (*parameter space*) to $\mathbf{R}^m$ (*object space*) :

$$F : \mathbf{R}^n \to \mathbf{R}^m$$

$$X = (x_1, x_2, \ldots, x_n)$$

$$F(X) = (F_1(X), F_2(X), \ldots, F_m(X)).$$

The variables $x_1, x_2, \ldots, x_n$ are called the *parametric variables* or *parametric coordinates*. The number of parametric coordinates on which F depends, n, is called the *input dimension* of the parametric function. The number of components in the result of F, m, is called the *output dimension* of the parametric function. The parameter space used for evaluation is a rectilinear region of $\mathbf{R}^n$ (also called a *hyper-rectangle*):

$$X = [a_1, b_1] \times [a_2, b_2] \times \ldots \times [a_n, b_n].$$

The image of F over X defines the shape of interest.

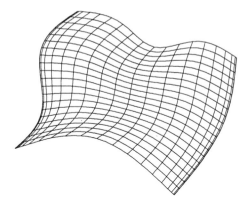

Figure 2.3: Rectilinear parametric function with $\mathbf{R}^2$ topology. A parametric function representing a warped sheet is defined over the rectilinear domain $[0, 1] \times [0, 1] \subset \mathbf{R}^2$. Its parameterization is one-to-one and hence is topologically identical to $\mathbf{R}^2$. The parameter lines over the surface are not periodic, and no singularities or "poles" exist. $\square$

Non-Cartesian Topology Using Parametric Functions

Many useful shapes have topologies other than that of a rectilinear subset of $\mathbf{R}^n$, such as the surfaces shown in Figures 2.4 through 2.6. As a basis for comparison, Figure 2.3 illustrates a surface whose topology is identical to rectangular subset of $\mathbf{R}^2$. These shapes can still be represented by parametric functions evaluated on rectilinear domains by using non-injective (not one-to-one) parameterizations. For example, a surface with spherical topology can be obtained with a parameterization that maps into a point at the limits of one parameter and is periodic in the other parameter. Similarly, a surface with cylindrical topology can be obtained by letting the parameterization be periodic in one parameter, while a surface with toroidal topology can be obtained by letting the parameterization be periodic in both parameters.

More complicated topologies, such as surfaces of arbitrary genus (i.e., with many holes or "handles"), or surfaces with boundary that branch, can be represented using connected sets of generative models. For example, Figure 2.7 shows a three-way branching tube surface. This surface cannot be defined by a continuous mapping from a single rectilinear domain. Instead, it is constructed from five separate, continuous parametric surfaces, each defined over a rectilinear domain. Data structures for connected sets of parametric functions that keep track of adjacency information are described in [THOM85].

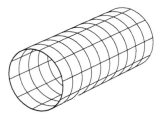

Figure 2.4: Rectilinear parametric surface with cylindrical topology. A parametric function representing a cylinder can be defined over the rectilinear domain $[0, 1] \times [0, 1] \subset \mathbf{R}^2$ using the parametric function

$$S(u, v) = \begin{pmatrix} \cos(2\pi u) \\ \sin(2\pi u) \\ v \end{pmatrix}.$$

This parametric function is periodic in the u parameter; that is, for a given v, $S(0, v) = S(1, v)$. $\square$

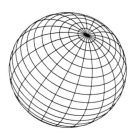

Figure 2.5: Rectilinear parametric surface with spherical topology. A parametric function representing a sphere can be defined over the rectilinear domain $[0, 1] \times [0, 1] \subset \mathbf{R}^2$ using the parametric function

$$S(u, v) = \begin{pmatrix} \cos(2\pi u) \sin(\pi v) \\ \sin(2\pi u) \sin(\pi v) \\ -\cos(\pi v) \end{pmatrix}.$$

This parametric function is periodic in the u parameter; that is, for a given v, $S(0, v) = S(1, v)$. The function has singularities at $v = 0$ and $v = 1$; that is, $S(u, 0)$ and $S(u, 1)$ are constants with respect to u. $\square$

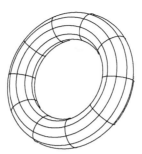

Figure 2.6: Rectilinear parametric surface with toroidal topology. A parametric function representing a torus can be defined over the rectilinear domain $[0, 1] \times [0, 1] \subset \mathbf{R}^2$ using the parametric function

$$S(u, v) = \begin{pmatrix} \cos(2\pi u)(R + r\cos(2\pi v)) \\ \sin(2\pi u)(R + r\cos(2\pi v)) \\ R + r\sin(2\pi v) \end{pmatrix}.$$

The parameter R controls the size of the torus hole, while the parameter r controls the thickness of the torus. This parametric function is periodic in the both the u and v parameters; that is, for a given v, $S(0, v) = S(1, v)$, and for a given u, $S(u, 0) = S(u, 1)$. $\square$

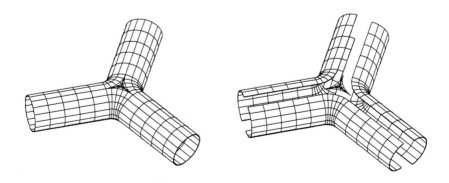

Figure 2.7: A three-way branching tube surface can be defined using connected sets of parametric surfaces, each defined over a rectilinear domain. In this example, five separate parametric surfaces are meshed together. $\square$

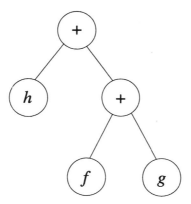

Figure 2.8: A parametric function $(f + g) + h$ is represented as a tree. Addition nodes have two subtrees. The f, g, and h nodes are parametric functions (e.g., constants or parametric coordinates). □

2.2.2   Using Symbolic Operators to Specify Parametric Functions

One way of specifying parametric functions is by selecting a set of *symbolic operators*. A symbolic operator is a function that takes a number of parametric functions as input and produces a parametric function as output. For example, addition is a symbolic operator that acts on two parametric functions, f and g, and produces a new parametric function, $f + g$. The addition operator is recursive in that we can continue to use it on its own results or on the results of other operators in order to build more complicated parametric functions (e.g., $(f + g) + h$).

A parametric function represented as the composition of symbolic operators can be viewed as a tree (see Figure 2.8). Each node of the tree is an operator. Each subtree is a lower-level parametric function used as an argument to its parent operator. The terminal nodes of the tree are parametric coordinates or constants.

Like the addition operator, all operators in the generative modeling approach are recursive; their results can be used as inputs to other operators.[2] Together with the closure property of parametric generators, this recursive nature of operators

---

[2] It should be noted that the result of an operator cannot always be used as input to another operator. Operators may constrain the output dimension of their arguments (e.g., an operator may accept only a scalar function as an argument and prohibit the use of functions of higher output dimension). In special circumstances, it may be desirable to constrain other properties of operator arguments. For example, the inversion operator expects its argument to be a monotonic scalar function. In this context, closure of the set of operators implies that an operator not arbitrarily prohibit any "reasonable" arguments, given the nature of the operator.

yields a modeling system with closure. That is, the designer is not prevented from using any reasonable combination of operations to specify shapes. For example, the addition operator can be applied to parametric functions of any input dimension (e.g., curves or surfaces). It can also be applied to parametric functions of any output dimension to perform vector addition, as long as the output dimension of its two arguments is identical.

Of course, it is not enough to represent parametric functions; we must also be able to compute properties about the parametric functions so that the shapes they represent can be rendered and analyzed. Such computations can be implemented by defining a set of *methods* for each operator. The method computes some property of a parametric function given the results of corresponding methods on the subtree parametric functions. Consider evaluation of a parametric function at a point in parameter space. For the addition operator, this can be implemented by evaluating the subtree parametric functions (by calling their respective evaluation methods) and adding the two intermediate results. By writing appropriate methods for each operator, we can compute properties of a parametric function formed by arbitrary composition of these operators.[3]

Why Aren't Rational Polynomials Enough?

Some geometric modeling systems specify parametric functions using *rational* parametric polynomials: functions formed by dividing one polynomial by another. The set of operators in such modeling systems is reduced to addition, subtraction, multiplication, and division of rational polynomials. Such a set of operators is attractive because it limits the complexity of computations required for analysis. Polynomials are very simple to evaluate and integrate (integration is especially easy for nonrational polynomials). Unfortunately, rational polynomials are a limited basis for modeling shapes.

Rational polynomials are not closed under many simple operations. For example, representing the distance between points on two polynomial curves requires a square root operator. Similarly, rotation of curves or surfaces by an exact angle requires operators, such as trigonometric functions, that cannot be expressed as rational polynomials. Even a simple arc that is parameterized by polar angle is not expressible as a rational polynomial. Most of the higher-level operations presented here, such as reparameterizing parametric curves by arclength and computation of intersections between curves and surfaces, are also not expressible using rational

---

[3]This is not to say that every conceivable property of parametric functions is computable in a completely modular fashion. For example, symbolic integration of a parametric function cannot be computed simply by integrating the subtree parametric functions and processing the result. Specifically, given two arbitrary parametric functions f and g, we cannot compute $\int f/g$ given only $\int f$ and $\int g$. Fortunately, many useful properties about parametric functions can often be computed using recursive evaluation of methods, including evaluation at a point in parameter space, symbolic differentiation, and inclusion functions.

parametric polynomials.

Modeling systems may solve these problems by approximation. That is, a rational parametric polynomial that is close to the desired shape is computed. This solution has two problems:

1. It implies the existence of a higher-level specification allowing operations that cannot be expressed as rational polynomials. Thus, the rational polynomials are reduced to a machine representation. The problem of identifying what types of operations are useful as a user representation remains. This is the central issue addressed by this book.

2. Even as a machine representation, rational parametric polynomials suffer problems. Systems using parametric polynomials control errors in a way that leads to numerical instability. Accuracy is achieved either by increasing the number of segments into which polynomial curves and surfaces are divided, or by increasing the degree of the approximating polynomial. As approximate results are fed back to the modeling system, error control quickly becomes intractable. On the other hand, when error control is done for higher-level operators, more appropriate algorithms can be used and better decisions concerning speed/accuracy tradeoffs can be made.

2.2.3 Specific Operators

In this section, we examine specific operators that form a basis for specifying a quite flexible variety of shapes. Many of the operators described here were found to be useful after experimentation in building example shapes. Techniques that seemed convenient in specifying examples were analyzed to extract a small, functionally independent set of operators.

It is not envisioned that the operators described here comprise a set fully adequate for all modeling tasks. Instead, operators that seem general purpose or immediately useful are described. This set of operators will be used in Chapter 3 to show the capability of the generative modeling approach for combining such low-level operators into complex and useful modeling tools.

Constants and Parametric Coordinates

Parametric coordinates and constants are terminal operators (operators that have no parametric function arguments) that specify the most basic parametric functions. The constant operator represents a parametric function with a real, constant value, such as $f = 2.5$. The parametric coordinate operator represents a particular parametric coordinate, such as $f = x_2$.

Arithmetic Operators

Arithmetic operators are addition, subtraction, multiplication, division, and negation of parametric functions. They are useful for such geometric operations as scaling and interpolation, and in many other, more complicated operations. For example, a cross-section curve can be multiplied by a constant to yield a scaled cross section. It can also be scaled by a parametric function that relates the amount of the scale to the inputs of the parametric function. Such a scaling parametric function can be used in a sweep surface where the scale of a cross-section curve is allowed to vary as a function of a sweep parameter.

Elementary Operators

Elementary operators include square root, trigonometric functions, exponentiation, exponential, logarithm, etc. The square root operator, for example, is useful for computing distance between points in space. The sine and cosine operators are useful in building parametric circles and arcs.

Vector and Matrix Operators

Vector operators include projection, cartesian product, vector length, dot product, and cross product. Projection and cartesian product allow extraction and rearrangement of coordinates of parametric functions. For example, given a 2D curve, an extrusion can be defined by appending an extrusion parameter to the curve as its third coordinate. That is, given a curve $\gamma(u)$ and an extrusion parameter v, we define a surface, $S(u, v)$, as

$$S(u, v) = \begin{pmatrix} \gamma_1(u) \\ \gamma_2(u) \\ v \end{pmatrix}.$$

The cylinder of Figure 2.1 is an example of such a surface. This extrusion definition uses projection to extract the first and second coordinates of the curve, and cartesian product to assemble the result into a 3D surface. Vector length, dot product, and cross product find many applications in defining geometric constraints on parameters of meta-shapes.

Vector operator analogs of the arithmetic operators are also useful for geometric modeling. These operators include addition and subtraction of vectors, and multiplication and division of vectors by scalars.

Matrix operators include multiplication and addition of matrices, matrix determinant, and inverse. Matrix multiplication is especially useful in defining affine transformations, which are used extensively in simple sweeps (see Section 3.2.1.4 on general affine transformations).

Differentiation and Integration Operators

The differentiation operator returns the partial derivative of a parametric function with respect to one of its parametric coordinates. This is useful, for example, in finding tangent or normal vectors on curves and surfaces. Tangent vectors are useful in defining sweeps where cross sections are moved along a plane curve or space curve, while remaining perpendicular to it. Normal vectors are necessary in computing offsets (see Section 3.2.2.2) and generating normals for shading.

The integration operator integrates a parametric function with respect to one of its parametric coordinates, given two parametric functions representing the upper and lower limits of integration. For example, the function

$$\int_{b(u)}^{a(u,v)} s(v, \tau) \, d\tau$$

can be formed by the integration operator applied to three parametric functions, where $s(v, \tau)$ is the integrand, $a(u, v)$ the upper limit of integration, and $b(u)$ the lower limit of integration.[4] Integration can be used to compute arclength of curves, surface area of surfaces, and volumes and moments of inertia of solids (see Section A.5.3).

Indexing and Branching Operators

A useful operation in geometric modeling is *concatenation*, the piecewise linking together of two shapes. For example, consider two curves, $\gamma_1(u)$ and $\gamma_2(u)$, that are both parameterized by $u \in [0, 1]$. It is often useful to define a new curve, $\gamma(u)$, that first follows γ_1 and then continues with γ_2. Mathematically, γ may be defined as

$$\gamma(u) = \begin{cases} \gamma_1(2u) & u \in [0, \, 0.5] \\ \gamma_2(2u - 1) & u \in (0.5, \, 1] \end{cases} .$$

Note that γ is continuous if

$$\gamma_1(1) = \gamma_2(0).$$

The concatenation of surfaces or functions with many parameters can be defined similarly, where the concatenation is done with respect to one of the coordinates. A further generalization is concatenation of more than two shapes. For example, the concatenation of the set of n curves $\gamma_1(u), \gamma_2(u), \ldots, \gamma_n(u)$, each defined over

---

[4] Of course, the integration operator is not limited to parametric function arguments of this form. The example only demonstrates that one is not limited to functions of a single parameter for the integrand or limits of integration. Furthermore, the functions representing the integrand and limits of integration may share input parameters.

the parametric variable $u \in [0,1]$, may be defined as

$$\gamma(u) = \begin{cases} \gamma_1(nu) & u \in [0, 1/n] \\ \gamma_2(nu-1) & u \in (1/n, 2/n] \\ \vdots & \\ \gamma_n(nu-(n-1)) & u \in ((n-1)/n, 1]. \end{cases}$$

This kind of concatenation is *uniform* concatenation, because each concatenated segment is defined in an interval of equal length $(1/n)$ in parameter space. It is commonly used in defining piecewise cubic curves such as B-splines.

Uniform concatenation can be implemented using an *indexing operator*, which takes as input an array of parametric functions and an index function that controls which function is to be evaluated. Given the same $\gamma_i(u)$ curves used in the previous example, and an index function $q(x)$, the index operator is defined as

$$\text{index}(q(x), \gamma_1(u), \ldots, \gamma_n(u)) = \gamma_{\lfloor q(x) \rfloor}(u),$$

where $q(x) = nu$ results in the uniform concatenation of the γ_i functions. In addition to the indexing operator, it is also useful to have a *substitution operator* to define uniform concatenation. The substitution operator symbolically substitutes a given parametric function for one of the parametric coordinates of another parametric function. For example, this can be used to represent $\gamma_i(nu-(i-1))$ given $\gamma_i(u)$, by substituting the function $nu-(i-1)$ for the parametric coordinate u.

The index operator is a special case of a *branching operator*, an operator that allows different parametric functions to be evaluated depending on some conditions. An if-then-else operator is another example of a branching operator useful in shape modeling. Given c, a condition parametric function that evaluates to 0 (false) or 1 (true), and two parametric functions to be evaluated, f_1 and f_2, the if-then-else operator can be defined as

$$\text{if-then-else}(c, f_1, f_2) = \begin{cases} f_1 & \text{if } c = 1 \\ f_2 & \text{otherwise} \end{cases}.$$

The if-then-else operator can be generalized to a multiway branch operator, which takes as input a sequence of conditional functions and evaluation functions. The result of the operator is the result of the first evaluation function whose corresponding conditional function is true. This multiway branch operator can be used to define a *nonuniform* concatenation of parametric functions where each concatenated segment need not be defined on an equal interval in the concatenated parameter (see Section A.4.2 for an example). Branching operators are also useful for implementing operators such as the minimum and maximum of a pair of functions, for defining deformations that act only on certain parts of space, and for detecting error conditions (e.g., taking the square root of a negative number, or normalizing a zero length vector).

Relational and Logical Operators

In order to support the definition of useful conditional expressions for the branching operators (and the constraint solution operator to be presented shortly), it is useful to have the standard mathematical relational operators, such as equality, inequality, greater than, etc., and the standard logical operators, such as "and," "or," and "not."

Curve and Table Operators

Curve and table operators allow shapes to be specified from data produced outside the system.

The curve operator specifies continuous curves such as piecewise cubic splines or sequences of lines and arcs. It is useful in combination with an interactive tool called a *curve editor*, which allows free-form creation of the curves.

The table operator is used to specify an interpolation of a multidimensional data set. For example, a simulation program may produce data defined over a discrete collection of points on a surface or solid. The table operator interpolates this data to yield a continuous parametric function, which can be used in definitions of more complex parametric functions. Additionally, the table operator can be used to approximate parametric functions whose evaluation is computationally expensive.

Inversion Operator

The inversion of monotonic functions is a useful operator for defining shapes. For example, one operation that requires such an inversion is the reparameterization of a curve by arclength, shown in Figure 2.9. This is often a useful operation in computer animation where some object is to move along a given trajectory at a constant speed. To specify the object's trajectory, a curve may be used that has the right geometric shape, but yields a nonconstant speed. In particular, a piecewise cubic spline curve can easily be edited by a human designer to give a desired shape, but cannot easily be modified to control the speed resulting from its use as a trajectory.

Let $\gamma(t)$ be a continuous curve specifying the object's trajectory, starting at $t = 0$ and ending at $t = 1$. The arclength along γ, $\gamma_{\text{arc}}(t)$, is given by

$$\gamma_{\text{arc}}(t) = \int_0^t \|\gamma'(\tau)\| \, d\tau.$$

The integration and differentiation operators mentioned previously serve to define γ_{arc}. The reparameterization of γ by arclength, γ_{new}, is then given by

$$\gamma_{\text{new}}(s) = \gamma \left(\gamma_{\text{arc}}^{-1} \left(s \, \gamma_{\text{arc}}(1) \right) \right).$$

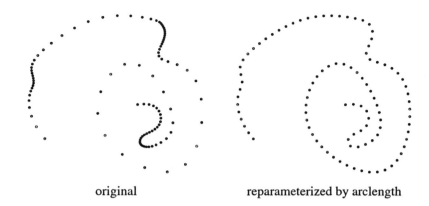

original   reparameterized by arclength

Figure 2.9: A parametric curve is reparameterized by arclength. Each dot represents a point on the curve along uniform increments of the curve's input parameter. □

The s parameter of γ_{new} actually represents normalized arclength, in that s varies between 0 and 1 to traverse the original curve γ, and equal distances in s represent equal distances in arclength on the curve. This reparameterization involves the inversion of the monotonic arclength function γ_{arc}.

Many other useful operations can also be formulated in terms of the inversion of monotonic functions. Most often, these operations involve reparameterizing curves and surfaces so that parameters are matched by arclength, polar angle, or output coordinate to some other curve or surface. For example, it is useful to reparameterize a given curve so that its x coordinate matches that of another curve.

Consider two curves that represent how two different parameters are to be varied in some sweep surface. In both curves, the first coordinate is the same sweep parameter, and the second coordinate is the value of the corresponding parameter to be swept. Let $\gamma(u)$ and $\delta(v)$ be two plane curves defined on $u, v \in [0, 1]$. Since the first coordinate of both curves is the sweep parameter, we assume that the first coordinate of both curves is a monotonic function of its input parameter and has an identical range.

Of course these curves may be defined so that their second coordinate is a function of the first, i.e.,

$$\gamma(u) = \begin{pmatrix} u \\ y_\gamma(u) \end{pmatrix}$$

$$\delta(v) = \begin{pmatrix} v \\ y_\delta(v) \end{pmatrix}.$$

In this case, the two curves are already tied together because $\gamma_1(w) = \delta_1(w)$. However, it may be easier for a human designer to specify the two curves as parametric functions in both the first and second coordinate, i.e.,

$$\gamma(u) = \begin{pmatrix} x_\gamma(u) \\ y_\gamma(u) \end{pmatrix}$$

$$\delta(v) = \begin{pmatrix} x_\delta(v) \\ y_\delta(v) \end{pmatrix}.$$

This kind of curve provides more flexibility in defining the desired relationship between sweep parameter and corresponding swept quantity. In this case, we no longer have that $\gamma_1(w) = \delta_1(w)$. One of the curves must be "tied" to the other: reparameterized so that its first coordinate is matched to the other curve. Tying the curve δ to γ can be accomplished using the inversion operator on the first coordinate of δ:

$$\delta_{\text{new}}(u) = \delta\left(\delta_1^{-1}\left(\gamma_1(u)\right)\right).$$

Inversion of monotonic functions in a single variable may be computed using fast algorithms, such as Brent's method [PRES86].

Constraint Solution Operator

The constraint solution operator takes a parametric function representing a system of constraints and produces either a solution to the constrained system or an indication that no solution exists.[5] Two forms of solution are useful: finding any point that solves the system, or finding all points that solve it, assuming there is a finite set of solutions. The operator also requires a parametric function specifying a rectilinear domain in which to solve the constraints.

For example, the constraint solution operator can be used to find the intersections between two planar curves. Let $\gamma^1(s)$ and $\gamma^2(t)$ be two curves in $\mathbf{R}^2$. These curves could be represented using the curve operator on page 39, or using any of the other operators. The appropriate constraint is then

$$F(s,t) \equiv (\gamma^1(s) = \gamma^2(t)),$$

which can be represented using the equality relational operator. The constraint solution operator applied to this constraint produces a constant function representing a point (s,t) where the two curves intersect.

The constraint system can also be solved over a subset of its parameters to yield a non-constant parametric function. For example, the constraint system $\gamma^1(r,s) = \gamma^2(t)$ can be solved over s and t, resulting in a function that depends on r. The user therefore specifies not only a parametric function representing the constraint

---

[5]Note that the inversion operator is a special case of the constraint solution operator.

system, but also a list of parametric coordinates over which the system should be solved. The rest of the constraint function's parametric coordinates parameterize the system.

Constraint solution has application to problems involving intersection, collision detection, and finding appropriate parameters for parameterized shapes. A robust algorithm for evaluating this operator will be presented in Chapter 5.

Constrained Minimization Operator

The constrained minimization operator takes two parametric functions representing a system of constraints and an objective function, and produces a point that globally minimizes the objective function, subject to the constraints. The operator also requires a parametric function specifying a rectilinear domain in which to perform the minimization. The minimization operator has many applications to geometric modeling, including

- finding intersections of rays with surfaces for ray tracing

- finding the point on a shape closest to a given point

- finding the minimum distance between shapes (illustrated in Figure 2.10)

- finding whether a point is inside or outside a region defined with parametric boundaries, called *point-set classification*

For example, consider a parametric surface $S(u, v)$ whose image over a 2D rectangle $D = [u_0, u_1] \times [v_0, v_1]$ forms the boundary of a compact 3D region. Assume further that this surface has a consistent normal vector, $N(u, v)$ (i.e., N always points outside the interior of the bounded region). The point-set classification problem involves determining whether a point $p \in \mathbf{R}^3$ is inside or outside the region. Let $d(u, v)$ be the distance between a point on S and p:

$$d(u, v) = \|S(u, v) - p\|.$$

Let $(u^{\min}, v^{\min})$ be a point in D that minimizes d, and let

$$S^{\min} = S(u^{\min}, v^{\min})$$
$$N^{\min} = N(u^{\min}, v^{\min}).$$

Note that $N^{\min}$ is either parallel or anti-parallel to the direction $S^{\min} - p$. We can therefore determine whether p is inside or outside the region bounded by S by

$$N^{\min} \cdot (S^{\min} - p) > 0 \quad \Rightarrow \quad p \text{ is inside } S$$
$$N^{\min} \cdot (S^{\min} - p) < 0 \quad \Rightarrow \quad p \text{ is outside } S$$

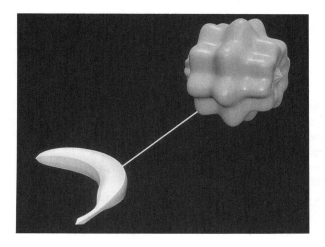

Figure 2.10: Using the constrained minimization operator to find the minimum distance between shapes. The minimum distance between two parametric surfaces can be computed by solving an unconstrained minimization problem minimizing $\|S(u,v) - T(r,s)\|$ where $S(u,v)$ and $T(r,s)$ are the two parametric surfaces. Finding the minimum distance is important to detect collisions in rigid body simulations, and in determining clearance in mechanical assemblies. $\square$

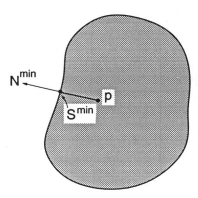

Figure 2.11: Point-set classification with the constrained minimization operator. To test whether a point p is inside or outside the shaded region, the point on the region's boundary closest to p, $S^{\min}$, is computed using minimization. Since the region's normal vector at this point, $N^{\min}$, is parallel to the direction $S^{\min} - p$, p is inside the region. $\square$

as shown in Figure 2.11. Thus, unconstrained global minimization can be used to solve point-set classification problems for parametrically bounded regions.

A robust algorithm for evaluating parametric functions that use the minimization operator will be presented in Chapter 5.

ODE Solution Operator

The ODE operator solves a first order, initial value ordinary differential equation (ODE). It is useful for defining limited kinds of physical simulations within the modeling environment. For example, we can simulate rigid body mechanics, or find flow lines through vector fields, as shown in Figure 2.12. Plate 5 illustrates the results of the ODE operator for a simple gravitational simulation specified entirely in GENMOD.

Let f be a specified parametric function of the form

$$f(t, y_1, y_2, \ldots, y_n) \colon \mathbf{R}^{n+1} \to \mathbf{R}^n.$$

The ODE operator returns the solution $y(t) \colon \mathbf{R} \to \mathbf{R}^n$ to the system of n first order equations

$$\frac{dy}{dt} = f(t, y)$$

with the initial condition

$$y(t_0) = y_0.$$

Parameterized ODEs, in which f and y_0 (and thus the result y) depend on an additional m parameters $x_1, \ldots, x_m$, are also allowed. The user supplies the ODE operator with an indication of which parametric coordinates of f are the t and y_i variables and which are the additional parameters x_i.

GENMOD implements the ODE operators using a Numerical Algorithms Group (NAG) ODE solver. Similar operators, for solution of boundary value problems and PDEs, are also useful in a geometric modeling environment, but have not been implemented in the present GENMOD system.

2.2.4   Operator Methods

An operator method is a function defined for each symbolic operator. It allows computation of a property of parametric functions formed using the operator, such as the value of the parametric function at a point in parameter space. The set of methods defined for each operator should be small, permitting convenient addition of new operators. At the same time, the set of methods should compute all the properties of parametric functions required for rendering and analysis. The GENMOD system includes three operator methods: evaluation of the parametric

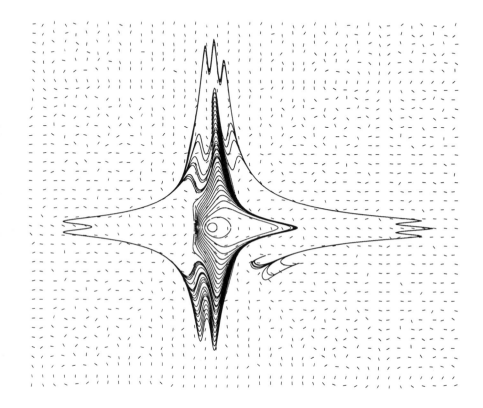

Figure 2.12: Results of the ODE solution operator to find the flow lines through a 2D vector field. The vector field is given by

$$V(x, y) = \begin{pmatrix} y + x^2 \sin(xy) \\ -x + y^2 \cos(xy) \end{pmatrix}.$$

Its direction is indicated with short lines. A family of integral curves of this vector field are shown, starting from points $p(y) = (0, y)$ for various values of y. These curves are computed using the ODE solution operator with a parameterized initial condition (see Section A.3.14). □

function at a point in parameter space, symbolic differentiation of the parametric function, and evaluation of an inclusion function for the parametric function. These methods will be discussed in more detail in the following sections.

Locally Recursive Operator Methods

In the following discussion, a distinction is made between methods that can be defined in a completely modular fashion and methods that cannot be so defined. An operator P that takes n parametric functions as inputs defines a parametric function $p = P(f_1, \ldots, f_n)$. A method on parametric functions is called *locally recursive for* P if its result on p is completely determined by the set of its results on each of the n parametric functions $f_1, \ldots, f_n$. Thus, a method to evaluate a parametric function at a point in parameter space is locally recursive for the addition operator because $f + g$ can be evaluated by evaluating f, evaluating g, and adding the result. A method to symbolically integrate a parametric function is not locally recursive for the division operator, because $\int f/g$ cannot be computed given only $\int f$ and $\int g$. Generally, a locally recursive method can be simply implemented and efficiently computed.

Evaluation at a Point

The generative modeling approach represents a shape as the image of a parametric function. Such a shape may be approximated by evaluating the parametric function over a series of points in parameter space and computing a new shape that interpolates the resulting points. The approximate shape is typically a collection of simple linked pieces, called a *tessellation*. For example, a surface is commonly approximated as a connected set of polygons. Approximate shapes can be used to transfer shape information to software that has no access to the generative representation, such as rendering and simulation modules.

A method to evaluate a parametric function at a point in parameter space is locally recursive for most of the operators discussed previously. Several operators are exceptions: the integration, inversion, and ODE solution operators.[6] All three of these operators require their input parametric function to be evaluated repeatedly over many domain points. For example, evaluation of the integration operator can be computed numerically using Romberg integration [PRES86, pages 123–125], which adds the value of the integrand parametric function over many points in its domain in order to produce an approximate integral.

Two forms of the evaluation method have proved useful: evaluation at a single, specified point in parameter space and evaluation over a multidimensional, recti-

---

[6]The differentiation, constraint solution, and constrained minimization operators are also exceptions. As we will discuss later, the evaluation method for the differentiation operator depends on the differentiation method, while the evaluation method for the constraint solution and constrained minimization operators uses the inclusion function method.

linear lattice of points in parameter space. Evaluation of a parametric function over a rectilinear lattice gives information about how the function behaves over a whole domain and is useful in "quick and dirty" rendering schemes. Although evaluation over a rectilinear lattice can be implemented by repeated evaluation at specified points, much greater computational speed can be achieved with a special method, as we will see in Chapter 4.

It has also proved useful to define the evaluation methods so that they return an error condition as well as a numerical result. The error condition signifies whether the parametric function has been evaluated at an invalid point in its domain (e.g., f/g where g evaluates to 0, or $\sqrt{h}$ where $h < 0$). Error checking during evaluation can be used to warn a designer that an interactively specified shape contains errors. It can also be explicitly included in a shape representation through the use of an error operator. The error operator returns the error condition result of evaluating a parametric function. It can be used, for example, as a conditional in a branching operator (e.g., if error($\sqrt{h}$) then $-\sqrt{-h}$ else $\sqrt{h}$).

Differentiation

The differentiation method is used to implement the derivative operator introduced on page 37. The differentiation method computes a parametric function that is the partial derivative of a given parametric function with respect to one of the parametric coordinates. The partial derivative is computed symbolically; that is, the partial derivative result

is represented using the same set of operators that represent the parametric function whose derivative is sought. For example, the partial derivative with respect to x_1 of the parametric function $x_1 + \sqrt{x_1 x_2}$ yields the parametric function $1 + x_2/(2\sqrt{x_1 x_2})$, which is represented with the addition, multiplication, division, square root, constant, and parametric coordinate operators.

Although the differentiation method is not locally recursive for most operators discussed previously, it is still relatively easy to compute. For example, the partial derivative of the parametric function $h = \cos(f)$ depends not only on the partial derivative of f, but also on f itself, since

$$\frac{\partial h}{\partial x_i} = -\sin(f)\frac{\partial f}{\partial x_i}.$$

The differentiation method is therefore not locally recursive for the cosine operator, but may be computed simply if a sine operator exists. Similar situations arise for many of the other operators. Fortunately, it is a simple matter to extend a set of operators such that the set is closed with respect to the differentiation method, meaning that any partial derivative may be represented in terms of available operators.[7]

---

[7] For example, this implies that if the cosine operator is included in the set of primitive operators,

In many respects, a symbolic integration method is similar to the differentiation method discussed here and could be used to implement the integration operator. The use of symbolic integration can result in much faster evaluation of parametric functions defined with the integration operator. Furthermore, symbolic integration obviates the need to write a special method for the integration operator to evaluate the integral at a point or evaluate its inclusion function. As for the differentiation operator, these methods result simply by using the already defined methods of the symbolic representation of the integral. We have chosen not to implement symbolic integration in GENMOD. Parametric functions that use the integration operator are evaluated using a numerical method, rather than by evaluating a new parametric function that is produced by symbolic integration.

Symbolic integration was avoided for two reasons. First, the set of operators discussed in Section 2.2.3 cannot be closed with respect to the symbolic integration method by adding a finite number of new operators. Second, symbolic integration requires complex and costly algorithms. A better implementation of the generative modeling approach may use existing mathematical symbolic manipulation tools, such as Mathematica [WOLF91]. Such a system could compute symbolic integrals when they are representable, reverting to numerical procedures when the symbolic manipulation fails to produce a result.

Evaluation of an Inclusion Function

An inclusion function computes a rectilinear bound for the range of a parametric function, given a rectilinear domain. It is used to evaluate parametric functions defined with the constrained minimization and constraint solution operators. Chapter 5 will explain how evaluation of these operators may be computed using inclusion functions.

Although an inclusion function computes a global property of a parametric function, it can often be computed using locally recursive methods. As we will see in Section 5.2.2, for example, an inclusion function method for the multiplication operator can be computed using interval arithmetic on the results of the inclusion functions for its parametric function multiplicands.

Computing solutions to nonlinear systems of equations and nonlinear, constrained optimization problems is a very difficult problem for systems of arbitrary functions. The approach advocated here restricts the set of allowable functions to those formed by composition of operators for which an inclusion function can be computed. It is quite surprising, but nonetheless true, that such a difficult problem can be solved for this special case, given only a set of methods to evaluate inclusion functions.

---

then the sine operator must be included as well. Some operators, such as the constrained minimization operator, do not have easily expressible partial derivatives. For these operators, the partial derivative must be computed numerically.

Other Operator Methods

The modeling system can be extended by adding a new method to each primitive operator. If the method is locally recursive, then its addition requires little implementation effort. Methods that are not locally recursive require more knowledge of the subtree parametric functions than simply the results of their methods.

Another useful operator method determines whether a parametric function is continuous or differentiable to a specified order over a given rectilinear domain. Many times, algorithms for rendering and analysis require that the functions accepted as input be differentiable (see Section 5.3.6). The differentiability operator can therefore be used to select whether an algorithm that assumes differentiability is appropriate, or if a less restrictive (and probably slower) algorithm should be used instead.

The differentiability/continuity method is locally recursive for most of the operators discussed previously, but there are exceptions. For example, the differentiability/continuity method for the division operator cannot simply check that the two parametric functions being divided are differentiable. It must also check whether the denominator equals 0 in the given domain. This is easily accomplished using an inclusion function method.

Other operator methods, whose implementation is still a research issue, include one-to-oneness over a rectilinear domain for functions $f : \mathbf{R}^n \rightarrow \mathbf{R}^n$. A similar method is *degree*, defined as

$$d(f, D, p) = \text{cardinality} \left\{ x \in D \mid f(x) = p \right\},$$

where $D \subset \mathbf{R}^n$.

2.3 Development of the Generative Modeling Representation

The representation of generative models proposed in this chapter is not the first representation we imagined or implemented. The representation is the final result of many implementation iterations. These implementation iterations have followed a natural progression starting with systems allowing relatively little interactivity and power of expression and progressing to much more powerful and interactive systems. This section traces the history of generative modeling representations implemented as part of this research.

It is hoped that this discussion will show that the generative modeling approach advocated here is mature, arrived at after rejection of simpler and more obvious possibilities. This historical treatment also identifies for future implementors considerations that are important in a modeling system.

2.3.1   System 1 – Nonrecursive Transformations and Generators

The first generative modeling system we implemented used a predefined, nonrecursive set of transformations. Nonrecursive in this context means that the result of a transformation could not be used as an input to another transformation. A transformation accepted one or more curves as input and performed a simple sweep, producing a surface as output. The input curves were used both to specify generators and to specify parameters for parameterized transformations.

For example, the set of transformations included a profile product transformation acting on two planar curves. One planar curve specified a generator, which was translated and scaled according to the second planar curve. Mathematically, the profile product transformation was an operator on two planar curves, $\gamma(u)$ and $\delta(v)$, that produced a surface given by

$$\text{profile\_product}(\gamma, \delta)(u, v) = \begin{pmatrix} \gamma_1(u)\delta_1(v) \\ \gamma_2(u)\delta_1(v) \\ \delta_2(v) \end{pmatrix}.$$

Another example of a transformation was the interpolate-and-sweep transformation. It accepted as input two planar cross-section curves, a scalar curve specifying how to interpolate between these cross sections, and three more scalar curves specifying scaling (in x and y) and translation (in z) of the cross section. This transformation was defined as an operator on two planar curves, $\gamma(u)$ and $\delta(u)$, and four scalar curves, $\alpha(v)$, $x(v)$, $y(v)$, and $z(v)$, that produced a surface given by

$$\text{sweep}(\gamma, \delta, \alpha, x, y, z)(u, v) = \begin{pmatrix} x(v)(\gamma_1(u)\alpha(v) + \delta_1(u)(1 - \alpha(v))) \\ y(v)(\gamma_2(u)\alpha(v) + \delta_2(u)(1 - \alpha(v))) \\ z(v) \end{pmatrix}.$$

Curve inputs to the transformations were selected from a set of parameterized families including constants, lines, arcs, and sinusoids. For example, a family of arcs was parameterized in terms of the arc origin, radius, and two angular limits. Piecewise cubic curves created with a curve editor program could also be used as transformation inputs. A representation of a piecewise cubic curve was transferred from the curve editor program to the modeling program through a file interface.

This early modeling system allowed testing of the generative modeling approach with a minimum of implementation effort, but was essentially unsatisfactory. The representation was limited to surfaces, and the set of transformations and curves was too limited. For example, one could not create a sweep surface where the cross section was translated, rotated, and then translated again. Nor could a curve be formed using useful operations such as the concatenation of several primitive curves. Finally, the modeling process was not sufficiently interactive. One could not see a shape change as the curves used in its specification were edited. Instead, significant time and user interaction were required to write to disk the modified curve files and reread them in the modeling program.

2.3.2   System 2 – Limited Recursive Transformations

We next implemented a generative modeling system whose transformations were expressed using recursive composition of simple, primitive transformations. A shape in this system was represented using an modeling entity called a *u-curve*, mathematically representable as a parametric surface, $S(u, v): \mathbf{R}^2 \rightarrow \mathbf{R}^3$. A u-curve was recursively defined as a primitive curve, or a transformation of a u-curve specified through a set of parameterized transformations. This recursive definition allowed an arbitrary series of transformations on a primitive curve.

For example, one transformation in this second system translated a u-curve along a coordinate axis. In particular, the translate-in-z transformation was defined as an operator on a u-curve, $T(u, v)$, and a scalar curve, $z(v)$, that produced the transformed u-curve:

$$\text{translate-in-}z(T, z)(u, v) = \begin{pmatrix} T_1(u, v) \\ T_2(u, v) \\ T_3(u, v) + z(v) \end{pmatrix}.$$

As another example, the set of transformations included interpolation, defined as an operator on two u-curves, $S(u, v)$ and $T(u, v)$, and a scalar curve $\alpha(v)$, that produced the u-curve:

$$\text{interpolate}(S, T, \alpha)(u, v) = \begin{pmatrix} S_1(u, v)\alpha(v) + T_1(u, v)(1 - \alpha(v)) \\ S_2(u, v)\alpha(v) + T_2(u, v)(1 - \alpha(v)) \\ S_3(u, v)\alpha(v) + T_3(u, v)(1 - \alpha(v)) \end{pmatrix}.$$

Parameterized transformations included many other types, including

- scaling of any coordinate of a u-curve

- rotation of the u-curve about any axis

- moving a u-curve perpendicular to a trajectory specified by a planar curve or a space curve

- simultaneous translation and scaling of a u-curve, specified by a planar profile curve

- simultaneous translation and scaling of a single coordinate of a u-curve, specified by two "rail" curves

- warping a u-curve by addition of a quadratic function of any of its coordinates to any other coordinate

In each case, transformation inputs were of two types: u-curves and primitive curves. One or more u-curves specified the generator of the transformation, while primitive curves specified other parameters of the transformation (e.g., the scale factor for the scale transformation, or the amount of rotation for the rotate transformation).

This second modeling system represented shape much more flexibly than the first. Composition of any number of transformations, in any order, was allowed. The new system could represent all the transformations in the first system, as well as an infinite variety of new ones. Nevertheless, the second system was lacking in several respects. As in the previous implementation, only 3D surfaces were represented.

Furthermore, the representation of curves in the system was not general enough. Curves were still specified as an instance of a parameterized family or with a curve editor, and could not be modified or operated upon. Curves could not be built using operations that computed distances or derivatives, found intersections between curves, or evaluated a u-curve over a curve in its parameter space. Transformations that could be applied to a u-curve could not be applied to other transformation inputs. For example, the scalar curve parameter of the translate-in-z transformation had to be a primitive curve rather than the interpolation of a pair of scalar curves, or some other transformation of a simpler scalar curve.

One enhancement to the curve specification part of the modeling program was implemented: a reparameterization operator. This operator reparameterized a planar curve based on arclength, x or y component, or polar angle, to produce a new planar curve. It was used to match curves that were used as transformation inputs in the same shape. Although crudely implemented, this operator gave rise to the idea that curves (or more generally, parameterized transformation inputs) should be recursively defined in the same way that transformations were.

While using this second system, we realized that it would be useful to allow users to define their own transformations by packaging a series of primitive transformations into a transformation "subroutine." As an example, the interpolate-and-sweep transformation discussed in Section 2.3.1 could be defined by an interpolation transformation, followed by scale-in-x, scale-in-y, and translate-in-z transformations. We suspected that many shapes could be defined using similar transformation sequences. Therefore, modeling time would be reduced if the modeler could select from a library of such transformation subroutines rather than redefining the subroutine for each new shape. The next implementation iteration addressed this issue as well as the lack of generality of the curve representation.

2.3.3   System 3 – Fully Recursive Transformations and Generators

The third system represented generative models with fully recursive transformations and generators, as this chapter proposes. Soon after the second system was completed, we realized that an improved modeling system should allow a rich set of operations, such as arithmetic operations, vector and matrix operations, differentiation, and integration. This set of operators should be used to specify both transformation subroutines and the inputs to these transformation subroutines. Transformations should apply equally well to shapes of any input dimension, including curves, surfaces, or solids. Thus, the u-curve of the previous system evolved into a multidimensional parametric function, while the set of primitive transformations on u-curves evolved into a set of primitive operators on parametric functions.

In order to implement a modeling system based on this approach, we added some new features to an existing modeling program. The modeling program accepted a simple command line language to specify surface geometry, associate shading characteristics with the surfaces, position surfaces in the scene, and specify lighting and camera positioning for the scene. We added several new commands to this modeling program to allow specification of curves and surfaces using the new recursive generative modeling approach.

The surface command caused the parametric function specified as an argument to be sampled, approximated with a polygonal mesh, and added to the rest of the scene. The specification of a parametric function in this command was aptly described by one user as "lisp without the parentheses." For example, the command

```
surface  output begin \
     cos mult u twopi  \
     sin mult u twopi  \
     v                 \
end
```

created a cylinder. The output begin ... end operator specified a cartesian product of all the arguments between the begin and end (three arguments in this case). The cos and sin operators specified cosine and sine, respectively, of the following argument. The mult operator specified multiplication of the next two arguments. Finally, the u and v operators specified parametric coordinates, and the twopi operator specified the constant 2π. These last three operators had no arguments. The surface specified in this example is therefore mathematically represented as

$$\begin{pmatrix} \cos(2\pi u) \\ \sin(2\pi u) \\ v \end{pmatrix}.$$

This third modeling system also included a facility for defining transformation subroutines. The define_operator command was used to define such subroutines by creating higher-level operators that combined the primitive operators. For example, the command

```
define_operator interp 3   a in1 in2 \
        add   in1    mult sub in2 in1 a
```

defined an interpolation operator, called interp, which took three arguments and used the primitive addition, multiplication, and subtraction operators. The operator specified can be mathematically represented as an operator on three parametric functions a, i_1, and i_2 that yields the parametric function

$$\text{interp}(a, i_1, i_2) = i_1 + (i_2 - i_1)a.$$

Once defined, an operator could be used in the same way as the primitive operators already present in the system (i.e., in later definitions of surfaces and operators).

We do not hesitate to admit that the language described here was extremely inelegant and hard to use. Most of the syntactic inelegance was caused by grafting the parametric function parsing on top of the crude lexical analysis provided by the original modeling program's interpreter. Still, we were satisfied that the representational approach of this third system was the right one, even if its syntax was inadequate. In addition, the operator definition facility, primitive though it was, proved to be very useful. An extensive library of user-defined operators was developed that defined many kinds of sweeps as well as general purpose mathematical operators that interpolated parametric functions, found normal vectors to surfaces, and reparameterized curves. Operators in this library were used repeatedly, saving the modeler the work of reinventing and reimplementing the operator.

Two aspects of this third system seemed particularly in need of improvement. First, the operator definition facility was too limited. It had no access to information about the parametric functions supplied as its arguments. Thus, user-defined operators could not perform error checking to test, for example, that an argument had an appropriate output dimension. Further, the operator definition could not accept arguments such as integers, floating point numbers, strings, or higher-level data structures; only parametric functions were allowed. Finally, operator definitions could not make use of programming language constructs such as loops or conditionals. Only recursive composition of primitive or previously defined operators could be used in the definition of a new operator.

Second, the connection between the generative modeling part and the rest of the modeling program was too restrictive. One could not define and render sets of generative models using programming constructs (e.g., a chain of links could not be specified using an iterative construct like a FORTRAN do statement). Information that could be computed about a generative model, such as its integral properties, could not easily be made available to the rest of the system.

2.3.4   System 4 – Using a General Purpose Language

It became clear that the problems with the third system could be solved if the user interacted with the modeling program through an interpreted, general purpose programming language. The modeling program would make available to the user, through interpreted function calls, predefined libraries including the generative modeling module, graphics library, curve editor, and multidimensional data visualization module. The user would then have all the modeling system's data structures and code accessible in a single environment, and processable using general programming constructs. In particular, user-defined parametric operators could be implemented as interpreted functions, solving the problems mentioned in Section 2.3.3.

This approach was used in the final implementation iteration, a system called GENMOD. Details of GENMOD's user interface can be found in Appendix A. Implementation of GENMOD was guided by the following principles:

- The modeling language should be derived from an already existing basis language. Users who already know the basis language would be spared some of the work required to learn the system. In addition, the programming constructs in the language would be "tried and true" constructs of an existing programming language.

- The modeling language should be interpreted. Users should be able to test and modify ideas for shapes as quickly as possible.

- The modeling language should allow a substrate of non-interpreted code. We expected that interpretation of the whole system, including the lowest-level code, would be very slow. Therefore, the system should allow some code sequences to be run as compiled units.

GENMOD's use of an interpreted, general purpose language has tremendously simplified the process of extending the system. For example, with only a modest implementation effort, we were able to tie together the shape visualization tool and the curve editor, so that the user can see a shape change as the curves used in its specification are modified.

Chapter 3

Shape Specification Examples

This chapter presents examples of generative shapes. It is not meant to be a complete catalog of techniques for specifying objects. Instead it shows how the generative modeling approach leads a designer to think about shape and the size of the domain of shapes that can be represented.

3.1   GENMOD Preliminaries

The examples in this chapter are specified using the GENMOD language for building parametric functions. This section provides an introduction to the GENMOD language by documenting a few of the heavily used symbolic operators; a complete description of the GENMOD language can be found in Appendix A.

The GENMOD language is based on the C programming language, with some operators overloaded to have a nonstandard meaning, and some new operators added. The basic data structure in GENMOD is the MAN type (for *manifold*), which represents a parametric function. The primitive operators described in Appendix A act on parametric functions (of type MAN) to produce new parametric functions.

For example, the code

```
MAN x = m_x(0);
MAN y = m_x(1);
MAN plane = @(x,y);
```

defines three parametric functions, x, y, and plane. The m_x operator takes an integer, i, and produces a parametric function that is simply the i-th parametric coordinate x_i. The first two manifolds, x and y, are therefore merely the parametric coordinates x_0 and x_1. The cartesian product operator, $\texttt{@()}$, combines a series of parametric functions, separated by commas, by concatenating their output coordinates. The $\texttt{plane}$ manifold uses the cartesian product operator to combine the parametric functions x and y into a manifold of output dimension 2. It can be mathematically expressed as the function

$$\text{plane}: \mathbf{R}^2 \rightarrow \mathbf{R}^2$$

where

$$\text{plane}(x_0, x_1) = \begin{pmatrix} x_0 \\ x_1 \end{pmatrix}.$$

Similarly, the definition

```
MAN plane2 = @(x@^2,x+y);
```

produces the parametric function

$$\text{plane2}(x_0, x_1) = \begin{pmatrix} x_0{}^2 \\ x_0 + x_1 \end{pmatrix}$$

where the primitive exponentiation operator, $\texttt{@\char94}$, squares the function x_0, and the primitive addition operator, $\texttt{+}$, adds the two parametric functions x_0 and x_1.

Output coordinates can also be extracted from a parametric function with the $\texttt{[]}$ operator, which, like the addition and exponentiation operators, has been overloaded when used with the $\texttt{MAN}$ type. Thus,

```
MAN a = plane2[0];
MAN b = plane2[1];
```

defines the manifolds a and b, which extract output coordinates 0 and 1, respectively, from the manifold $\texttt{plane2}$, yielding the parametric functions

$$\begin{aligned} a(x_0) &= x_0{}^2 \\ b(x_0, x_1) &= x_0 + x_1. \end{aligned}$$

Note that coordinates are numbered starting with index 0 for the first coordinate, index 1 for the next, etc.

Another commonly used operator is the curve operator $\texttt{m\_crv}$. This operator takes a filename representing a curve file (usually produced using the curve editor program) and creates a parametric function representing the curve. Figure 3.1 illustrates an example curve file, $\texttt{example.crv}$, in the standard display format used to illustrate all curve files in this book. The code

```
MAN c = m_crv("example.crv",m_x(0));
```

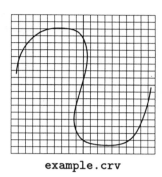

example.crv

Figure 3.1: Curve file example. An example curve file called example.crv is illustrated. The curve file contains control points that define, in this case, a B-spline curve having an "S" shape. Curve files are used in many of the shape specification examples that follow in this chapter. They are drawn, unless otherwise noted, in a 2D square having extent -1 to 1 in both the x and y dimensions. □

```
MAN c = m_crv("example.crv",m_x(0));
MAN d = m_crv("example.crv",m_x(0)@^2);
```

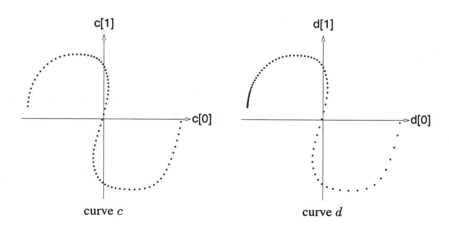

Figure 3.2: Curve manifold example. Two different manifolds, c and d, are formed in GENMOD using the same curve file, example.crv. On the left, the curve is parameterized by x_0; on the right, by x_0^2. The dots show samples on the curve along equally spaced increments of x_0, as it ranges from 0 to 1. All curves in this book are drawn with their first coordinate (coordinate 0) on the x axis, and their second (coordinate 1) on the y axis. □

forms the parametric function $c(x_0)\colon \mathbf{R}^1 \to \mathbf{R}^2$, which follows the curve shape shown in Figure 3.1 as x_0 goes from 0 to 1. A curve with the same shape, but with a different parameterization, can be created by supplying a different manifold as the second argument of m_crv. Figure 3.2 compares two curves, both using the curve file example.crv, with one parameterized by x_0 and the other by $x_0{}^2$.

3.2   Generative Surfaces

A useful class of generative shapes is the set of 3D surfaces formed by a 1-parameter transformation acting on a curve generator. The curve generator may be thought of as the "cross section" of the generative surface. This section first examines modeling with generative surfaces using simple affine transformations of the generator curve. Next, more complicated and powerful transformations are discussed.

3.2.1   Affine Cross Section Transformations

Many shapes can be modeled as a generative surface formed by an affine transformation of a single cross section. Affine transformations refer to transformations like translation, rotation, and scaling in 3D space, but will be precisely defined on page 66.

3.2.1.1   Profile Products

A profile product [BARR81] is perhaps the simplest nontrivial generative surface. It is formed by scaling and translating a 2D cross section according to a 2D profile. More precisely, a profile product surface, $S(u, v)$, is defined using a cross-section curve, $\gamma(u) = (\gamma_1(u), \gamma_2(u))$, and a profile curve, $\delta(v) = (\delta_1(v), \delta_2(v))$, where

$$S(u, v) = \begin{pmatrix} \gamma_1(u)\delta_1(v) \\ \gamma_2(u)\delta_1(v) \\ \delta_2(v) \end{pmatrix}.$$

A profile product may be defined in the GENMOD language as follows:

```
MAN m_profile(MAN cross,MAN profile)
{
     return @(cross[0]*profile[0],
              cross[1]*profile[0],
              profile[1]);
}
```

```
MAN cross = m_circle(m_x(0)*2*pi);
MAN profile = m_crv("profile.crv",m_x(1));
MAN doorknob = m_profile(cross,profile);
```

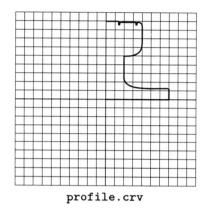
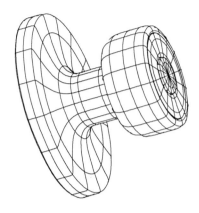

profile.crv

Figure 3.3: Doorknob example. A doorknob shape is represented by a profile surface. The cross section used is a circle; the doorknob is therefore a surface of revolution. The graph of the profile curve is plotted in a square whose extent is from -1 to 1 in x and y. □

Many shapes are conveniently represented as profile products. Cups, vases, and doorknobs, for example, are surfaces of revolution — profile products with circular cross sections. Figure 3.3 shows an example of a profile product doorknob. Profile products need not be surfaces of revolution. Figure 3.4 shows how a profile product can represent a polyhedron, in this case, a patio tile. Figure 3.5 presents an example of a profile product surface for a lamp stand shape.

Although profile products can represent a variety of shapes, they are more limited than one might expect. If the cross section is not *star-shaped* (not single-valued in polar coordinates), then the profile product surface may self-intersect.[1] This is because smaller scales of the cross section do not remain in its interior. A different technique must therefore be used to sweep non-star-shaped cross sections. Profile products also have the undesirable property that points on the cross section move outwards at a rate proportional to their original distance from the origin and along rays from the origin. A technique for sweeping cross sections so that each point on the cross section moves outwards at the same rate and in a direction normal to the cross section will be discussed in the section on offset products on page 80.

---

[1] Problems also occur if the profile curve self-intersects or crosses the y axis.

```
MAN cross = m_crv("cross.crv",m_x(0));
MAN profile = m_crv("profile.crv",m_x(1));
MAN block = m_profile(cross,profile);
```

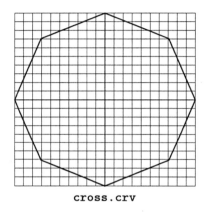
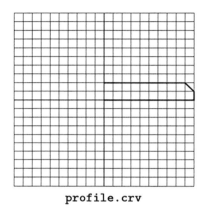

cross.crv   profile.crv

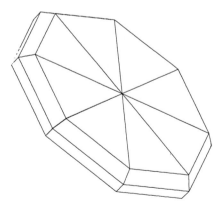

Figure 3.4: Patio tile example. A patio tile shape is represented by a profile surface. In this case, the two curves used in the profile product are composed of straight line segments. The resulting shape is therefore a polyhedron. □

```
MAN cross = m_crv("cross.crv",m_x(0));
MAN profile = m_crv("profile.crv",m_x(1));
MAN lampstand = m_profile(cross,profile);
```

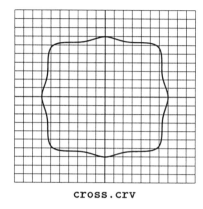

cross.crv

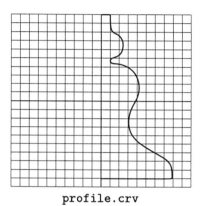

profile.crv

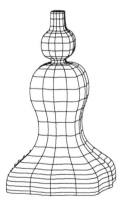

Figure 3.5: Lamp stand example. A lamp stand shape is represented by a profile surface. The GENMOD definition of a lamp stand is shown, followed by graphs of the two curves used in the definition, and a solid shaded image of the shape. □

3.2.1.2 Wire Products

A wire product is formed by translating a 2D cross-section curve along a 2D wire curve, so that the cross section remains perpendicular to the wire. Let $\gamma(u)$ be a cross-section curve, and $\delta(v)$ be a wire curve. The normalized tangent vector, t, of δ is given by

$$\tilde{t}(v) = \frac{d\delta}{dv}$$

$$t(v) = \frac{\tilde{t}}{\|\tilde{t}\|}.$$

A normal vector to the wire curve, n, may be defined by

$$n(v) = \begin{pmatrix} -t_2(v) \\ t_1(v) \end{pmatrix}.$$

The wire product surface, $S(u,v)$, may then be defined by sweeping the cross section so that its x axis aligns with n, its y axis aligns with the z axis of the wire, and its origin moves onto the wire:

$$S(u,v) = \begin{pmatrix} n_1\gamma_1 + \delta_1 \\ n_2\gamma_1 + \delta_2 \\ \gamma_2 \end{pmatrix}.$$

A wire product may be defined in the GENMOD language as follows:

```
MAN m_wire(MAN cross,MAN wire)
{
        MAN that = m_derivative(wire,wire->input_list[0]);
        MAN t = m_normalize(that);
        MAN n = @(-t[1],t[0]);
        return @(n*cross[0] + wire, cross[1]);
}
```

Here, the m_derivative operator produces the derivative of the wire curve wire with respect to its first parametric coordinate, which is stored in wire->input_list[0] (see Section A.2). The m_normalize operator divides that by its length, resulting in the normalized tangent vector $t(v)$.

Like profile products, wire products are a quite general meta-shape. Figure 3.6 shows an example of a wire product surface representing a tennis racket head frame. Wire products self-intersect if the wire curve's radius of curvature is too small in relation to the size of the cross section.

```
MAN cross = m_crv("cross.crv",m_x(0));
MAN wire = m_crv("wire.crv",m_x(1));
MAN racket_frame = m_wire(cross,wire);
```

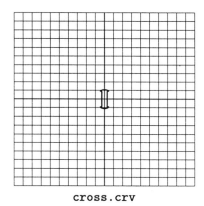

cross.crv

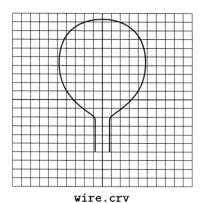

wire.crv

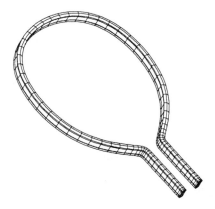

Figure 3.6: Tennis racket example. A tennis racket head frame is represented by a wire product surface. The graphs of the cross section and wire curves are both plotted in a square whose extent is from −1 to 1 in x and y. The cross section cross.crv has been scaled by a factor of three for display purposes. □

3.2.1.3   Rail Products

A rail product is formed by sweeping a 2D cross section so that it falls between two 2D rail curves. Let $\gamma(u)$ be the cross-section curve, and $\delta^1(v)$ and $\delta^2(v)$ be the two rail curves. The orientation vector, t, between the two rail curves is

$$t(v) = \begin{pmatrix} t_1 \\ t_2 \end{pmatrix} = \delta^2 - \delta^1.$$

The rail product surface, $S(u, v)$, may then be defined by sweeping the cross section so that its x axis aligns with t (note that this involves a scale by the length of the orientation vector), its y axis aligns with the z axis of the rail, and its origin moves onto the midpoint of the two rail curves, m, where

$$m = \frac{\delta^1 + \delta^2}{2}.$$

We then have

$$S(u, v) = \begin{pmatrix} t_1 \gamma_1 / 2 + m_1 \\ t_2 \gamma_1 / 2 + m_2 \\ \gamma_2 \end{pmatrix}.$$

If the first coordinate of γ is in the range $[-1, 1]$, then the resulting rail product surface falls between the two rail curves.

A rail product may be defined in the GENMOD language as follows:

```
MAN m_rail(MAN cross,MAN rail1,MAN rail2)
{
        MAN t = rail2 - rail1;
        MAN m = 0.5*(rail1 + rail2);
        return @(0.5*t*cross[0] + m, cross[1]);
}
```

Figure 3.7 shows an example of a rail product surface representing a briefcase handle.

Note that the parameterizations, not just the shapes, of the two rail curves in a rail product are important. A particular cross section in a rail product surface is determined by a point on each of the two rail curves. Therefore the way points on the two rail curves are matched affects the shape of the resulting surface. The section on matching parameter schedules (Section 3.2.4.1) discusses techniques for matching parameterizations.

3.2.1.4   General Affine Transformations

The ideas of the previous sections can be simply generalized with an affine transformation. Affine transformations can combine sweep techniques including scaling, translating, twisting, and skewing. They can be used to move a cross section

```
MAN cross = m_crv("cross.crv",m_x(0));
MAN rail1 = m_crv("rail1.crv",m_x(1));
MAN rail2 = m_crv("rail2.crv",m_x(1));
MAN handle = m_rail(cross,rail1,rail2);
```

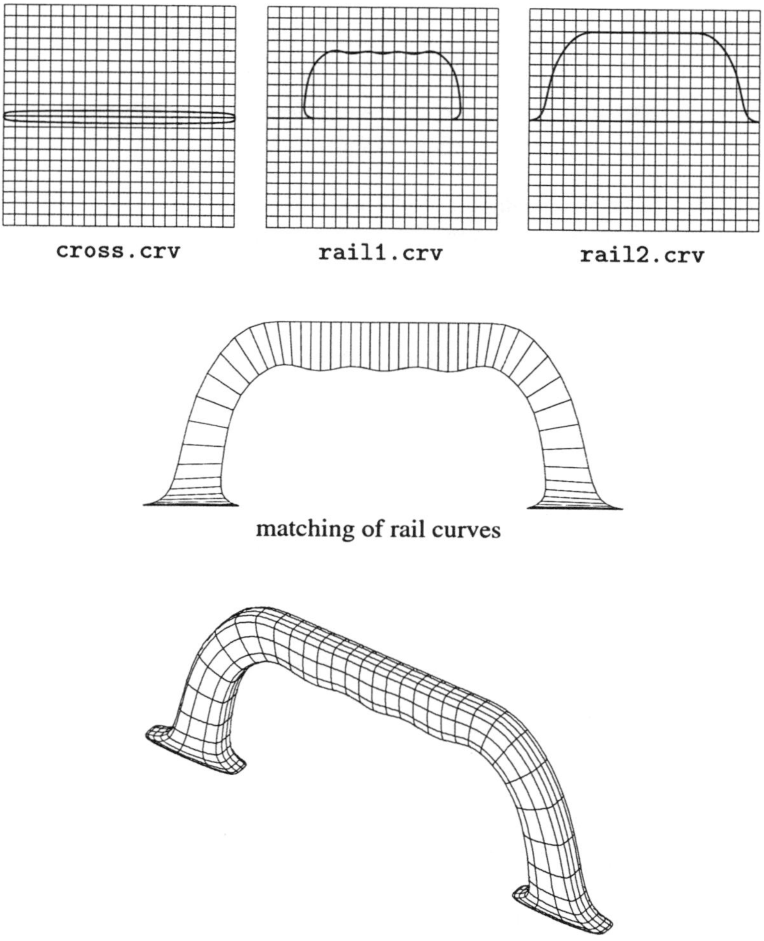

cross.crv   rail1.crv   rail2.crv

matching of rail curves

Figure 3.7: Briefcase handle example. A briefcase handle shape is represented by a rail product surface. The middle figure shows how the parameterizations of the two rail curves match up. □

along a given space curve while maintaining perpendicularity of cross section to space curve. They can be used to specify profile products, wire products, and rail products discussed previously,

An affine transformation shape uses a 2D or 3D curve generator and a transformation represented by a linear transformation and a translation. Let $\gamma(u)$ be a 3D curve. Let $M(v)$ be a linear transformation on 3D space, and let $T(v)$ be a 3D curve. An affine transformation surface, $S(u, v)$, is given by

$$S(u, v) = M(v)\gamma(u) + T(v).$$

Figure 3.8 presents an example of an affine transformation that represents a banana surface. Figure 3.9 presents an example of an affine transformation representing a turbine blade.

One method of representing affine transformations is to use 4×4 matrices. This is the same technique used in computer graphics, called *homogeneous transformations*, to represent 3D transformations including translation and perspective. The 4×4 matrix is defined with M as the upper 3×3 part of the matrix, T as the fourth column of the matrix, and the fourth row the same as in the identity matrix. A 3D point is transformed by appending a fourth vector element equal to 1, postmultiplying it as a column vector with the 4×4 transformation matrix, and eliminating the fourth coordinate, which is always equal to 1. Mathematically, the affine transformation is expressed as

$$\begin{pmatrix} S_1 \\ S_2 \\ S_3 \\ 1 \end{pmatrix} = \begin{pmatrix} & M & & T \\ 0 & 0 & 0 & 1 \end{pmatrix} \begin{pmatrix} \gamma_1 \\ \gamma_2 \\ \gamma_3 \\ 1 \end{pmatrix}.$$

The advantage of this representation is that it allows affine transformations to be composed using the matrix multiply operator.

Using this technique, we can define an affine transformation in the GENMOD language as follows:

```
MAN m_transform3d(MAN cross,MAN_MATRIX m)
{
    MAN_MATRIX S = m*m_matrix(@(cross,1),4,1);
    return @(S.m[0], S.m[1], S.m[2]);
}
```

The MAN_MATRIX type is a parametric function representing a matrix. It is identical to the type MAN except that the matrix size (number of rows and columns) is also stored (see Section A.2). The m_matrix operator forms a 4×1 matrix from the

```
MAN u = m_x(0);
MAN v = m_x(1);
MAN cross = m_crv("bancross.crv",u);
MAN scale = m_crv("banscale.crv",v)[1];
MAN banana = m_transform3d(@(cross,0),
    m_roty(m_interp(v,0.0,-0.4*pi)) *
    m_transz(m_interp(v,-1,1)) *
    m_scalex(scale) * m_scaley(scale)
);
```

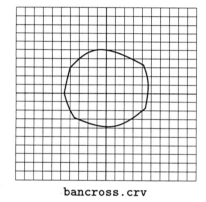
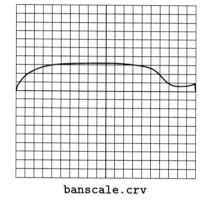

bancross.crv   banscale.crv

Figure 3.8: Banana example. A banana is represented by an affine transformation surface. The cross section is scaled, translated along z from -1 to 1, and rotated around the y axis.
□

```
MAN u = m_x(0);
MAN v = m_x(1);
MAN cross = m_crv("bladecross.crv",u);
MAN blade = m_transform3d(@(cross,0),
    m_transz(m_interp(v,-1,1)) *
    m_transx(-0.5) *
    m_rotz(pi*m_crv("bladerot.crv",v)[1]) *
    m_transx(0.5) *
    m_scalex(m_crv("bladexscl.crv",v)[1]) *
    m_scaley(m_crv("bladeyscl.crv",v)[1]) *
);
```

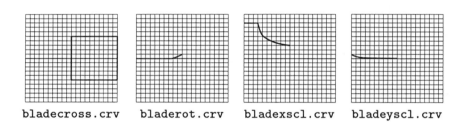

bladecross.crv   bladerot.crv   bladexscl.crv   bladeyscl.crv

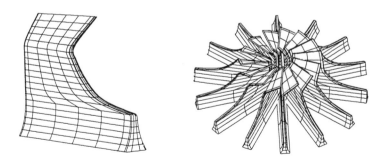

Figure 3.9: Turbine blade example. A turbine blade-like surface is represented by an affine transformation surface. The cross section is scaled separately in x and y, translated in x, rotated around z, translated back in x, and extruded along the z axis. □

cross section to be transformed, cross, corresponding to the vector

$$\begin{pmatrix} \gamma_1 \\ \gamma_2 \\ \gamma_3 \\ 1 \end{pmatrix}$$

in the above equation. The * operator is overloaded to perform matrix multiplication with arguments of type MAN_MATRIX. It is used to produce the affine transformation surface by multiplying the 4×4 matrix m with a 4×1 matrix, resulting in the 4×1 matrix S. The final result is the first three components of S.

The operators used in the two examples, such as m_transz, m_roty, and m_scalex, form various types of affine transformations representing translation in z, rotation around y, and scaling about x, respectively. They are completely defined in Section A.5.1. Each produces a result of type MAN_MATRIX. Note that because the matrix transforms the cross section by premultiplying it, the transformations in Figures 3.8 and 3.9 must occur in reverse order (i.e., transformations that affect the cross section first must appear last in the sequence of multiplied transformations).

3.2.2   Non-Affine Cross Section Transformations

Although an affine transformation of a cross section is quite useful as a modeling primitive, it is too inflexible to represent many common shapes. This section presents some sweep techniques that involve non-affine transformations; that is, transformations that cannot be expressed as an affine transformation of a single cross section.

3.2.2.1   Interpolating Cross Sections

Many times we want a cross section to change as it is swept in a generative surface. One of the simplest ways to specify this change is to specify two or more cross sections and interpolate between them [BINF71]. This interpolation can be a straightforward linear interpolation or a higher-order interpolation. For example, hermite interpolation, where tangent vectors as well as points are interpolated, is often useful in yielding a smooth interpolation between cross sections.

Linear Interpolation

Let γ_1 and γ_2 be two points, and let α be a scalar between 0 and 1. A linear interpolation of these points, linear_interp($\alpha, \gamma_1, \gamma_2$), is given by

$$\text{linear\_interp}(\alpha, \gamma_1, \gamma_2) = \gamma_1 + \alpha(\gamma_2 - \gamma_1).$$

When α is 0, linear_interp is equal to γ_1. When α is 1, linear_interp is equal to γ_2. For α values between 0 and 1, linear_interp yields a point on the line segment joining γ_1 and γ_2.

The linear interpolation operator can be applied to curves as well as points. For example, we can define a linearly interpolated cross section using two curves and an interpolation scalar. Let $\gamma_1(u)$ and $\gamma_2(u)$ be the two cross-section curves, and let $\alpha(v)$ be a scalar function that varies from 0 to 1. A linear interpolation of these cross sections, $R(u, v)$, is defined by

$$R(u, v) = \text{linear\_interp}(\alpha(v), \gamma_1(u), \gamma_2(u)).$$

When $\alpha(v)$ is 0, R is equal to the first cross section. When $\alpha(v)$ is 1, R is equal to the second cross section. For $\alpha(v)$ values between 0 and 1, R is an interpolated cross section such that each point moves on a line joining the corresponding points of the two cross sections.

It is often convenient to use a curve to specify the interpolation function, α, thus relating the interpolation to other sweep parameters. For example, Figure 3.10 shows a gear with a round hole that is formed using linear interpolation. The cross section in this example is a linear interpolation between a gear-shaped curve and a circle. An interpolation curve is used to relate the extrusion of the cross section out of its plane to the amount of interpolation. Plate 7 is a more complicated example, which uses linear interpolation to change the cross section of a steering arm from a circle to an ellipse, and then to an ellipse with a flared rectangular projection.

Hermite Interpolation

Hermite interpolation is an interpolation in which the ending tangent vectors, as well as the ending positions, are specified. Let p^1 and p^2 be two points in $\mathbf{R}^n$, t^1 and t^2 be two vectors of the same dimension, and α be a scalar between 0 and 1. The hermite interpolation, $H(\alpha) \colon \mathbf{R} \to \mathbf{R}^n$, of these points and vectors satisfies

$$\begin{aligned} H(0) &= p^1 \\ H(1) &= p^2 \\ \frac{dH}{d\alpha}(0) &= t^1 \\ \frac{dH}{d\alpha}(1) &= t^2. \end{aligned}$$

A cubic polynomial is the lowest degree polynomial for which these constraints can be satisfied. Letting $H(\alpha)$ be a cubic polynomial in α, we have

$$H(\alpha) = a\alpha^3 + b\alpha^2 + c\alpha^1 + d,$$

```
MAN u = m_x(0);
MAN v = m_x(1);
MAN cross1 = m_crv("cross.crv",u);
MAN cross2 = m_normalize(cross1)*0.25;
MAN interp = m_crv("interp.crv",v);
MAN gear = @(m_interp(interp[1],cross1,cross2),interp[0]);
```

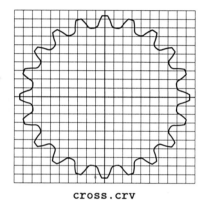

cross.crv

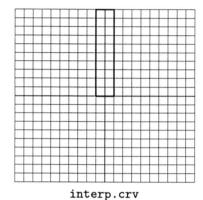

interp.crv

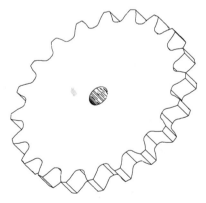

Figure 3.10: Gear example. A gear with a round hole is represented as a linear interpolation of a gear-shaped cross section and a circular cross section. The curve interp.crv relates, on its y axis, the interpolation between a circle of radius 0.25 and the gear-shaped curve cross.crv to form the cross section and, on its x axis, the extrusion of this cross section.
□

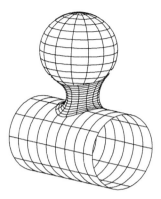

Figure 3.11: Sphere/cylinder fillet using hermite interpolation. A cylindrical fillet between a cylinder and sphere can be accomplished using hermite interpolation. The GENMOD code for this example is given in Section B.1. $\Box$

where $a, b, c, d \in \mathbf{R}^n$. Solving for a, b, c, and d in the above constraints yields

$$
\begin{aligned}
a &= t^2 + t^1 + 2(p^1 - p^2) \\
b &= 3(p^2 - p^1) - 2t^1 - t^2 \\
c &= t^1 \\
d &= p^1.
\end{aligned}
$$

We can now define a hermite interpolation operator as

$$\text{hermite\_interp}(\alpha, p^1, p^2, t^1, t^2) = a\alpha^3 + b\alpha^2 + c\alpha + d,$$

where a, b, c and d are defined as before.

As in the case of linear interpolation, the hermite interpolation operator can be applied to curves as well as points. In other words, the arguments to hermite_interp can be functions of a parameter instead of constants. In this case, we can use hermite interpolation to define a surface that interpolates between two curves with specified tangents on these curves. This is useful in defining a fillet surface between two surfaces.

For example, Figure 3.11 shows a fillet between a cylinder and a sphere that was specified using hermite interpolation. The two curves being interpolated are the curves of intersection of a fillet cylinder with the sphere, S, and cylinder, C. Let these intersection curves be parameterized by $c_C(u)$ and $c_S(u)$, respectively. To maintain the fillet's smoothness, the direction of the fillet's normal vector must equal that of S and C where it intersects these surfaces. Let the unit normal vectors on S and C at each point on the curves of intersection be given by $n_C(u)$ and $n_S(u)$, and let $F(u, v)$ be the fillet surface. Constraining the fillet surface to be on the two surfaces being filleted yields the equations

$$
\begin{aligned}
F(u, 0) &= c_C(u) \\
F(u, 1) &= c_S(u).
\end{aligned}
$$

Constraining the fillet surface normal to have the same direction as the normals on the two intersection curves yields the equations

$$
\begin{aligned}
\frac{\partial F(u, v)}{\partial u}(u, 0) \times \frac{\partial F(u, v)}{\partial v}(u, 0) &= \lambda n_C(u) \\
\frac{\partial F(u, v)}{\partial u}(u, 1) \times \frac{\partial F(u, v)}{\partial v}(u, 1) &= \kappa n_S(u)
\end{aligned}
$$

for arbitrary scalars λ and κ.

For the hermite interpolation surface $F(u, v)$ defined as

$$F(u, v) = \text{hermite\_interp}(v, c_C(u), c_S(u), t_C(u), t_S(u)),$$

we therefore have

$$
\begin{aligned}
\frac{\partial F(u, v)}{\partial u}(u, 0) &= \frac{dc_C(u)}{du}(u) \\
\frac{\partial F(u, v)}{\partial u}(u, 1) &= \frac{dc_S(u)}{du}(u) \\
\frac{\partial F(u, v)}{\partial v}(u, 0) &= t_C(u) \\
\frac{\partial F(u, v)}{\partial v}(u, 1) &= t_S(u).
\end{aligned}
$$

Thus the constraints can be solved by setting the tangent vectors $t_C(u)$ and $t_S(u)$ to the following:

$$
\begin{aligned}
t_C(u) &= \eta n_C(u) \times \frac{dc_C(u)}{du} \\
t_S(u) &= \nu n_S(u) \times \frac{dc_S(u)}{du}
\end{aligned}
$$

for arbitrary scalars η and ν. The choice of η and ν control how much the fillet bends inward near the intersection of the fillet with the cylinder and sphere, respectively. They may be thought of as indirect controls over the fillet "radius." It is even possible to specify η and ν as functions of u.

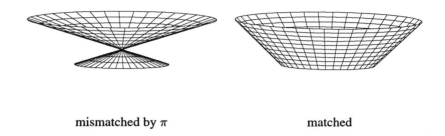

mismatched by π matched

Figure 3.12: Mismatching cross section problem. Two circles, of radius 1 and 2, are interpolated to form a cone. On the left, the circles are parameterized so that one is π radians out of phase with the other, causing a singularity. On the right, the circles are parameterized in the same way, forming the desired cone whose radius linearly changes from 1 to 2. The example illustrates that the parameterizations as well as the shapes of the cross sections are important when these cross sections are interpolated. □

Matching Interpolated Cross Sections

A significant problem involved in defining surfaces by interpolating cross-section curves is that the cross sections can be mismatched. This problem is similar to *inbetweening* in computer animation — the automatic generation of many interpolatory points or curves between a small specified (or *keyframed*) set (see for example [BART89]). Consider defining a conical segment by interpolating between two circles, one of radius 1 and the other of radius 2. Let the two circles be given by two parametric functions from $\mathbf{R}$ to $\mathbf{R}^2$, $c(u)$ and $d(u)$, respectively. Simply interpolating $c(u)$ and $d(u)$ as a function of v yields the surface

$$S(u, v) = \begin{pmatrix} c_1(u)(1 - v) + d_1(u)v \\ c_2(u)(1 - v) + d_2(u)v \\ v \end{pmatrix}.$$

$S(u, v)$ is not necessarily a cone along the z axis whose radius varies linearly from 1 to 2 as a function of z. For example, if the circles c and d are parameterized by polar angle, but c starts at $\theta = 0$, while d starts at $\theta = \pi$, then a cone with a singularity at $z = 1/3$ will result, since points on the circle c are matched to points on the opposite side of the circle d. Figure 3.12 illustrates this problem.

Typically, we would like to parameterize the cross-section curves to be interpolated so that the projection of the first two parametric coordinates of S forms an invertible map from $(u, v) \in [0, 1) \times [0, 1]$ to the 2D region contained between the

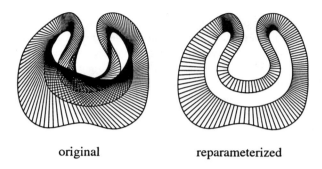

original   reparameterized

Figure 3.13: Reparameterizing cross sections based on minimum distance. Two closed cross sections are linearly interpolated. On the left, the curves are interpolated without reparameterization. On the right, the inner curve is reparameterized so that each point on it is matched to the nearest point on the outer curve. The linear segments show the matching of points on the two curves. Note that reparameterization is necessary to ensure that the interpolated cross section falls in the region between the two cross sections. □

two curves.[2] While this is a hard problem in general, it can be handled in several ways:

- by ad hoc control point matching

- by reparameterizing based on polar angle for star-shaped cross sections

- by reparameterizing based on minimum distance

- by a PDE-solving technique described in [THOM85]

The first technique gives the modeler the responsibility of specifying matched cross-section curves. This is often very inconvenient. If the cross sections are star-shaped, then one can be reparameterized to match the polar angle of the other, using the inversion operator of Section 2.2.3. Alternatively, the first cross section can be reparameterized so that each point is matched to a point on the second cross section closest to it, using the constrained minimization operator, as shown in Figure 3.13. Although this technique does not work in every situation, it is useful if the two curves to be interpolated are similar.

The PDE-solution technique is a very robust, computationally expensive method. It has not yet been implemented in the GENMOD system, but points out the need for a PDE-solution operator as a primitive in the system.

---

[2]Because the cross sections are closed, the map is necessarily not invertible everywhere because $S(0, v) = S(1, v)$ for all v. Thus, we restrict the u interval to $[0, 1)$ rather than $[0, 1]$.

3.2.2.2   Cross Section Offsetting

The offset to a smooth[3] planar curve is the curve formed by moving each point on
the original curve a given distance along the curve normal. Alternatively, a curve
offset may be viewed as the envelope of centers of circles of a given radius tangent
to the curve. Two distinct offset curves may be defined for a given planar curve
corresponding to the choice of normal vector (e.g., a non-self-intersecting closed
curve has an inside offset and an outside offset). Figure 3.14 illustrates offsets of
planar curves.

Let $\gamma(u)$ be a 2D curve. Let $n(u)$ be the unit normal of γ:

$$\tilde{n}(u) = \left(\begin{array}{c} -\dfrac{d\gamma_2}{du} \\ \dfrac{d\gamma_1}{du} \end{array} \right)$$

$$n(u) = \frac{\tilde{n}}{\|\tilde{n}\|}.$$

In this case, n points outward from a closed, non self-intersecting curve if the curve
is traversed counterclockwise.

The unit normal to a given 2D curve can be defined in GENMOD as follows:

```
MAN m_normal2d(MAN curve)
{
        int parm = curve->input_list[0];
        MAN d = m_normalize(m_derivative(curve,parm));
        return @(-d[1],d[0]);
}
```

The offset of radius r of γ, offset(γ, r), is an operator that takes as input a 2D
curve γ, and a radius r, and yields a 2D curve. It is defined by

$$\text{offset}(\gamma, r) = \gamma + rn.$$

In GENMOD, this offset operator can be defined as

```
MAN m_offset(MAN curve,MAN r)
{
        MAN n = m_normal2d(curve);
        return curve + r*n;
}
```

The m_offset operator was used to create the offset curves in Figure 3.14.

The next two sections show examples of the use of curve offsetting in modeling.

---

[3] *Smooth* means that a well-defined, nonvanishing tangent vector exists at each point on the curve.

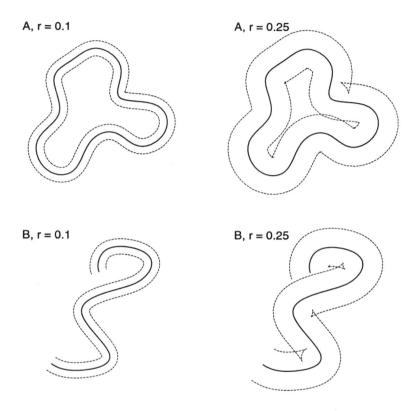

Figure 3.14: Planar curve offsets. Two smooth curves, A and B, are offset with offset radii equal to 0.1 and 0.25. Each curve has two offsets of a given radius, corresponding to the choice of normal vector. Curve A, for example, has an offset corresponding to the inward and outward pointing normals. Note that the offset curves self-intersect and cease to be smooth when the radius of the offset becomes larger than the radius of curvature of the curve, for positive radius of curvature. □

Offset Products

Offset products are similar to profile products presented in Section 3.2.1.1. In an offset product, a closed cross-section curve is changed by offsetting rather than scaling about the origin as in a profile product.

An offset product surface, $S(u, v)$, is formed given a cross-section curve, $\gamma(u)$, and a profile curve, $\delta(v)$. The profile curve relates the radius of offset, r, with the translation of the cross section normal to its plane. Let n be the unit normal to the cross-section curve γ. $S(u, v)$ is defined by

$$S(u, v) = \begin{pmatrix} \gamma_1(u) + \delta_1(v)n_1(u) \\ \gamma_2(u) + \delta_1(v)n_2(u) \\ \delta_2(v) \end{pmatrix}.$$

An offset product may be defined in the GENMOD language as follows:

```
MAN m_offset_prod(MAN cross,MAN prof)
{
    MAN n = m_normal2d(cross);
    return @(cross[0] + prof[0]*n[0],
             cross[1] + prof[0]*n[1],
             prof[1]);
}
```

Offset products are convenient for defining extruded surfaces with rounded corners. Figure 3.15 shows an example of an offset surface that represents a thin plate with semicircular cuts and rounded corners.

Cross Section Formation Using Offsetting

Curve offsetting can also be used to define a cross section with a given thickness that surrounds a given non-closed curve (see Figure 3.16). The resulting cross section is composed of four segments: two offsets of a given radius (using the curve normal of both senses) and two semicircular arcs around the endpoints of the curve. Under certain conditions,[4] the resulting curve is the boundary of the set of points whose distance from the curve does not exceed some constant. This constant is equal to the radius of the offset. Section A.4.4 defines an operator, m_closed_offset, that forms the closed offset to a given planar curve.

Figure 3.17 shows a spoon whose cross section was formed using this technique. In this case, the curve that was offset was a circular arc whose endpoints and radius are varied.

---

[4] The radius of the offset must not exceed the absolute value of the radius of curvature of the original curve.

```
MAN cross = m_crv("cross.crv",m_x(0));
MAN profile = m_crv("profile.crv",m_x(1));
MAN plate = m_offset_prod(cross,profile);
```

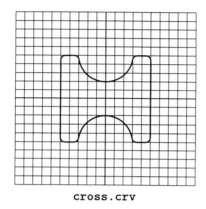

cross.crv

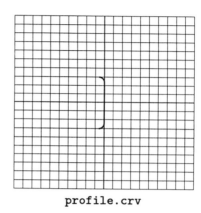

profile.crv

Figure 3.15: Offset product example. A thin plate with semicircular notches is formed using an offset product. The GENMOD definition is actually for the surface forming the sides of plate; the top and bottom are created by drawing two regions bounded by the cross-section curve. The profile curve has been scaled by a factor of three for display purposes.
□

Figure 3.16: Defining a cross section using offsets and circular end caps. A closed cross section may be defined in terms of a non-closed curve by concatenating two offset curves and two circular end caps. □

3.2.2.3 Cross Section Deformations

Deformations such as warps, bends, and tapers are useful in defining shapes. They are particularly powerful when deformation parameters (such as the amount of bending) are allowed to vary as the cross section is swept. For example, consider a parabolic warping of the z coordinate of a cross section as a function of the x coordinate. This deformation may be defined as

$$\text{warp}(a,b)(\begin{pmatrix} x \\ y \\ z \end{pmatrix}) = \begin{pmatrix} x \\ y \\ z + ax^2 + b \end{pmatrix}.$$

The amount of warping is controlled by the parameters a and b, which define a parabola. This warp deformation can be defined in the GENMOD language as follows:

```
MAN m_warp_z_by_x(MAN cross,MAN a,MAN b)
{
    MAN x = cross[0];
    MAN y = cross[1];
    MAN z = cross[2];
    return @(x,y,z + a*x@^2 + b);
}
```

Figure 3.18 illustrates the use of this warping deformation to define a key shape from a computer keyboard.

```
MAN u = m_x(0), v = m_x(1);
MAN shape = m_crv("shape.crv",v);
MAN bowl = m_crv("bowl.crv",v);
MAN bend = m_crv("bend.crv",v);
MAN p1 = @(-shape[1],0);
MAN p2 = @(shape[1],0);
MAN arc = m_arc_2pt_height(p1,p2,bowl[1],u);
MAN carc = m_closed_offset(arc,0.01);
MAN spoon = @(shape[0],carc[0],carc[1] + bend[1]);
```

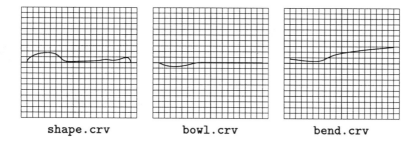

shape.crv   bowl.crv   bend.crv

Figure 3.17: Spoon example. A spoon surface is formed using a cross section formed by the closed offset of an arc. A closed offset with circular end caps gives the spoon its thickness. The curve that is offset is deformed as it is extruded — its radius is increased to give the spoon its bowl, and its length is changed to shape the width of the spoon. The operator m_arc_2pt_height, which is defined in Section A.5.2, forms a circular arc connecting two points having a specified height above their line of connection. □

```
MAN u = m_x(0), v = m_x(1);
MAN cross = m_crv("cross.crv",u);
MAN yz_l = m_crv("yz_left.crv",v);
MAN yz_r = m_crv("yz_right.crv",v);
MAN xz = m_crv("xz.crv",v);

MAN cross_sides = (cross + @(MAN)(1,1)) * 0.5;

MAN warp_scale = 0.2, warp_offset = -0.05;
MAN _sides = @(m_interp(cross_sides[0],-xz[0],xz[0]),
               m_interp(cross_sides[1],yz_l,yz_r));
MAN sides = m_warp_z_by_x(_sides,warp_scale*v,warp_offset*v);
```

| cross.crv | xz.crv | yz_left.crv | yz_right.crv |

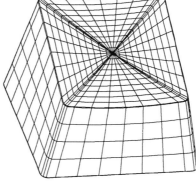

Figure 3.18: Key example. A key shape from a computer keyboard is represented by deforming a rounded-square cross section. This cross section is transformed so that it lies between specified curves in the yz and xz planes. The cross section is also deformed using a parabolic warping deformation that causes the top of the key to curve as a function of x. The amount of this warping increases towards the top of the key: at the bottom there is no warping, and at the top there is maximum warping. The GENMOD definition of the sides of the key is shown; the key top can be defined by scaling the cross section to a point and applying the same warping deformation. □

3.2.3 Boolean Operations on Planar Cross Sections

Constructive planar geometry (CPG) is the analog of constructive solid geometry for 2D areas. It is a modeling operation that uses Boolean set operations on closed planar areas to produce new planar areas. Figure 3.19 shows some examples of CPG operations.

CPG is simpler to reason about than CSG because the set operations take place in a lower-dimensional space, on lower-dimensional entities. It is also less costly to compute than CSG operations. Yet CPG can be an extremely useful modeling paradigm. For example, many objects can be represented as surfaces where each cross section is a Boolean set subtraction of one closed area from another. The fact that the two planar areas may be swept according to different schedules before being subtracted makes the operation more powerful. Figure 3.20 shows two screwdriver blade tips specified using CPG. The Phillips blade, for example, is specified by sweeping a circle with a varying radius, from which is subtracted a notch of varying size. The GENMOD code for both examples is given in Section B.2.

CPG operations in the generative modeling approach are handled most easily when the resulting planar area is connected, so that a single parametric curve describes its boundary.[5] In this case, computing CPG operations may be accomplished by finding intersections between planar curves that bound the planar areas. These intersections separate the boundary curves into a number of segments. The boundary of the resulting planar area may then be found by concatenating an appropriate set of these segments.

Often, the intersections between boundary curves can be computed analytically. Consider regions whose boundary is represented as a piecewise series of line segments. Intersections between such regions can be computed by solving for intersections between line segments, which can be done analytically. When intersections cannot be analytically computed, the constraint solution operator can be used.[6] The resulting segments can then be combined by concatenation, as described starting on page 37.

3.2.3.1 CPG with Filleting

The CPG operations described previously result in cross sections that are not smooth, even if the planar regions operated on have smooth boundaries. Smooth-

---

[5]Note that this is not always the case: the union of two disjoint closed areas is an obvious exception. If the result of the CPG operation is not connected, its boundary is described by a collection of parametric curves.

[6]The intersections of two planar curves, $\gamma_1(u_1)$ and $\gamma_2(u_2)$, are found by solving $\gamma_1(u_1) = \gamma_2(u_2)$. The constraint solution operator should be applied to this system of two equations (for equality of the first and second coordinates of the two curves) and two variables (u_1 and u_2).

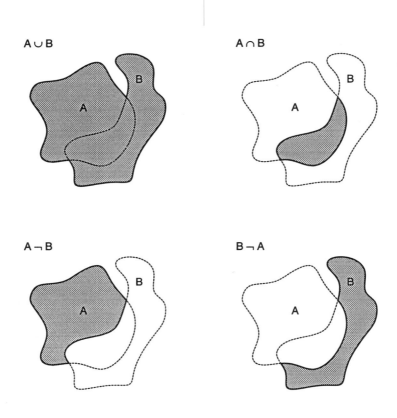

Figure 3.19: Constructive planar geometry. Two planar regions, A and B, are used in four binary CPG operations. The top left figure is the union of the two regions, the top right is the intersection, the bottom left is the subtraction of B from A, and the bottom right is the subtraction of A from B. The boundary curves of the regions are naturally separated into four segments: the boundary of A inside B, the boundary of A outside B, the boundary of B inside A, and the boundary of B outside A. The boundary of the result of each CPG operation is formed by the concatenation of two of these boundary segments. We can compute the boundary of the result of a CPG operation by computing the intersections of the boundaries of the regions, dividing the boundaries into segments at these intersections, and concatenating appropriate segments. □

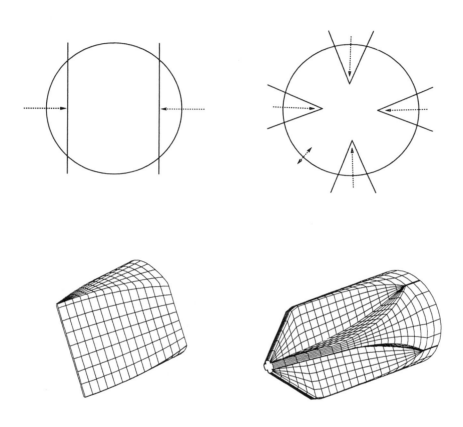

Figure 3.20: Screwdriver example. The tips of two screwdriver blades are constructed using CPG. The regular screwdriver on the left is generated using a cross section formed by subtracting two half-plane regions from a circle. The two half-planes are gradually moved toward each other as the cross section is translated to the tip of the screwdriver. The circle from which the half-planes are subtracted remains constant. The Phillips screwdriver on the right has a cross section formed by subtracting four wedge-shaped regions from a circle. In this case, the wedge-shaped regions are moved toward the circle's center as the cross section is translated to the tip of the screwdriver. The circle from which the wedges are subtracted is scaled down near the tip to yield a pointed blade. The GENMOD code for both examples is given in Section B.2. □

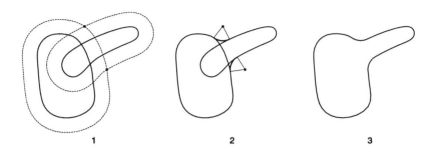

Figure 3.21: CPG with filleting. CPG operations can be done with filleting to produce
smooth boundary curves. In this example, we wish to compute a smooth curve that bounds
the union of two planar regions. To do this, we first compute the intersections of the offsets
of the two curves (step 1). The radius of the offset controls how large a fillet will be used.
Next, we compute circular arcs whose centers lie on the intersections of the offset curves
(step 2). Each arc endpoint lies on a point on a boundary curve that corresponds to the
intersection point on its offset curve. Finally, we concatenate the curve boundary segments
and fillet arcs together to produce a filleted curve (step 3). □

ness is not maintained whenever a transition occurs between region boundaries;
that is, at points of intersection between region boundaries. To maintain smoothness, we can add *fillets* to the boundary — small segments, such as circular arcs,
that allow a smooth transition from one boundary to another. Figure 3.21 shows
how this can be accomplished.

3.2.4   Parameterizing Cross Sections

Up to now, we have discussed surfaces formed by simple operations on a cross section, including affine transformations, interpolation, offsets, warps, and Boolean
operations. The generative modeling operators allow a much greater range of operations than these. The idea of parameterized cross sections is a useful way of
conceptualizing surface shape that takes advantage of the full power of the generative modeling approach.

The modeler designs a cross-section curve, γ, given by

$$\gamma(u, x_1, x_2, \ldots, x_n)\colon \mathbf{R}^{n+1} \to \mathbf{R}^3.$$

The curve γ is parameterized by u and n additional parameters that affect its shape.

A simple example is a circle, parameterized by radius, r,

$$\gamma(u,r) = \begin{pmatrix} r\cos(u) \\ r\sin(u) \end{pmatrix}.$$

Of course, the modeler is free to design quite arbitrary cross sections with many parameters, which can control the shape in convenient ways. A surface can then be formed using this parameterized cross section by letting the parameters $x_1, \ldots, x_n$ become functions of a single parameter, v, yielding the surface

$$S(u,v) = \gamma(u, f_1(v), \ldots, f_n(v)).$$

Figure 3.22 illustrates an example of a shape formed in this way. In this case, a bottle is constructed using a cross section shaped like the top half of a square rotated 45 degrees. At three points on the cross section, the curve is rounded out. The curve is parameterized in terms of the radius of these rounds. Another curve is then used to relate this radius with other parameters of the cross section, including its scale, translation out of its plane, and warping out of its plane. Plate 4 shows a solid shaded image of the bottle shape.

3.2.4.1   Matching Parameter Schedules

The most difficult part of representing surfaces using parameterized cross sections is choosing the functions f_i that relate cross-section parameters to the single surface parameter v. As an example, consider a cross section parameterized by three variables: x_1, which controls the translation of the cross section in z, and x_2 and x_3, which control some specialized properties of the cross section (e.g., the radius of a circle). The surface is formed by simultaneously changing these variables as a function of v.

Assuming the variables x_2 and x_3 have a functional relationship with x_1, one method of accomplishing this is to let x_1 vary linearly with v, and to specify x_2 and x_3 with two curves, as shown in Figure 3.23. One curve, $c_2(t)$, relates x_1 (on the x axis) with x_2 (on the y axis). The second curve, $c_3(t)$, relates x_1 (on the x axis) with x_3 (on the y axis). Of course, if c_2 or c_3 is not parameterized by its x coordinate, this requires an inversion operation to find the y value of c_2 or c_3 that corresponds to a given x value (i.e., value of x_1). Such an operation is called *matching* the x_2 and x_3 parameter schedules, and can be achieved with the inversion operator discussed on page 39.

Alternatively, the variables x_1 and x_2 can be related using an arbitrary 2D parametric curve, $c_2(t)$, so that we are not limited to a functional relationship between x_1 and x_2. A second curve, $c_3(t)$, can then be used to specify the functional relationship between x_3 and either x_1 or x_2. Again, the inversion operator can be used to match the x_3 schedule to either x_1 or x_2. Figure 3.24 illustrates this form of parameter matching.

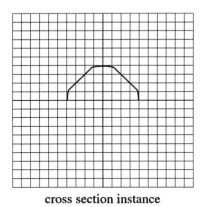

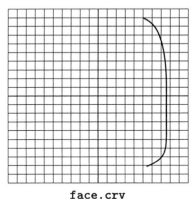

cross section instance   `face.crv`

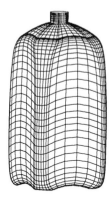

Figure 3.22: Bottle example. A bottle surface is represented by constructing a parameterized cross section. The cross section, for which one instance is illustrated, is parameterized in terms of several parameters. One parameter controls the radius of the circular segments at the left, top, and right of the cross section. The second curve, `face.crv`, controls how this radius parameter is varied as the cross section is translated out of its plane. The result is one half of the bottle surface, which, when added to its mirror image about the xz plane, forms the whole bottle. The GENMOD code for the bottle example is given in Section B.3.
☐

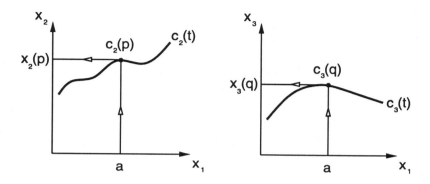

Figure 3.23: Matching parameter schedules. Two curves, $c_2(t)$ and $c_3(t)$, determine how three parameters, x_1, x_2, and x_3, are matched. For any given value of x_1, say a, the c_2 curve is inverted to determine a p such that the x coordinate of $c_2(p)$ is a. The y coordinate of $c_2(q)$ then yields the value of x_2 that corresponds to $x_1 = a$ (left diagram). Similarly, the c_3 curve is inverted to obtain q where the x coordinate of $c_3(q)$ is a. The y coordinate of $c_3(q)$ then yields the value of x_3 that corresponds to $x_1 = a$ (right diagram). $\square$

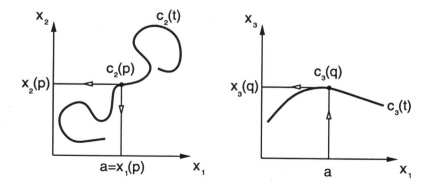

Figure 3.24: Matching parameter schedules continued. In this case, a value of the t parameter of the curve $c_2(t)$, say p, is chosen. This yields a matching between x_1 and x_2 as the x and y coordinates, respectively, of $c_2(p)$ (left diagram). The x coordinate of $c_2(p)$ is labeled a. To obtain the corresponding x_3 parameter, the c_3 curve is inverted to obtain q where the x coordinate of $c_3(q)$ is a. The y coordinate of $c_3(q)$ then yields the value of x_3 (right diagram). $\square$

Finally, we note that a function, $c(v)$,

$$c: \mathbf{R} \to \mathbf{R}^3$$

can be used to match the three parameters x_1, x_2 and x_3, where

$$\begin{pmatrix} x_1 \\ x_2 \\ x_3 \end{pmatrix} = \begin{pmatrix} c_1(v) \\ c_2(v) \\ c_3(v) \end{pmatrix}.$$

The advantage of this approach is that a functional relationship is not enforced between any pair of the parameters. The disadvantage is that a 3D curve must be specified, which is much more difficult for designers to control than two 2D curves.

3.3   Other Generative Shapes

The generative modeling approach allows many types of shapes other than surfaces to be specified. This is achieved by building parametric functions of different input and output dimensions. For example, a time-dependent surface may be represented as the parametric function

$$S(u, v, t): \mathbf{R}^3 \to \mathbf{R}^3.$$

Another example is a vector field defined over a surface, represented as the parametric function

$$V(u, v): \mathbf{R}^2 \to \mathbf{R}^6.$$

In this case, the output of V is a 3D point and a 3D direction. This section examines some examples of specifying "multidimensional" generative shapes such as S and V.

3.3.1   Solids

A generative solid can be represented with a parametric function

$$S(u, v, w): \mathbf{R}^3 \to \mathbf{R}^3.$$

Essentially, the solid S is represented as a 3D deformation of a 3D "brick." Such a representation has two advantages. First, even if we require only the surface boundary of the solid for rendering or simulation, it is often convenient to model the entire solid at once, rather than separately modeling the six faces of the deformed brick. Second, we may need to parameterize the interior of the solid for

```
MAN beam = m_wire(s,c);
```

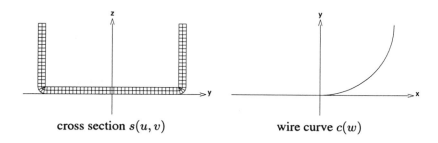

cross section $s(u, v)$ wire curve $c(w)$

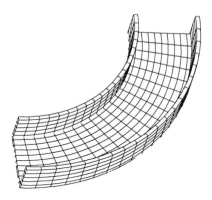

Figure 3.25: Circular beam example. A circular beam solid is modeled using the wire product of Section 3.2.1.2. In this case, a planar region rather than a boundary curve is used as the cross section. The region $s(u, v)$ is swept along the 2D wire curve $c(w)$ to form a parametric solid with three input coordinates. Note that the same definition of m_wire given in Section 3.2.1.2 suffices to sweep the area cross section $s(u, v)$, as well as a simple curve. □

simulation purposes. For example, a cubic lattice approximating the solid S may be required for finite element analysis. Furthermore, by parameterizing the solid S, we can easily associate with each point additional quantities such as a scalar representing temperature, or a direction representing a force.

Figure 3.25 illustrates an example of a generative solid.

3.3.2   Time-Dependent Shapes

Time-dependent shapes can be represented by including a time parameter in the parametric function representing the shape. For example, a time-varying curve, $c(v, t)$, was used to produce the wing motion of a creature included in a computer graphics animated sequence. The creature is pictured in Plate 3.

The curve c is a damped sinusoid that has a time-varying phase and that is truncated at a specific arclength, λ. Mathematically, c is given by

$$c(u, t) = \left(\begin{array}{c} u \\ \dfrac{\sin(2\pi(t - 0.1u))}{2u^2} \end{array} \right).$$

The parametric range of the u parameter is from 0 to u_t, where u_t is determined by finding where the arclength of $c(u, t)$ is λ, i.e.,

$$u_t \ni \lambda = \int_0^{u_t} \left\| \frac{\partial c}{\partial u} \right\| du.$$

Note that this formula can be computed using the integration and inversion operators in Section 2.2.3. Figure 3.26 shows the time-varying behavior of $c(u, t)$.

The time-varying curve $c(u, t)$ can then be used to produce a time-varying surface, representing the wing of the animated creature. In this case, $c(u, t)$ is used as the wire curve in the wire product of Section 3.2.1.2. The cross section of this wire product is an ellipse, one of whose axes is scaled and translated to produce the wing shape. The result is shown in Figure 3.27.

3.3.3   Vector Fields on Surfaces

In the previous section, shapes were produced with an extra input dimension representing time. The generative modeling approach can also represent shapes with "extra" output dimensions (i.e., more than three output dimensions). For example, a vector field defined over a surface can be represented with a parametric function of output dimension 6. This shape was useful in modeling a furry teddy bear [KAJI89], which was rendered using a new 3D texturing technique. The rendering method required not only the shape of the "skin" of the bear, but also the behavior of the hairs on the bear's skin. The hairs were modeled as straight segments whose

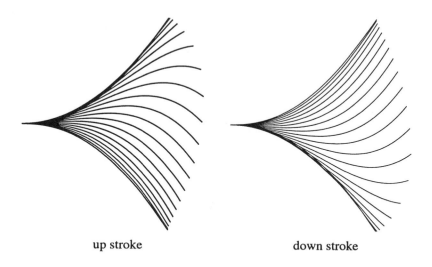

up stroke   down stroke

Figure 3.26: Time-varying curve example. The left side shows the behavior of the curve $c(u, t)$ for $t \in [-0.1, 0.4]$ (the up stroke). The right side shows its behavior for $t \in [0.4, 0.9]$ (the down stroke). □

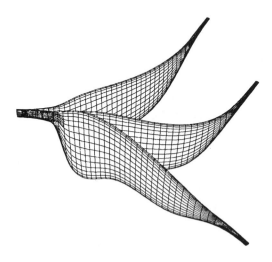

Figure 3.27: Time-varying wing surface. A wing surface is constructed with a wire product using the curve $c(u, t)$ as the wire. The wing is shown at three instants of time. □

orientation varied with respect to the skin normal, simulating a combing of the hair. The hair was therefore modeled as a vector field over a surface representing the bear skin. The surface model for the bear and the furry final result are illustrated in Plate 2.

Mathematically, the teddy bear fur (see also the vector field of Figure 4.4 for another example) was modeled as a parametric surface $S(u, v)$,

$$S: \mathbf{R}^2 \rightarrow \mathbf{R}^3$$

and a vector field direction function $f(x, y, z)$,

$$f: \mathbf{R}^3 \rightarrow \mathbf{R}^3.$$

At each point on the surface, $S(u, v)$, a coordinate frame is constructed using the surface tangents and normals at that point. Three mutually perpendicular, unit length vectors, $U(u, v)$, $V(u, v)$, and $N(u, v)$, are constructed via

$$U(u, v) = \frac{\dfrac{\partial S}{\partial u}(u, v)}{\left\| \dfrac{\partial S}{\partial u}(u, v) \right\|}$$

$$N(u, v) = \frac{\dfrac{\partial S}{\partial u}(u, v) \times \dfrac{\partial S}{\partial v}(u, v)}{\left\| \dfrac{\partial S}{\partial u}(u, v) \times \dfrac{\partial S}{\partial v}(u, v) \right\|}$$

$$V(u, v) = N(u, v) \times U(u, v).$$

The vector originating from the point $S(u, v)$ is then given by

$$f_1(S(u, v))\, U(u, v) + f_2(S(u, v))\, V(u, v) + f_3(S(u, v))\, N(u, v).$$

That is, the function f specifies the coordinates of the vector in the $\{U, V, N\}$ basis of $\mathbf{R}^3$. Note that the substitution and differentiation operators are indispensable in specifying such a definition. In the case of the vector field over a sphere from Figure 4.4,[7] f is given by

$$f(x, y, z) = 0.6 \begin{pmatrix} x \\ y \\ z^2 \end{pmatrix}.$$

---

[7] It is impossible to construct a smooth, well-defined coordinate frame on a sphere where two of the frame vectors remain tangent to the sphere. We defined $N(u, v) = S(u, v)$, eliminating the problem of normalizing a zero length vector. Further, the particular direction function f is such that it ignores (scales by 0) the ill-defined frame vectors (e.g., $f_1(S(u, v)) = 0$ whenever $\left\| \dfrac{\partial S}{\partial u}(u, v) \right\| = 0$).

Chapter 4

Shape Rendering

Rendering is the production of "images" of shapes, where images are synthetic pictures produced using computer graphics, or approximations of the shape suitable for postprocessing (e.g., manufacturing and simulation). The need for the latter form of rendering is obvious in a CAD/CAM system whose ultimate goal is the production of physical parts. It is less clear why pictures are necessary in a shape design system.

Pictures provide information that is important for checking the design's validity. This information is presented in a way that is easy for a human being to assimilate. A picture can illustrate how close two objects are, where they are close, whether they intersect, and where the intersections occur. This information is more complete than a single bit telling the designer whether or not the shapes intersect.

Pictures allow the designer to be more "connected" with his or her design. That is, the designer can see that a selection of certain shape parameters yields a certain observable shape. As the parameters are varied, the shape's appearance changes correspondingly. Interactivity of the parameter selection/rendering cycle enhances this connectedness. In some cases, such as in designing a shape for a computer animation sequence, the parameter selection/rendering cycle is the preferred form of searching the parameter space. Once the shape looks right, there is no need to check it further. In other cases, the shape must be simulated as part of a larger assembly. It must fit together with other parts and have the right physical properties. Choosing the right shape and verifying its suitability in the larger assembly cannot be done solely with visual tools. Yet visual tools are extremely useful in debugging the choice of shape.

This chapter examines methods for rendering shapes represented as generative models. We first categorize generative shapes based on how they can be rendered. Methods for sampling of generative models, a necessary component of almost all the rendering methods, is also presented. Lastly, this chapter describes how visualization of shapes is specified and implemented in GENMOD.

4.1   Categorizing Generative Models for Rendering

Generative shapes may be broken down into two categories: low-dimensional shapes and high-dimensional shapes. Low-dimensional shapes are the familiar points, curves, surfaces, and solids in 3D space, which form the bulk of the shapes of interest in CAD systems and computer graphics. Currently existing rendering methods are directly applicable to these low-dimensional shapes.

High-dimensional shapes do not fit into these simple categories. Shapes of high input dimension include curves, surfaces, and solids that change as a function of time, or as a function of many parameters. Shapes of high output dimension are embedded in a space of dimension greater than 3, such as vector fields defined over surfaces or 3D transformations. High-dimensional shapes must be projected, animated, or otherwise transformed into low-dimensional shapes before they can be rendered.

This section examines rendering methods for low-dimensional shapes and discusses ways for visualizing high-dimensional shapes by converting them into renderable, low-dimensional shapes.

4.1.1   Curves

Much graphics hardware available today is designed to draw 3D vectors quickly. Graphics workstations now commonly achieve speeds of hundreds of thousands of vectors per second. Given this available hardware, the most attractive rendering method for curves is to convert them to a sequence of 2D or 3D vectors. Since curves in the generative modeling approach are represented as parametric functions, we require a method of approximating parametric functions as a sequence of vectors.

Let $\gamma(u)$ be a parametric curve where $u \in [0, 1]$. Converting γ into a sequence of line segments involves sampling γ: choosing a sequence of n values for u, $u_1 = 0, u_2, \ldots, u_n = 1$, and evaluating γ at each, yielding a sequence of points

$$\gamma(u_1), \gamma(u_2), \ldots, \gamma(u_n).$$

Each pair of consecutive points determines a vector to be rendered with the graphics hardware (see Figure 4.1). The choice of the number of samples, n, and the sample locations, $u_1, u_2, \ldots, u_n$, trade off speed of curve rendering with the accuracy of the line segment approximation.

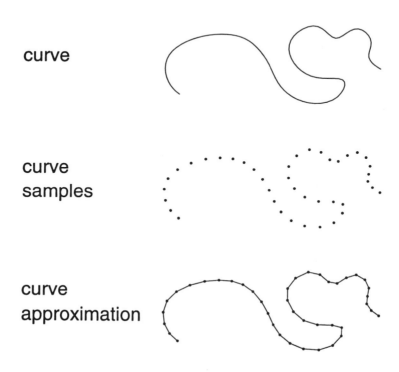

Figure 4.1: Approximating a parametric curve. A parametric curve is approximated by generating a sequence of points on the curve and interpolating between these points. In this example, the curve is approximated by a series of line segments joining adjacent samples on the curve. □

A curve approximation consisting of a series of line segments does not preserve smoothness of the original curve. To obtain a smooth approximation, a higher-order interpolant, such as a quadratic or cubic curve, must be used. To compute such an approximation, derivatives of various orders can be sampled, as well as points on the curve. The resulting higher order curves can then be directly rasterized using recursive subdivision and/or forward differencing [FOLE90, SHAN87, SHAN89].

4.1.2 Surfaces

Surfaces in 3D space can be rendered using a variety of methods, including:

1. Line drawing

2. Z-buffering

3. Ray tracing

4. Radiosity methods

Plate 6 compares some of these rendering methods.

Line drawing of surfaces involves drawing curves on the surface, approximated by a series of line segments. Typically, the parameter lines of the surface are drawn, in which one of the parameters of the parametric surface varies while the other is held constant. Such line drawings give a reasonable idea of the surface's shape, especially if the user can rotate the surface interactively. The technique of hidden line elimination can also be used in order to eliminate parts of the curves that are occluded in a given view. This technique is much more costly than simple line drawing, even with depth cueing.[1]

Z-buffering produces a solid shaded image of the surface. Rendering is accomplished by *tessellating* the surface into simple pieces, usually polygons. These polygons are scan converted (i.e., the pixels in the raster grid covered by the polygon's screen projection are visited), and a z value is computed at each pixel. This z value represents the depth of the surface from the screen, so that a surface with a smaller z value will occlude a surface with a larger z value. Graphics hardware is now available to do real-time z-buffering of large numbers of polygons.

Ray tracing produces a solid shaded image of a surface by simulating geometric optics. Light rays are traced backwards from the film plane or eye and into the collection of surfaces. Effects such as shadows, reflections, and refractions can be realized. The fundamental operation in ray tracing is the intersection of a ray with a surface. This can be accomplished in two ways: the renderer can directly compute such intersections [BARR86, JOY86, TOTH85], or tessellate the surface and compute intersections with the resulting collection of simple pieces [SNYD87]. The latter method, while approximate, is attractive because direct ray/surface intersections may be very costly to compute. Both ray tracing methods are applicable to generative surfaces discussed in this book. Surface tessellation will be

---

[1] The hidden line eliminated drawings in this book, such as in Figure 4.3, were made using z-buffer hardware. The technique involves rendering into the z-buffer both a traditional line drawing of the surface and a solid shaded version of the surface in the same color as the background. The background colored surface effectively removes occluded lines. The line drawing should be a slightly enlarged version of the surface (i.e., an offset surface) to prevent immediate erasure of all lines. Other hidden line elimination techniques exist that avoid using special purpose graphics hardware [FOLE90, pages 665-668].

further discussed in the next section. Plate 1 shows two example images that contain generative surfaces rendered by tessellating the surfaces into polygons and ray tracing the resulting polygons. Direct intersection of a ray with a generative surface can be computed using the constrained minimization operator, as discussed in Section 4.1.2.2.

Radiosity methods attempt to balance light energy within an environment composed of surfaces [GORA85, COHE85]. Surfaces are tessellated, and *form factors* are computed between each pair of tessellation elements. These form factors represent the proportion of energy emitted by one element that reaches the other. Assuming each surface is perfectly diffuse (scatters incident light energy in all directions equally), the energy balance can be accomplished by solving a large linear system. Radiosity methods can simulate diffuse interreflections between surfaces, an effect not realizable with standard ray tracing. Research is continuing to enhance radiosity methods with the ability to simulate non-diffuse surfaces [IMME86]. At the same time, ray tracing methods are being enhanced to handle interreflection of light between surfaces [KAJI86].

4.1.2.1 Surface Tessellation and Sampling

Many of the rendering methods discussed previously require surfaces to be tessellated — approximated by a set of connected pieces. Most often, surfaces are tessellated into a polygonal mesh. Other tessellation units can be used that allow more faithful approximation of the surface at the expense of slower rendering. For example, bicubic polynomial patches approximate a smooth surface better than a polygonal mesh, but are more difficult to z-buffer or ray trace directly.

Just as a curve is approximated by generating a sequence of points over the curve, a surface is tessellated by generating a network of points over the surface. An approximation to the surface results from interpolating this network of points using polygons, bicubic patches, or some other interpolation scheme. The simplest algorithm for generating a network of points over a parametric surface is called *uniform sampling*. It involves evaluating the surface over a rectangular, 2D lattice of points in parameter space.

Let $S(u, v)$ be a parametric surface where the domain of S is $[0, 1] \times [0, 1]$. To sample S uniformly, we choose the number of subdivisions in u and v (n_u and n_v) and evaluate S on $n_u n_v$ points given by

$$\begin{pmatrix} u_i \\ v_j \end{pmatrix} = \begin{pmatrix} i/(n_u - 1) \\ j/(n_v - 1) \end{pmatrix}$$
$$i = 0 \ldots n_u - 1$$
$$j = 0 \ldots n_v - 1.$$

Given a uniform grid of points on S, a polygonal mesh can be constructed by

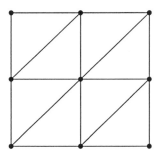

Figure 4.2: Triangular surface approximation from a uniform sample grid. A collection of triangles approximating a parametric surface can be generated from a regular 2D grid of samples by forming two triangles for each group of four corner samples. Each triangle's vertices result from evaluating the parametric surface at a point in its parameter space. □

generating a pair of triangles for each group of four adjacent points, as shown in Figure 4.2.

We can also tessellate S using *adaptive sampling*. In this case, samples of S can have an arbitrary distribution over its parameter space, rather than a uniform rectilinear distribution. One method of adaptive sampling is to partition the parameter space of S into a collection of rectangles. Each rectangle determines a small number of tessellation units, such as triangles. The rectangles are chosen small enough to guarantee a bound on some aspect of the behavior of the surface, using criteria such as:

1. Size (e.g., volume or maximum side length) of a bounding box on the surface

2. Area of the surface

3. Maximum variation of the surface's normal vector

4. Maximum distance of the tessellation unit from the surface

Section 6.3 discusses an algorithm to sample parametric surfaces using general criteria such as the above.

Figure 4.3 and Plate 10 compare uniform and adaptive sampling. Adaptive sampling allows samples to be chosen that guarantee certain properties about the resulting surface approximation. For example, using criterion 1 from the previous paragraph, an approximation can be generated that is no farther than a given distance from the original surface. Uniform sampling, in contrast, guarantees nothing about the quality of the approximation. The user merely chooses two integers controlling the fineness of sampling in the two parametric coordinates.

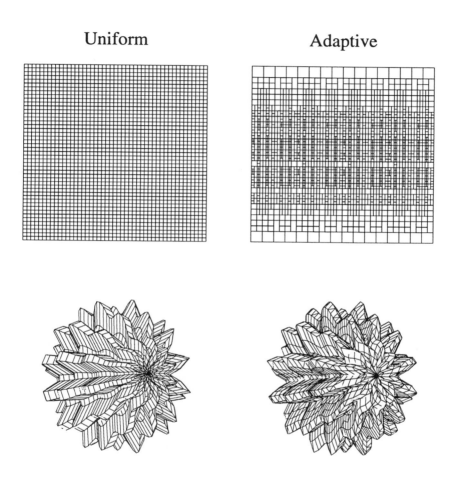

Figure 4.3: Uniform vs. adaptive sampling of a parametric surface. The left side of the figure illustrates uniform sampling of a parametric surface. In the top left, the parameter space of the surface is drawn. Samples are evaluated at each crossing of the parameter lines. The bottom left shows the resulting surface in $\mathbf{R}^3$, where each set of four adjacent points is used to define a tessellation element. Rendered lines correspond to the sampled parameter lines. The right side of the figure illustrates the same surface, adaptively sampled. The number of tessellation units is approximately the same, but samples are distributed so as to limit the size of a bounding box around each tessellation unit. There are therefore fewer samples at the poles of the surface, and more near the equator. □

On the other hand, adaptive sampling is usually much slower than uniform sampling. Computation is used both to check the adaptation criteria and to generate the tessellation mesh for the more complicated network of samples. In creating a polygonal mesh, for example, care must be exercised so that cracks do not form in the tessellation. Eliminating such cracks is trivial for uniform sampling, but much more complicated for adaptive sampling [VONH89]. In addition, the section on uniform sampling speedup on page 109 presents a speedup that increases the attractiveness of uniform sampling.

4.1.2.2 Surface Ray Tracing

Rendering with ray tracing can also be accomplished by intersecting rays with the continuous, parameteric representation of the surface, rather than with a tessellated approximation. Let a ray in $\mathbf{R}^3$ is defined as

$$a + bt,$$

where $a, b \in \mathbf{R}^3$ and $t \in [0, \infty)$. The vector a is the ray origin, b is the ray direction, and t is the ray parameter. To intersect this ray with the parametric surface $S(u, v): \mathbf{R}^2 \to \mathbf{R}^3$, we minimize t subject to the constraint system

$$a + bt = S(u, v).$$

Minimization is used because we require the first (minimum t) intersection of the ray with the parametric surface, in order to perform hidden surface elimination. An algorithm for solving such a system will be given in Chapter 5.

In fact, as pointed out in [TOTH85], a simpler 2D minimization problem can be used to compute ray intersections with parametric surfaces. We minimize

$$t(u, v) = \min \left\{ \frac{S_1(u, v) - a_1}{b_1}, \frac{S_2(u, v) - a_2}{b_2}, \frac{S_3(u, v) - a_3}{b_3} \right\}$$

subject to the constraint

$$(S(u, v) - a) \times b = 0.$$

Minimizing the objective function ensures that the minimum t intersection is returned; the constraint ensures that the point $S(u, v)$ lies on the ray.

4.1.3 Solids

A parametric solid can be represented by a function $d: \mathbf{R}^3 \to \mathbf{R}$ which associates a scalar $d(x, y, z)$ with a 3D point (x, y, z). For example, $d(x, y, z)$ can represent temperature or mass density at a point in the solid. Such solids can be visualized with the technique of *volume rendering*, a relatively new area of computer graphics (see [FOLE90, pages 1034-1039] for a brief survey and list of references). Most volume rendering techniques act on a discrete set of samples of the scalar function d. These techniques range from the simple summing of samples projecting onto the same pixel, to complicated simulation using light-scattering models. As in the case of surface and curve rendering, volume rendering a continuous function d requires sampling of the solid, which will be discussed in Section 4.2.

A solid in 3D space can also be represented and rendered as a collection of surfaces that form its boundaries, using any of the surface rendering techniques of Section 4.1.2. Such solids may be directly represented as a collection of boundary surfaces (termed a b-rep). A different approach which is sometimes convenient is to represent a solid as a parametric function $S(u, v, w): \mathbf{R}^3 \to \mathbf{R}^3$. The set of points in the solid is formed by the image of S over the rectilinear domain

$$D_S = [u_0, u_1] \times [v_0, v_1] \times [w_0, w_1]$$

If S is differentiable and invertible, and its Jacobian determinant is nonzero in D_S, then S defines a solid whose boundaries are given by the transformation of the boundaries of the domain of S. The solid represented by S can therefore be rendered by rendering the six surfaces forming the boundary of S, i.e.,

$$S_1(v, w) = S(u_0, v, w)$$
$$S_2(v, w) = S(u_1, v, w)$$
$$S_3(u, w) = S(u, v_0, w)$$
$$S_4(u, w) = S(u, v_1, w)$$
$$S_5(u, v) = S(u, v, w_0)$$
$$S_6(u, v) = S(u, v, w_1).$$

4.1.4   Shapes of High Input Dimension

An example of a shape of high input dimension is the time-varying surface:

$$S(u, v, t): \mathbf{R}^3 \to \mathbf{R}^3.$$

The time parameter t is called a *variable input parameter*, while the parameters u and v are called the *intrinsic input parameters*. More variable input parameters can also be added to create a surface that is a function of several parameters. Such a surface is represented by the parametric function

$$T(u, v, x_1, \ldots, x_n): \mathbf{R}^{n+2} \to \mathbf{R}^3,$$

where the variable input parameters are $x_1, \ldots, x_n$. For rendering purposes, the variable input parameters can be used to define a set of surfaces to be visualized.

Curves or solids can be similarly parameterized in terms of intrinsic input parameters and variable input parameters.

There are two main techniques for the visualization of such continuous sets of shapes: superimposition and animation. Both techniques first sample the shape at various points in the variable input parameter space. We will use the term *instance* to refer to a single sample of the shape at a point in the variable input parameter space (e.g., the surface $S(u, v, t_0)$). Superimposition renders the shape by rendering the entire collection of instances in a single image. Animation renders a sequence of instances, one at a time. Superimposition thus allows simultaneous visualization of the whole set of shapes, but often creates cluttered images where instances can occlude one another.

Animation solves this problem, but requires real-time rendering of each instance. Alternatively, we can use a medium, such as a single frame tape recorder, that allows each image to be added to the animation after it is rendered. The entire animation can then be played back in real-time after it is recorded. In either case, user interaction is useful as a means of ordering the sequence of instances, especially if there is more than one variable input parameter. For example, the user can attach each of the variable input parameters to a 1D graphics input device, such as a dial. Changing a dial changes the value of the parameter to which it is attached, and, consequently, the instance displayed on the screen.

4.1.5 Shapes of High Output Dimension

An example of a shape of high output dimension is a vector field defined over a surface. Such a shape can be represented using the parametric function

$$S(u, v): \mathbf{R}^2 \rightarrow (p, q) \in \mathbf{R}^6,$$

where $p \in \mathbf{R}^3$ represents a 3D point, and $q \in \mathbf{R}^3$ represents a 3D direction. Another example of a shape of high output dimension is an affine transformation defined as a function of time:

$$R(t): \mathbf{R} \rightarrow (M, T) \in \mathbf{R}^{12},$$

where $M \in \mathbf{R}^9$ represents a linear transformation of a 3D point, and $T \in \mathbf{R}^3$ represents a 3D translation. The resulting transformation of a point $p \in \mathbf{R}^3$ by R is given by

$$R(t; p) = M(t)p + T(t).$$

The output of S is therefore embedded in a 6D space, while the output of R is embedded in a 12D space.

We note that a color image is a 5D entity — two spatial dimensions and three color dimensions. How can entities such as S and R be visualized in this 5D image

Figure 4.4: Visualization of a vector field defined over a surface. A parametric function of input dimension 2 and output dimension 6 can be visualized by rendering a surface, representing the vector field origin, and a set of line segments, representing the vector field direction. □

space? A natural way of visualizing S is to render both the surface $p(u, v)$ and a collection of line segments from the point p to the point $p + q$, as in Figure 4.4. R can be visualized by selecting a surface in $\mathbf{R}^3$, such as a sphere, and applying R to it. The surface can even be parameterized. For example, we can apply R to a sphere parameterized by three coordinates for its origin and one for its radius,

$$p(\theta, \phi, x, y, z, r) = \begin{pmatrix} x + r \cos(\theta) \cos(\phi) \\ y + r \sin(\theta) \cos(\phi) \\ z + r \sin(\phi) \end{pmatrix}.$$

We can then visualize the resulting shape $R(t)(p(\theta, \phi, x, y, z, r))$ as a surface with five variable input parameters (t, x, y, z, r), using the ideas already discussed in the previous section.

In general, the method of visualization appropriate for a shape depends on the interpretation of the shape. We cannot expect a single visualization method to be appropriate for two different shapes, even if their output dimension is the same. Nevertheless, several general techniques exist for visualizing shapes of high output dimension:

1. Use of projection — the user can specify a transformation of the shape that projects it into a lower-dimensional embedding. This transformation can even be parameterized, allowing the user to change the projection using the techniques found in the previous section.

2. Use of color — the three color dimensions of the image can be used to convey information rather than to enhance the realism of the rendering. The technique of *texture mapping*, for example, allows the color of a surface or solid to vary as a function of the parametric coordinates.

3. Use of graphics output devices — images of a shape can be augmented by the output of devices that stimulate nonvisual senses of the user. For example, force feedback output devices allow the user to feel a varying force that can be attached to the outputs of a shape.

The generative modeling approach allows the user to specify different projection functions and methods of mapping shape outputs into color space. Although GENMOD does not currently support output devices other than displays, such output devices would be a natural extension of the system. Specific implementation of these ideas will be discussed in Section 4.3.

4.2   Sampling Generative Models

As we have seen, many methods of rendering shapes require approximation of the shape into units such as cubes, polygons, or line segments. Such approximation, in turn, requires *sampling* — computation of points over the shape. In the generative modeling approach, a shape is represented by a parametric function

$$S : \mathbf{R}^n \to \mathbf{R}^m$$

parameterized by the n variables $(x_1, \ldots, x_n)$. The shape is generated by the image of S over a rectilinear domain

$$(x_1, \ldots, x_n) \in [a_1, b_1] \times \ldots \times [a_n, b_n].$$

This section discusses two methods for sampling such parametric functions: uniform sampling and adaptive sampling.

4.2.1   Uniform Sampling

Uniform sampling of a parametric function involves evaluating the function over a rectilinear lattice of domain points. For each parametric coordinate x_i, we pick a number of samples, N_i. The parametric function S is then evaluated over the $\prod_{i=1}^{n} N_i$ samples given by

$$\left(a_1 + \frac{i_1(b_1 - a_1)}{N_1 - 1}, \ldots, a_n + \frac{i_n(b_n - a_n)}{N_n - 1} \right).$$

Each of the indices i_j independently ranges from 0 to $N_j - 1$. This evaluation is done by calling the uniform evaluation method of S (see the section on operator methods on page 44).

Uniform Sampling Speedup Using Table Lookup

A substantial speedup of uniform parametric evaluation can be accomplished by constructing evaluation tables for subfunctions [FRAN81]. As discussed in Section 2.2.2, a subfunction is a subtree in the tree of symbolic operators representing a parametric function. For example, let $f : \mathbf{R}^3 \to \mathbf{R}$ be the function

$$f(x_1, x_2, x_3) = (x_1 x_2 + x_2 x_3) e^{x_2}$$

which we wish to uniformly sample using n_i samples for x_i. This can be done by evaluating f at each of the $n_1 n_2 n_3$ lattice points in parameter space. Alternatively, we can construct evaluation tables for the subfunctions

$$
\begin{aligned}
f_1(x_1, x_2) &= x_1 x_2 \\
f_2(x_2, x_3) &= x_2 x_3 \\
f_3(x_2) &= e^{x_2}
\end{aligned}
$$

so that these subfunctions are not reevaluated at each lattice point. Here is a table of the number of operations required for the two methods of evaluating f:

function	$*$ ops	$+$ ops	e^x ops
evaluation point by point			
$f = (x_1 x_2 + x_2 x_3) e^{x_2}$	$3 n_1 n_2 n_3$	$n_1 n_2 n_3$	$n_1 n_2 n_3$
evaluation using tables			
$f_1 = x_1 x_2$	$n_1 n_2$	0	0
$f_2 = x_2 x_3$	$n_2 n_3$	0	0
$f_3 = e^{x_2}$	0	0	n_2
$f = (f_1 + f_2) * f_3$	$n_1 n_2 n_3$	$n_1 n_2 n_3$	0
total	$n_1 n_2 n_3 + n_1 n_2 + n_2 n_3$	$n_1 n_2 n_3$	n_2

The table shows that substantial computational savings result when the lower-dimensional subfunctions are evaluated and stored in tables. In general, **evaluation tables should be constructed for each subfunction that has an input dimension smaller than its parent.** For example, the subfunction e^{x_2}, of input dimension 1, should be tabulated because its parent function f has input dimension

3. Such a subfunction should be tabulated at the lattice points of its particular input variables. For example, evaluations from the subfunction e^{x_2} are stored in a 1D table of size n_2, while evaluations from the subfunction $x_1 x_2$ are stored in a 2D table of size $n_1 \times n_2$. The tabulated results can then be retrieved rather than computed when the parent parametric function is evaluated. This process can be applied recursively. That is, in evaluating the table of results for a subfunction, evaluation tables can be computed for any of its subfunctions whose input dimension is smaller than its parent. GENMOD implements this uniform sampling speedup in its "evaluate over a uniform rectilinear lattice" method for parametric evaluation.

Some unnecessary evaluation can be avoided without the use of tables (and the memory necessary for their storage) by simply saving the last computed value of a subfunction rather than recomputing it. For example, consider the problem of uniformly sampling the function

$$f(x_1, x_2) = g(x_1) h(x_2)$$

in order to construct a list of values of f, in which the x_2 variable varies most rapidly. We can evaluate g at some value of the 1D x_1 lattice, say at a_1. This result, $g(a_1)$, may then be multiplied by each value of h on the appropriate 1D lattice for the x_2 variable. Thus, $f(x_1, x_2)$ can be computed without evaluating g once for each point in the 2D lattice. However, without a table to store values for the evaluation of h over the x_2 lattice, these evaluations must be recomputed when they are multiplied with the value of g at the next x_1 lattice point, a_2. The table approach described here avoids these needless evaluations.

Uniform Sampling and Uncoupled Transformations

Uniform sampling evaluates a parametric function at equally spaced points in each of the parametric coordinates. This might seem like a severe restriction when the samples are to be used in a shape approximation, requiring many samples for a reasonable approximation. The use of "uncoupled transformations" can redistribute these uniform samples to improve the resulting approximation without unduly increasing computation. An *uncoupled transformation* is a function $T: \mathbf{R}^n \to \mathbf{R}^n$ that transforms each input coordinate independently, i.e.,

$$T(x_1, \ldots, x_n) = (f_1(x_1), \ldots, f_n(x_n)).$$

Uncoupled transformations can be applied to the domain of a parametric function S to independently adjust the sampling densities in each of the domain coordinates. Uniform sampling of the adjusted function still allows the table lookup optimization just discussed. We can evaluate the n functions f_i into 1D tables. Uniform evaluation of $S(T(x))$ then requires the same number of function evaluations as did the uniform evaluation of $S(x)$.

As an example of the usefulness of uncoupled transformations, consider a surface defined by sweeping a circle of radius r perpendicular to a space curve $s(v): \mathbf{R} \to \mathbf{R}^3$. Let $n(v)$ and $b(v)$ be differentiable vectors along this curve that are mutually perpendicular and perpendicular to the tangent vector of s, given by

$$\frac{ds}{dv}(v).$$

The sweep surface $S(u, v): \mathbf{R}^2 \to \mathbf{R}^3$ is then given by

$$S(u, v) = s(v) + r(n(v)\cos(u) + b(v)\sin(u)).$$

Depending on its parameterization, a uniform sampling of the space curve $s(v)$ may not yield a good approximation with a reasonable number of samples. However, we can reparameterize $s(v)$ by arclength, or so that the sampling density increases in areas of high curvature. Let the function $t(v): \mathbf{R} \to \mathbf{R}$ be such a reparameterization, yielding a new curve $\tilde{s}(v) = s(t(v))$. The sweep surface can incorporate this reparameterization of v using the uncoupled transformation:

$$T \quad : \quad \mathbf{R}^2 \to \mathbf{R}^2$$
$$(u, v) \mapsto (u, t(v)).$$

4.2.2   Adaptive Sampling

Adaptive sampling can be used to generate approximations that satisfy criteria [VONH87]. For example, we may wish to bound the maximum distance of the approximation from the original parametric shape. To accomplish this in a reasonable number of samples, it is probable that some areas of parameter space should be sampled more finely than others. While uniform sampling could be used, it would probably require an inordinate number of samples since the sampling is constant and independently fixed for each input coordinate.

An algorithm for adaptively sampling parametric shapes according to user specified criteria will be presented in Section 6.3. This algorithm requires evaluation of the shape at a fairly unstructured collection of points. Evaluation is done by calling the shape's point evaluation method (see page 46).

Adaptive Sampling Speedup Using Caching

Adaptive sampling can be enhanced by caching the last computed value of a subfunction. Both the input point and the subfunction result are stored. If, in a future evaluation, the input point matches the cached point, then the cached function result may be used without reevaluation. Candidate subfunctions are those that have lower input dimension than their parent or that are repeated (i.e., shared subexpressions). Caching can be used for inclusion function evaluation as well as point evaluation.

Consider the following three examples. First, let $f(x_1)$ be given by

$$f(x_1) = x_1 + \int_0^1 g(x_2)\, dx_2.$$

In sampling f for various values of x_1, the constant subfunction $\int_0^1 g(x_2)\, dx_2$ can be cached. It is then evaluated only once, rather than reevaluated for each value of x_1. Second, let $f(x_1)$ be given by

$$f(x_1) = g(x_1)^{1/2} + g(x_1).$$

Let $g(x_1)$ be some non-trivial expression, such as

$$g(x_1) = e^{2x_1{}^2 + 3x_1 + 1}.$$

In this case, the subfunction $g(x_1)$ is repeated in f so that caching saves an evaluation of g. Repeated subfunctions are common, especially when symbolic derivatives are used in defining the function f. Finally, consider the function $f(x_1)$ defined by

$$f(x_1) = \int_0^1 g(x_1, x_2)\, dx_2.$$

To compute the integral, the function g must be evaluated at many values of x_2 while the value of x_1 stays fixed. For example, if $g(x_1, x_2) = h(x_1) + s(x_1, x_2)$, then the result of the subfunction $h(x_1)$ can be cached, saving many evaluations in calculating the value of the integrand.

A limited form of this caching enhancement is part of the GENMOD system. That is, the system does not actually find common subexpressions in a parametric formula, but relies on the designer to use the same subexpression rather than redefine it. For example, in the second example discussed above, caching will not increase speed unless the designer defines a parametric function (i.e., a MAN type) representing $g(x_1)$ and uses this result in two places, as in

```
MAN g = m_exp(2*m_x(1)@^2 + 3*m_x(1) + 1);
MAN f = m_sqrt(g) + g;
```

A more sophisticated system could take advantage of common subexpressions without requiring the user to point them out in this way.[2] The speedup implied by the first and third examples is effective without user attention.

---

[2] We note that the evaluation of parametric functions in the approach is free of side effects, making caching for common subexpression effective.

4.3   Controlling Visualization of Generative Models

As we have seen, rendering of generative models involves directly applying one of the various rendering methods to low-dimensional shapes, or transforming high-dimensional shapes to sets of low-dimensional shapes, which can then be rendered. Often, a network of point samples on the shape is required for rendering, forming an intermediate data structure between parametric function and renderer. On the other hand, some rendering methods, like ray tracing, can accept the shape directly, given a method of computing intersections of rays with the shape.

There are, of course, many ways for the user of a geometric modeling system to control how shapes are visualized. The availability of different types of renderers, that accept different kinds of descriptions or approximations of the shape, make control of the visualization process even more difficult for the user. This section discusses how a user controls visualization in GENMOD. Admittedly, GENMOD does not present the user with an ideal interface for shape visualization. It does not support all the rendering methods discussed in Section 4.1, but instead concentrates on interactive, z-buffer rendering. The system is noteworthy, however, in its ability to flexibly combine a small set of primitive visualization methods. The result is a powerful, user-controllable means of visualizing any generative model, including the high-dimensional shapes examined in Sections 4.1.4 and 4.1.5.

4.3.1   Visualization Methods

A *visualization method* takes a shape and produces a renderable object or produces a transformation that can be applied to a renderable object. Shapes in the GENMOD system are parametric functions represented as a tree of symbolic operators. Visualization methods in GENMOD approximate such shapes, converting them into a form suitable for interactive manipulation using z-buffer graphics hardware.

There are four kinds of interactively renderable objects in GENMOD: points, curves, planar areas, and surfaces. A point is rendered as a dot in 2D or 3D space.[3] A curve is rendered as a sequence of line segments. A planar region is rendered as a single polygon formed by the interior of an approximated curve.[4] A surface is rendered as a collection of triangles. A transformation can be applied to any of the other renderable objects, deforming them via a 4×3 affine transformation (i.e., R

---

[3] A point visualization method was used to make the sequence of points on the curves in Figures 2.9 and 3.2, for example.

[4] The curve must not self-intersect, and must lie in a plane. Planar regions are convenient for forming end caps of generalized tubes, where the tube cross section is bounded by an arbitrary planar curve. Surfaces can also be used for this purpose, but are less convenient, since they require a 2D parameterization of the region's interior, rather than a simple boundary curve.

of Section 4.1.5).

Each of the visualization methods expects a shape of a given output dimension (e.g., a function $S(u, v)$ must have output dimension 3 to be used as input to the surface visualization method). Each visualization method also expects an input dimension at least as large as the intrinsic input dimension of the shape. For example, a function $C(t): \mathbf{R} \rightarrow \mathbf{R}^3$ can be used in the curve visualization method, as can $D(t, s): \mathbf{R}^2 \rightarrow \mathbf{R}^3$, since C and D have input dimension at least 1. On the other hand, a constant function is not appropriate for the curve method, nor is a function of a single coordinate appropriate for the surface method. The following table shows the number of intrinsic input parameters and output parameters of GENMOD's visualization methods:

name	intrinsic dim.	output dim.
point	0	2 or 3
curve	1	2 or 3
planar area	1	2 or 3
surface	2	3
transformation	0	12

Functions that have an input dimension greater than the visualization method's intrinsic dimension (e.g., a surface that deforms in time) are still valid input to the visualization method. The extra input coordinates, termed variable input coordinates in Section 4.1.4, can be visualized by animating or superimposing. The visualization method therefore requires an argument specifying which of the variable input coordinates are to be superimposed. The rest of the variable input coordinates are attached to dials and animated in the interactive visualization tool.

For example, consider a function $C(s, x_1, x_2)$ that is visualized using the curve method with s as the intrinsic parameter, x_2 as an animated parameter, and x_1 as a superimposed parameter. C will be rendered as a 1D family of curves that changes as the dial attached to x_2 is turned. If instead both x_1 and x_2 are chosen as superimposed parameters, then a 2D family of curves is rendered, leaving no animation parameters. Finally, both x_1 and x_2 can be chosen as animated parameters, in which case a single curve is rendered, changing shape as either of two dials, representing x_1 and x_2, is turned. As another example, a parametric function $Q(t): \mathbf{R} \rightarrow \mathbf{R}^{12}$ can be used as an input to the transformation visualization method in order to specify rigid body motions of a shape over time.

Since visualization methods can be applied to arbitrary parametric functions (as long as they satisfy input and output dimension restrictions), the modeler can visualize shapes of high output dimension by applying a projection transformation to his or her shape to produce a shape with a smaller output dimension. The GEN-MOD language allows the modeler to build such projection functions easily. The projection function can be parameterized, as in the example of Section 4.1.5.

The designer can also use combinations of the primitive visualization methods as an effective tool. For example, consider a vector field over a surface, defined as a function $V(u, v)$

$$V: \mathbf{R}^2 \rightarrow \mathbf{R}^6$$

where the first three output coordinates of V are a point on the surface, and the last three output coordinates are the direction of the vector field at that point. The surface visualization method can be applied to the surface $S(u, v)$

$$S(u, v) = \begin{pmatrix} V_1(u, v) \\ V_2(u, v) \\ V_3(u, v) \end{pmatrix}.$$

The designer can also form a parameterized 3D curve, $L(t, u, v)$ via

$$L(t, u, v) = \begin{pmatrix} V_1(u, v) \\ V_2(u, v) \\ V_3(u, v) \end{pmatrix} + t \begin{pmatrix} V_4(u, v) \\ V_5(u, v) \\ V_6(u, v) \end{pmatrix}$$

where t is the intrinsic input parameter of the parameterized curve L. The curve visualization method can then be applied to L, where u and v are variable input parameters. These parameters can be superimposed, to produce an image in which a 2D family of line segments represents the vector field (see the vector field representation in Figure 2.12 for an example). Alternatively, the designer can create a shape $L(s, t, u, v)$ representing a family of cylinders originating on S whose central axis is along

$$\begin{pmatrix} V_4(u, v) \\ V_5(u, v) \\ V_6(u, v) \end{pmatrix}.$$

By similarly superimposing the u and v parameters, the vector field can be visualized as a collection of cylinders rather than line segments. This technique was used to create the image in Figure 4.4.

The next sections discuss the use and implementation of particular visualization methods in GENMOD. These methods involve different tradeoffs between interactivity and accuracy.

4.3.2 Fast Visualization

Figure 4.5 illustrates the simplest and fastest form of visualization in the GENMOD system. Parameteric functions are uniformly sampled, including the variable input coordinates. Further, the variable input coordinates are sampled before the visualization takes place.

An example GENMOD specification of the fast visualization process is the following:

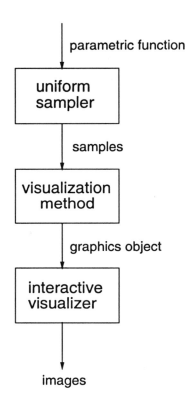

Figure 4.5: Fast visualization in GENMOD. Parametric functions (of type MAN) are uniformly sampled using their uniform evaluation method. The resulting samples are sent to a visualization method which creates a graphics object using calls to a graphics library. The resulting object is then visualized using an interactive visualizing tool that renders the graphics object, allowing interactive control of camera and lighting information, and selection of animated input parameters of parameterized shapes. Other forms of visualization are also available in GENMOD that use adaptive sampling rather than uniform sampling to produce more accurate shape approximations. These forms also produce a graphics object which can be visualized using the same interactive visualizer tool. □

```
int precision[] = {200};
MAN' c = m_crv("foo.crv",m_x(0));

object_object("foo");
m_curve(c,0,canonical_parm_space,precision);
close_object();

view_object("foo");
```

In this case, the parametric function c, a 2D curve, is used in the curve visualization method to create the graphics object foo. The m_curve operator is the curve visualization method. It takes four arguments. The first specifies the parametric function to be visualized. The second specifies the number of extra input coordinates to be superimposed — the rest of the extra input coordinates are animated as discussed previously.[5] In this example, the parametric function c has no extra input coordinates; it is a single 2D curve. The third argument specifies the parameter space over which to sample the curve. The argument canonical_parameter_space can be used for any parametric function and specifies a parameter space from 0 to 1 in each parametric coordinate. Finally, the precision argument specifies the number of samples in each of the parametric coordinates. In this example, 200 samples will be computed on the curve. After the object foo is defined, the view_object routine invokes the interactive visualization tool to view the curve.

Similar visualization methods exist for surfaces, points, planar areas, and transformations as well as for curves. The use of the surface visualization method, m_surface, is demonstrated in Section B.4. In fact, the surface visualization method has four distinct forms allowing surface normals and/or colors to be specified as well as points. The simplest form (m_surface) takes a parametric function of output dimension 3 and forms a collection of polygons. Normals, necessary for the rendering algorithm, are computed with a finite difference approximation.

Another surface visualization method takes a parametric function of output dimension 6 in which the surface normals are included in the samples as the last three coordinates. A third surface visualization method allows the definition of texture mapped surfaces where the color can vary over the surface. Surface colors are included in the samples as the last three coordinates. Again, a parametric function of output dimension 6 is required. Finally, both normals and colors can be included with a final surface visualization method, which takes a parametric

---

[5]To determine which parametric coordinates are intrinsic, animated, or superimposed, the visualization method uses a sorted list of the parametric variables used in the parametric function to be visualized. Assume the method has n intrinsic parameters and m variable input parameters are to be superimposed. Assume further that the parametric function has N input variables. The first n of these are thus the intrinsic parameters, the next m are the superimposed parameters, and the rest ($N - n - m$ parameters) are animated.

function of output dimension 9.

The user is free to place any calls to the graphics library between the open_object and close_object invocations. This includes various 3D transformations that affect the renderable objects defined, additional renderable objects (e.g., more curves or surfaces), or rendering parameters such as the color of the curve. The teddy bear definition in Section B.4 provides an example of how visualization methods and graphics library calls can be combined in a graphics object definition. We note that the full power of a general purpose language such as C becomes quite useful here, allowing the user to define quite complicated assemblies of objects with different spatial relationships, colors, and parameterized behaviors.

The visualization methods described here approximate shapes using uniform sampling. For example, the surface visualization method takes samples that form a set of 2D grids, one for each value of the variable input parameters. Let $S(u, v, t)$ be a time-varying surface, uniformly sampled with n_u samples in u, n_v samples in v, and n_t samples in t. The uniform samples of S thus form a collection of n_t 2D grids, each $n_u \times n_v$, representing S at a single t value. For each 2D grid, we form a collection of triangles, simply by forming two triangles for each adjacent group of four uv samples. This scheme has the advantage that real-time animation is possible, even when the shape is represented using complicated functions. The disadvantage is that much memory is required to store the precomputed samples, especially when there are many input coordinates. Another disadvantage is that the modeler must choose the sampling densities before the shape is visualized. An alternative technique that addresses these problems is discussed in the next section.

4.3.3   Non-Precomputed Visualization

For shapes with variable input parameters, precomputing the shape samples and then dialing through them is useful but very restrictive. GENMOD provides a more dynamic alternative using a curve editor interface. This alternative calls the visualization method during the visualization process rather than as a preprocessing step. Parameters to be varied are attached to 2D points or curves. Changing a point or curve in the curve editor then causes a new shape to be approximated and rendered.

For example, consider a 1D family of curves $C(s, t)\colon \mathbf{R}^2 \to \mathbf{R}^3$. The visualization method of the previous section samples C over a 2D lattice, with a pre-specified number of samples in s and t. The non-precomputed visualization method attaches the variable input parameter t to, for example, the x coordinate of a point in the curve editor. Changing this point causes a new curve, $C(s, t_0)$, to be approximated, where t_0 is computed from the x coordinate. Of course, performance may be poor if approximation of C requires extensive computation.

4.3.4   Non-Uniformly Sampled Visualization

GENMOD also provides visualization methods that do not use uniform sampling. These methods use adaptive sampling with criteria selected by the user and expressed using the GENMOD symbolic operators. Section 6.3 describes how these methods are implemented.

The resulting graphics object (e.g., a collection of line segments for a curve, or polygons for a surface) can be placed between open_object and close_object and viewed with view_object, along with the renderable objects discussed previously. Significant time is usually required to perform the adaptive sampling, compared with simple uniform sampling. Rendering time for the resulting graphics object, however, can be similar to that for the uniform sampling methods, since this time is related to the number of tessellation units, regardless of how they were produced.

Adaptively sampled objects can also be written to files and used in programs outside the GENMOD system, such as high quality rendering programs or simulation programs. In these cases, the extra time spent computing an accurate approximation is usually warranted.

4.3.5   Interactive Rendering Implementation

GENMOD provides a tool for interactively visualizing a collection of renderable objects once they have been created with the visualization methods. This is the tool invoked with the line

```
view_object("foo");
```

in the example in Section 4.3.2.

The modeler uses a 3D track ball to interactively rotate the objects in three dimensions. Three 1D dial devices are used to translate the objects along each of the coordinate axes, and another dial is used to scale the objects. Dial devices can also be attached to animated input variables. Different shapes with the same animated input variable are simultaneously changed when the dial attached to that variable is turned. This allows parameterized assemblies of objects to be visualized.

The track ball and dial devices are used to position the whole collection of objects as a group, or to move an individual object with respect to the others. The tool also has modes to allow the user to change the lighting and camera characteristics. Finally, the user can interactively change the following rendering characteristics:

1. How the tessellation units are derived from the uniform lattice of samples — the user can reduce the number of polygons or line segments that are derived from the uniform sampling of the shape, to increase rendering speed. This is done simply by disregarding some of the samples.

2. Whether surfaces are solid shaded or drawn with lines — the user can switch between these rendering modes, using line drawing to improve rendering speed.

3. Whether line drawings are depth-cued — depth cueing enhances interpretation of line drawings, at a slightly increased rendering cost.

Chapter 5

Interval Methods for Shape Synthesis and Analysis

In Chapter 2 we introduced the constraint solution and constrained minimization operators and enumerated some of their uses in a geometric modeling system. This chapter discusses two basic algorithms that use interval methods to compute solutions to systems of constraints and constrained global minimization problems. We will refer to such problems as *global problems* in the following text.

Interval analysis is a new and promising branch of applied mathematics. A general treatment of interval analysis can be found in [MOOR66] and [MOOR79] by R. E. Moore, the "inventor" of interval analysis as a tool for error analysis on digital computers. More recently, interval analysis has been used in a variety of algorithms to compute solutions to global problems (see, for example, [RATS88]). The ideas presented in this section are not new but find new application in the area of geometric modeling.

The interval analysis approach to solving global problems can be summarized as follows:

1. Inclusion functions are constructed which bound the ranges of functions used in the constraining equations and inequalities and the objective function (function to be minimized).

2. These inclusion functions are used in a branch and bound algorithm. An initial region of parameter space is recursively subdivided into smaller regions. Inclusion functions are used to test whether a particular region can be a solution to the global problem. For example, to test whether a region X may include a solution to the equation $f(x) = 0$, an inclusion function for f is evaluated over the region X. If the resulting bound on f does not contain 0, then X may be rejected. Similarly, an inclusion function bound

on the objective function in a minimization problem can reject a region if the objective function is too large to contain a global minimum. Subdivision proceeds until all regions are either rejected or accepted as solution regions.

In addition, such subdivision methods can be augmented by local techniques (e.g., Newton and quasi-Newton methods for constraint problems, steepest descent and conjugate gradient methods for minimization problems). Incorporation of these techniques can often dramatically improve the solution algorithm's performance.

5.1   Why Interval Analysis?

The interval analysis approach has several advantages over other solution approaches to global problems. Interval analysis controls approximation errors that result from doing imprecise floating point computation on a digital computer. Control of error is accomplished by ensuring that inclusion functions are valid bounds, even though these bounds must be represented with the machine's discrete set of floating point numbers. Interval analysis is an exhaustive technique; that is, all regions of the problem's input space are examined for solutions. The interval analysis approach thus allows global minima to be found, not just a local minimum that may be close to the global minimum. Furthermore, all minima or all solutions to a constraint system can be found, rather than a single solution.[1]

Interval analysis algorithms have two main problems as well. First, interval bounds tend to become very large as the "complexity" of the bounded function grows. By complexity, we mean, roughly, the number of primitive operations required to evaluate the function. This problem results because, in order to control approximation error and reduce computation, bounds are computed that are larger than the ideal, theoretical bounds. The excess size is added to and magnified with each operation. Although an interval analysis approach will not lose areas that contain solutions, it may fail to converge to adequately small regions if there is too much excess in the inclusion function bound. In particular, interval analysis approaches are often unacceptable for iterated solution methods, such as for ODEs, because intermediate results of the algorithm are incrementally updated, giving a very complex result as the computation progresses.

Second, interval analysis approaches, because they are exhaustive, tend to be slow, especially as the dimension of a problem's input space grows. Even when enhanced with non-interval techniques, interval approaches are not applicable to problems with large numbers of variables. For example, we would not expect

---

[1] Actually, the interval analysis algorithms presented here yield a set of intervals that bound the solutions.

interval methods to be appropriate for solving problems for which statistical optimization methods are commonly employed.

For the generative modeling approach advocated here, we believe the benefits of interval methods far outweigh their disadvantages. Functions can be represented with simple, noniterated formulae for which relatively tight inclusion functions can be computed. Also, the global problems that arise tend to be defined in terms of a small number of parameters (e.g., two to compute the intersection of two curves, four to compute the intersection of two surfaces or to compute a CSG operation on two surfaces). For problems with such small numbers of variables, satisfactory performance has been achieved with interval methods in a prototype implementation. At the same time, interval methods have allowed robust control of error. They have allowed computation of all solutions to global problems, a property employed in many of the algorithms that follow.

5.2   Inclusion Functions

An inclusion function produces a bound for the range of a function, given a bound on its domain. These bounds take the form of a vector of real intervals; a more precise definition will follow in Section 5.2.1. The goal of an inclusion function is to bound a function as tightly as possible, using as little computation as possible. Tight bounds allow domain regions to be rejected earlier in algorithms to solve global problems, saving further computation to subdivide the region and bound its subregions.

This section defines inclusion functions and describes some of their mathematical properties. Methods are presented for computing inclusion functions of functions represented as the composition of operators like those introduced in Section 2.2.3.

5.2.1   Terminology and Definitions

An *interval*, $A = [a, b]$, is a subset of $\mathbf{R}$ defined as

$$[a, b] \equiv \{x \mid a \leq x \leq b, \ x, a, b \in \mathbf{R}\}.$$

The numbers a and b are called the *bounds* of the interval; a is called the *lower bound* and b, the *upper bound*. The lower and upper bounds of an interval are written as

$$\begin{aligned} \mathrm{lb}[a, b] &\equiv a \\ \mathrm{ub}[a, b] &\equiv b. \end{aligned}$$

The symbol $\mathbf{I}$ denotes the set of all intervals. A *point interval* is a special interval in which the lower and upper bounds are equal; i.e.,

$$A = [a, a].$$

A *vector-valued interval of dimension n*, $A = (A_1, A_2, \ldots, A_n)$, is a subset of $\mathbf{R}^n$ defined as

$$A \equiv \{x \mid x_i \in A_i \text{ and } A_i \in \mathbf{I} \text{ for } i = 1, 2, \ldots, n\}.$$

For example, a vector-valued interval of dimension 2 represents a rectangle in the plane, while a vector-valued interval of dimension 3 represents a "brick" in 3D space. An interval A_i that is a component of a vector-valued interval is called a *coordinate interval of A*. The symbol $\mathbf{I}^m$ denotes the set of all vector-valued intervals of dimension m.

The *width* of an interval, written $w([a, b])$, is defined by

$$w([a, b]) \equiv b - a.$$

The *midpoint* of an interval, written $\text{mid}([a, b])$, is defined by

$$\text{mid}([a, b]) \equiv \frac{a + b}{2}.$$

Similarly, the width and midpoint of a vector-valued interval, $A \in \mathbf{I}^n$, are defined as

$$
\begin{aligned}
w(A) &= \max_{i=1}^{n} w(A_i) \\
\text{mid}(A) &= (\text{mid}(A_1), \text{mid}(A_2), \ldots, \text{mid}(A_n)).
\end{aligned}
$$

Hereafter, we will use the term interval to refer to both intervals and vector-valued intervals; the distinction will be clear from the context.

Given a subset D of $\mathbf{R}^m$, let $\mathbf{I}(D)$ be defined as the set of all intervals that are subsets of D:

$$\mathbf{I}(D) \equiv \{Y \mid Y \in \mathbf{I}^m \text{ and } Y \subset D\}.$$

Let $f: D \to \mathbf{R}^n$ be a function and $Y \in \mathbf{I}(D)$. An *inclusion function* for f, written $\square f$, is defined as

$$\square f: \mathbf{I}(D) \to \mathbf{I}^n$$

satisfying the property that

$$x \in Y \Rightarrow f(x) \in \square f(Y) \quad \text{for all } Y \in \mathbf{I}(D).$$

Thus, $\square f$ is a vector-valued interval bound on the range of f over a vector-valued interval bound on its domain.

An inclusion function $\Box f$ is called *isotone* (also termed *inclusion monotonic*) if

$$Y \subset Z \Rightarrow \Box f(Y) \subset \Box f(Z).$$

An inclusion function $\Box f$ is called *convergent* if

$$w(X) \to 0 \;\Rightarrow\; w(\Box f(X)) \to 0.$$

Note that f must be continuous for its inclusion function to be convergent. In fact, convergent inclusion functions can never actually be implemented on real computers having finite precision. Nevertheless, they are a useful tool for the analysis of interval algorithms (see, for example, the proofs of convergence of the constraint solution and minimization algorithms in Sections C.2 and C.3).

The *ideal inclusion function* of a function f, written $\overset{\text{idl}}{\Box} f$, is an inclusion function for f that results in the "tightest" interval possible. That is, for any domain interval, the resulting range interval consists of a vector of real intervals for which no lower bound may be increased or upper bound decreased, while the result remains a bound on the range of f. We note that the ideal inclusion function is always isotone. The quality of an inclusion function, $\Box f$, may be measured by its *excess width*, defined as the difference in width between the inclusion function and an ideal inclusion function for the same function:

$$w(\Box f(Y)) - w(\overset{\text{idl}}{\Box} f(Y)) \text{ for } Y \in \mathbf{I}(D).$$

An inclusion function, $\Box f$, is called *order* α if its excess width is of the order[2] of its domain width, raised to the power α, i.e.,

$$w(\Box f(Y)) - w(\overset{\text{idl}}{\Box} f(Y)) = \mathcal{O}(w(Y)^\alpha).$$

A high order means that the inclusion function rapidly becomes a tight bound as the width of the domain interval shrinks.[3]

A function f is called *Lipschitz* if there exists an inclusion function for f and a real constant K such that

$$w(\Box f(Y)) \leq K w(Y) \quad \forall Y \in \mathbf{I}(D).$$

---

[2] A function, $u(t)$ is *order* another function $v(t)$ over a domain $t \in S$, written $u = \mathcal{O}(v)$, if there exists a constant $B > 0$ such that $\|u(t)/v(t)\| < B$ for all $t \in S$.

[3] Contrary to what one might expect, an excess width of 0 does not imply that an inclusion function is identical to the ideal inclusion function. In order for an inclusion function to have excess width 0, it must only be identical to the ideal inclusion function in whatever coordinate interval has the maximum width. To restore our mathematical intuition, many other widths can be defined (analogous to vector norms in $\mathbf{R}^n$), such as the sum of the widths of the coordinate intervals, the square root of the sum of their squares, and so forth. Theorems like Theorem C.1 on page 277 are easily amended for such definitions of the width of a vector-valued interval.

5.2.2   Inclusion Functions for Arithmetic Operations

To see how inclusion functions can be evaluated on a computer, let us first consider functions defined using arithmetic operations. Let g and h be functions from $\mathbf{R}^m$ to $\mathbf{R}$, and let $X \in \mathbf{I}^m$. Let inclusion functions for g and h be given and evaluated on the interval X:

$$\square g(X) = [a, b]$$
$$\square h(X) = [c, d].$$

Given these interval bounds on g and h, we can bound an arithmetic combination, $g \star h$, where $\star$ represents addition, subtraction, multiplication or division. This bound may be computed by bounding the set $Q_\star$, defined as

$$Q_\star = \{ x \star y \mid x \in [a, b], y \in [c, d] \} .$$

$Q_\star$ can be bounded within an interval using the well-known technique of *interval arithmetic*. Interval arithmetic defines the operators $+_\square$, $-_\square$, $*_\square$, and $/_\square$ according to the rules

$$
\begin{aligned}
[a, b] +_\square [c, d] &= Q_+ &= [a + c, b + d] \\
[a, b] -_\square [c, d] &= Q_- &= [a - d, b - c] \\
[a, b] *_\square [c, d] &= Q_* &= [\min(ac, ad, bc, bd), \max(ac, ad, bc, bd)] \\
[a, b] /_\square [c, d] &= Q_/ &= [\min(\tfrac{a}{c}, \tfrac{a}{d}, \tfrac{b}{c}, \tfrac{b}{d}), \max(\tfrac{a}{c}, \tfrac{a}{d}, \tfrac{b}{c}, \tfrac{b}{d})] \\
& & \text{provided } 0 \notin [c, d].
\end{aligned}
$$

These rules lead to the following inclusion functions for $f \star g$ over the interval X:

$$
\begin{aligned}
\square(g + h)(X) &= \square g(X) +_\square \square f(X) \\
\square(g - h)(X) &= \square g(X) -_\square \square f(X) \\
\square(g * h)(X) &= \square g(X) *_\square \square f(X) \\
\square(g/h)(X) &= \square g(X) /_\square \square f(X).
\end{aligned}
$$

Therefore, we can evaluate an inclusion function for $f \star g$, given inclusion functions for the functions f and g.

Unfortunately, the inclusion functions defined above are only "theoretically" valid; they rely on an infinitely precise representation for real numbers and arithmetic operations. Of course, such infinite precision cannot be achieved using the floating point hardware of a digital computer. To perform interval analysis on a computer, an interval $A = [a, b]$ must be approximated by a *machine interval* $A_M = [a_M, b_M]$ that contains A and that is representable on the computer (i.e., a_M and b_M are members of the machine's set of floating point numbers). A computer implementation of an inclusion function must ensure that machine intervals are produced that contain the range of the function.

Specifically, to perform interval arithmetic on a computer, we must be careful computing the arithmetic operations on the interval bounds. We cannot assume that an inclusion function for $g + h$ can be constructed by producing the interval $[a +_M c, b +_M d]$, where the $+_M$ operator denotes the hardware addition operator. Hardware addition yields rounding errors, so it is possible that

$$a +_M c > a + c,$$

in which case the interval $[a +_M c, b +_M d]$ might not be a valid bound for $g + h$. This problem can be solved on machines that support round-to-$-\infty$ and round-to-$+\infty$ rounding modes, such as those that conform to the IEEE floating point standard [ANSI/IEEE Std 754-1985, IEEE Standard for Binary Floating-Point Arithmetic]. Hardware operations that are performed in round-to-$-\infty$ mode result in a lower bound for the result of the operation, rather than a result that is close to the theoretical result, but may be greater or less. Hardware operations performed in round-to-$+\infty$ mode result in an upper bound for the result. A valid inclusion function for an arithmetic operator can therefore be computed using the round-to-$-\infty$ mode for computation of interval lower bounds (e.g., the addition $a +_M c$ for the lower bound of $g + h$) and round-to-$+\infty$ mode for computation of interval upper bounds (e.g., the addition $b +_M d$ for the upper bound of $g + h$).

5.2.3 Natural Interval Extensions

In the previous section we showed how inclusion functions may be evaluated for functions defined using arithmetic operators. In summary, given inclusion functions $\Box g$ and $\Box h$, we can construct an inclusion function for any arithmetic combination, $g \star h$. Symbolically, we have

$$\Box(g \star h) = \Box g \star_\Box \Box h,$$

where $\star_\Box$ is an operator that takes the results of two inclusion functions and produces a bound on their arithmetic combination. For example, the $+_\Box$ operator is defined by

$$[a, b] +_\Box [c, d] = [a + c, b + d].$$

It is clear that this technique can be recursively applied to yield an inclusion function for an arbitrary nested combination of arithmetic operators on a set of functions with known inclusion functions. For example, an inclusion function for $f + (g + h)$ is given by

$$\Box(f + (g + h)) = \Box f +_\Box (\Box g +_\Box \Box h). \tag{5.1}$$

Furthermore, this notion can be extended to non-arithmetic operators. For each operator $P(f_1, f_2, \ldots, f_n)$ that produces a function given n simpler functions, we define a method, $P_\square$, that evaluates an inclusion function for P, depending only on the interval results of the inclusion functions $\square f_i$. In fact, this method is locally recursive, as defined on page 46. Let each of the functions f_i be defined on a domain D and let $X \in I(D)$. An inclusion function for $P(f_1, \ldots, f_n)$ is then given by

$$\square P(f_1, f_2, \ldots, f_n)(X) = P_\square(\square f_1(X), \square f_2(X), \ldots, \square f_n(X)).$$

In a generalization of Equation 5.1, given a set of operators like P, say $P_1, P_2, \ldots, P_N$, an inclusion function can be evaluated for any function formed by their composition, such as

$$P_1(P_2(f_1, f_2), P_3(f_3)).$$

Inclusion functions that are constructed with this recursive approach are called *natural interval extensions*.

Construction of an operator's inclusion function method may not be difficult if the operator's monotonicity intervals are known. Such inclusion functions are often ideal (i.e., have an excess width of 0). For example, an inclusion function evaluation method can be defined for the cosine operator. This definition is based on the observation that the cosine function is monotonically decreasing in the interval $[\pi 2n, \pi(2n + 1)]$ and monotonically increasing in the interval $[\pi(2n + 1), \pi(2n + 2)]$, for integer n. Let f be a function from $\mathbf{R}^m$ to $\mathbf{R}$, and let $X \in \mathbf{I}^m$. Let an inclusion function for f be given and evaluated on the interval X, yielding an interval $[a, b]$. An inclusion function for $\cos(f)$ can be evaluated on X according to the following rules:[4]

$$\cos_\square([a, b]) =$$
$$\begin{cases} [-1, 1], & \text{if } 1 + \lceil \frac{a}{\pi} \rceil \leq \frac{b}{\pi} \\ [-1, \max(\cos(a), \cos(b))], & \text{if } \lceil \frac{a}{\pi} \rceil \leq \frac{b}{\pi} \text{ and } \lceil \frac{a}{\pi} \rceil \bmod 2 = 1 \\ [\min(\cos(a), \cos(b)), 1], & \text{if } \lceil \frac{a}{\pi} \rceil \leq \frac{b}{\pi} \text{ and } \lceil \frac{a}{\pi} \rceil \bmod 2 = 0 \\ [\min(\cos(a), \cos(b)), & \\ \quad \max(\cos(a), \cos(b))], & \text{otherwise.} \end{cases}$$

Similar inclusion functions can be constructed for operators such as sine, square root, exponential, and logarithm.

As another example, the "square" operator, which raises its argument to the second power, has an easily constructed inclusion function. In this case, if the

---

[4] As in the case of the arithmetic operators, care should be exercised in computing the interval result for the cosine inclusion function. The numerical cosine evaluations implied by $\min(\cos(a), \cos(b))$, for example, must be computed so that they are a lower bound for the theoretical result.

function f is defined as before, we have

$$\Box f^2(X) = \begin{cases} [a^2, b^2], & \text{if } a \geq 0 \\ [b^2, a^2], & \text{if } b \leq 0 \\ [0, \max(a^2, b^2)], & \text{otherwise} \end{cases}$$

where $\Box f(X) = [a, b]$ as before. Interestingly, an inclusion function for the square operator can also be defined using the multiply inclusion function, $*_\Box$, via

$$\Box f^2(X) = \Box f(X) *_\Box \Box f(X).$$

Such an inclusion function is not as tight as the one described above if the interval to be squared straddles 0. For example, given $a > 0$,

$$[-a, a] *_\Box [-a, a] = [-a^2, a^2]$$

but

$$[-a, a]^2 = [0, a^2].$$

This is typical of the behavior of inclusion functions, in that looser bounds are achieved when functionally dependent entities are combined as independent intervals.

Inclusion functions for the vector and matrix operations discussed in Section 2.2.3 are also easy to construct. For example, consider the dot product operator, which takes two functions of output dimension n, f and g, and produces a function, $f \cdot g$, of output dimension 1, defined by

$$f \cdot g = \sum_{i=1}^{n} f_i g_i.$$

An inclusion function method for the dot product operator can be defined using the interval arithmetic already discussed. To compute $\Box(f \cdot g)$, we compute

$$(\Box f_1 *_\Box \Box g_1) +_\Box (\Box f_2 *_\Box \Box g_2) +_\Box \ldots +_\Box (\Box f_n *_\Box \Box g_n).$$

Note that the interval $\Box f_i$ or $\Box g_i$ is trivially computed by extracting the i-th coordinate interval of the vector-valued interval produced by $\Box f$ and $\Box g$, respectively. Similarly, interval arithmetic can be used to define inclusion function methods for the matrix multiply, inverse and determinant operators, and for vector operators like addition, subtraction, length, scaling, and cross product.

5.2.4   Inclusion Functions for Relational and Logical Operators

Inclusion functions can also be defined for relational and logical operators. These definitions allow natural interval extensions for functions that employ relational and logical operations (e.g., functions used as constraints).

A relational operator produces a result in the set $\{0, 1\}$, 0 for "false" and 1 for "true." The operators **equal to, not equal to, less than,** and **greater than or equal to** are all binary relational operators. Inclusion functions for these operators must bound the result of the operator. For example, an inclusion function for **less than** can be easily defined. Let f and g be functions from $\mathbf{R}^n$ to $\mathbf{R}$. Let $\Box f$ and $\Box g$ be inclusion functions for f and g respectively. Let $X \in \mathbf{I}^n$, and

$$\begin{aligned}
\Box f(X) &= [a, b] \\
\Box g(X) &= [c, d].
\end{aligned}$$

Then we have

$$\Box (f < g)(X) = \begin{cases} [0, 0], & \text{if } d \leq a \\ [1, 1], & \text{if } b < c \\ [0, 1], & \text{otherwise.} \end{cases}$$

Similarly, an inclusion function for the equality operator is given by

$$\Box (f = g)(X) = \begin{cases} [0, 0], & \text{if } d < a \text{ or } b < c \\ [1, 1], & \text{if } a = b = c = d \\ [0, 1], & \text{otherwise.} \end{cases}$$

Three results of a relational operator's inclusion function can be expected:

- $[0, 0]$ — the relation is false over the entire domain interval

- $[1, 1]$ — the relation is true over the entire domain interval

- $[0, 1]$ — the relation may be true or false in the domain interval

Logical operators combine results of the relational operators in Boolean expressions. The operators **and, or,** and **not** are examples of logical operators. An inclusion function for a logical operator must be defined with respect to the ternary output of the relational inclusion functions. For example, if r_1 and r_2 are two relational functions from $\mathbf{R}^n$ to $\{0, 1\}$, and $\Box r_1$ and $\Box r_2$ are their corresponding inclusion functions, then an inclusion function for the logical **and** of the relations, $r_1 \wedge r_2$, is given by

$$\Box (r_1 \wedge r_2) = \begin{cases} [0, 0], & \text{if } \Box r_1 = [0, 0] \text{ or } \Box r_2 = [0, 0] \\ [1, 1], & \text{if } \Box r_1 = [1, 1] \text{ and } \Box r_2 = [1, 1] \\ [0, 1], & \text{otherwise.} \end{cases}$$

An inclusion function for the logical **or** of the relations, $r_1 \vee r_2$, is given by

$$\Box(r_1 \vee r_2) = \begin{cases} [0,0], & \text{if } \Box r_1 = [0,0] \text{ and } \Box r_2 = [0,0] \\ [1,1], & \text{if } \Box r_1 = [1,1] \text{ or } \Box r_2 = [1,1] \\ [0,1], & \text{otherwise.} \end{cases}$$

An inclusion function for the logical **not** of a relation, $\neg r_1$, is given by

$$\Box(\neg r_1) = \begin{cases} [0,0], & \text{if } \Box r_1 = [1,1] \\ [1,1], & \text{if } \Box r_1 = [0,0] \\ [0,1], & \text{otherwise.} \end{cases}$$

5.2.5 Mean Value and Taylor Forms

Given a differentiable function $f: \mathbf{R}^m \to \mathbf{R}^n$, with parameters $x_1, x_2, \ldots, x_m$, an inclusion function, called the *mean value form*, can be constructed for f as follows:

$$\Box f(Y) = f(c) +_\Box \Box f'(Y) \cdot_\Box (Y -_\Box c) \tag{5.2}$$

where $c \in Y$, $Y \in \mathbf{I}^m$ and $\Box f'$ is an inclusion function for the Jacobian matrix of f, i.e.,

$$\Box f'(Y) = \left[\Box \frac{\partial f_i}{\partial x_j}(Y) \right].$$

The $\cdot_\Box$ operator denotes an inclusion function method for the matrix multiply operator. The above formula represents a valid inclusion function for f because of Taylor's theorem. Note that the addition, subtraction and matrix–vector multiplication operations implied by this definition are computed using interval arithmetic.[5] The rest of the treatment of interval analysis in this book will drop the $\Box$ subscripts for interval arithmetic operations; it should be clear by the context whether the standard operations or their interval analogs are appropriate. We also note that this mean value form can be easily implemented in the generative modeling approach by using the natural interval extension for the Jacobian matrix, which may be symbolically computed using the partial derivative operator.

If f' is Lipschitz, then the mean value form is order 2, a result proved in Section C.1. This result means that a mean value form can result in very tight bounds as the width of the domain interval shrinks. On the other hand, the quadratic convergence of the mean value form implies that a poor bound will result for large intervals, Y. In this case, it may be better to use the natural interval extension for f, which may be order 1, and switch to a mean value form when the domain regions become small enough.

---

[5]It should also be noted that to implement this mean value form on a computer, the interval $\Box f([c, c])$ should replace $f(c)$. This is because the computer cannot *exactly* compute $f(c)$ and must instead bound the result.

Choosing $c = \text{mid}(Y)$ in Equation 5.2 simplifies the calculations. This is because the interval subtraction result $Y - \text{mid}(Y)$ leads to symmetric intervals of the form

$$([-y_1, y_1], \ldots, [-y_n, y_n]).$$

The matrix–vector interval multiplication implied by Equation 5.2 then requires multiplication of intervals (from the Jacobian inclusion function, $\Box f'$) by symmetric intervals (from $Y - c$), which can be computed by

$$[-y, y] *_\Box [a, b] = [-\max(|a|, |b|)\, y, \max(|a|, |b|)\, y].$$

Hence, the mean value form can be computed by finding the maximum of the absolute values of the Jacobian interval bounds, and computing simple scales of the symmetric intervals rather than the more costly computation implied by the interval multiplication rule in Section 5.2.2. On the other hand, choosing a specific c not necessarily equal to $\text{mid}(Y)$ can lead to a tighter bound for f [BAUM87].

The idea of a mean value form can be generalized to produce inclusion functions that incorporate more terms of a function's Taylor expansion. For example, an inclusion function called a *Taylor form of order 2* is defined by

$$\Box f(Y) = f(c) + f'(c)(Y - c) + \frac{1}{2}(Y - c)^T \Box f''(Y)(Y - c)$$

where $\Box f''$ is an inclusion function for the Hessian operator of f and the T superscript denotes the transpose operator. Taylor forms of order n are treated in more detail in [RATS84] and [RATS88].

Under certain conditions, a mean value form can also be used as an inclusion function for a function that is not differentiable, using the concept of a *generalized gradient*. For example, the scalar function $f(x) = |x|$ is not differentiable at $x = 0$. Nevertheless, an inclusion function exists for its generalized gradient $\Box f'(X)$, given by

$$\Box f'([a, b]) = \begin{cases} [1, 1] & \text{if } a > 0 \\ [-1, -1] & \text{if } b < 0 \\ [-1, 1] & \text{if } 0 \in [a, b]. \end{cases}$$

A mean value form that uses this generalized gradient inclusion function is a valid inclusion function for f. A more complete definition and treatment of generalized gradients and their inclusion functions can be found in [RATS88].

5.2.6   An Inclusion Function for the Integration Operator

We can use the idea of the mean value form from the previous section to define a convergent inclusion function for the integration operator. Let $F(x)$ be defined by

$$F(x) \equiv \int_{b(x)}^{a(x)} f(\tau, x) \, d\tau$$

where $x = (x_1, \ldots, x_n)$. We would like to define an inclusion function for F, $\Box F$. Let $X \in \mathbf{I}^n$ and let inclusion functions for $a(x)$ and $b(x)$ be given and evaluated over X yielding

$$\Box a(X) = A = [a_1, a_2]$$
$$\Box b(X) = B = [b_1, b_2].$$

We thus require an interval bound on the set

$$Q(X) = \left\{ \int_b^a f(\tau, x) \, d\tau \mid a \in A, \, b \in B, \, x \in X \right\}.$$

There are two interesting cases for the intervals $A = [a_1, a_2]$ and $B = [b_1, b_2]$; either $b_2 \le a_1$ (Case I), or the two intervals overlap (Case II). Without loss of generality, if $a_2 \le b_1$, then we can switch the upper and lower limits of integration and negate the result, thus obtaining Case I again.

Case I: Disjoint Intervals

Since $b_2 \le a_1$, breaking up the integral into parts, we have

$$Q(X) = \left\{ \int_{b_2}^{a_1} f(\tau, x) \, d\tau + \int_b^{b_2} f(\tau, x) \, d\tau + \int_{a_1}^a f(\tau, x) \, d\tau \right.$$

$$\left. \mid a \in A, \, b \in B, \, x \in X \right\}$$

$$= Q_1(X) +_\Box Q_2(X) +_\Box Q_3(X).$$

$Q_1(X)$ may be bounded by choosing N points in the interval $[b_2, a_1]$, $\tau_1, \tau_2, \ldots, \tau_N$ such that

$$\tau_1 = b_2$$
$$\tau_N = a_1$$
$$\tau_i < \tau_{i+1} \quad \text{for all } i = 1, 2, \ldots, N - 1.$$

We then have

$$Q_1(X) \subset \sum_{i=1}^{N-1} \Box f([\tau_i, \tau_{i+1}], X)$$

where the sum refers to interval addition. $Q_2(X)$ and $Q_3(X)$ can be bounded via

$$Q_2(X) \subset [0, w(B)] *_\Box \Box f(B, X)$$
$$Q_3(X) \subset [0, w(A)] *_\Box \Box f(A, X).$$

Thus, for Case I, $\Box F(X)$ may be defined as

$$\Box F_I(X) \equiv \sum_{i=1}^{N-1} \Box f([\tau_i, \tau_{i+1}], X) +_\Box [0, w(B)] *_\Box \Box f(B, X)$$
$$+_\Box [0, w(A)] *_\Box \Box f(A, X).$$

Case II: Overlapping Intervals

In this case, $Q(X)$ may be expressed as the union of two sets, one in which the lower limit of integration is less than the upper limit, and the other in which the lower limit is greater than the lower

$$Q(X) = \left\{ \int_b^a f(\tau, x) \, d\tau \mid b \leq a, \, a \in A, \, b \in B, \, x \in X \right\} \bigcup$$
$$\left\{ -\int_a^b f(\tau, x) \, d\tau \mid a \leq b, \, a \in A, \, b \in B, \, x \in X \right\}$$
$$= Q_4(X) \bigcup Q_5(X).$$

Define the intervals

$$R_L = [b_1, \, \min(b_2, a_2)]$$
$$R_U = [\max(a_1, b_1), \, a_2]$$

and

$$S_L = [a_1, \, \min(a_2, b_2)]$$
$$S_U = [\max(b_1, a_1), \, b_2].$$

Using these definitions, we can restrict the interval domains of a and b in the above definitions of Q_4 and Q_5 via

$$Q_4(X) = \left\{ \int_b^a f(\tau, x) \, d\tau \mid b \leq a, \, a \in R_U, \, b \in R_L, \, x \in X \right\}$$
$$Q_5(X) = \left\{ -\int_a^b f(\tau, x) \, d\tau \mid a \leq b, \, a \in S_L, \, b \in S_U, \, x \in X \right\}.$$

Defining the merged intervals $R = R_L \vee R_U$ and $S = S_L \vee S_U$, where the merge operator $\vee$ is defined in Section 5.3.3, we then have

$$Q_4(X) \quad \subset \quad [0, w(R)] *_\square \square f(R, X)$$
$$Q_5(X) \quad \subset \quad -[0, w(S)] *_\square \square f(S, X)$$

so that

$$Q(X) \subset [0, w(R)] *_\square \square f(R, X) \vee -[0, w(S)] *_\square \square f(S, X).$$

Thus, for Case II, $\square F(X)$ can be defined as

$$\square F_{\mathrm{II}}(X) \equiv [0, w(R)] *_\square \square f(R, X) \vee -[0, w(S)] *_\square \square f(S, X).$$

A complete inclusion function for F is then given by

$$\square F(X) \equiv \begin{cases} \square F_{\mathrm{I}}(X), & \text{if } A \cap B = \emptyset \\ \square F_{\mathrm{II}}(X), & \text{otherwise.} \end{cases}$$

Achieving Convergence

Unfortunately, this definition of an inclusion function for F is typically not convergent. In the definition of $\square F_{\mathrm{I}}$ in Case I, we choose N points in the interval $[b_2, a_1]$. In order to guarantee that $\square F$ be convergent, we must have

$$N \to \infty \quad \text{as} \quad w(X) \to 0.$$

Not only does this require that an unbounded amount of computation be performed, but sloppiness in the bounds returned for $\square f$ to compensate for numerical imprecision will soon overwhelm the computation, prohibiting convergence.

To solve this problem, we can use a mean value form to define an inclusion function for F that takes advantage of the non-convergent inclusion function we have already defined. We first note that

$$\frac{\partial F}{\partial x_i}(x) = \int_{b(x)}^{a(x)} \frac{\partial f}{\partial x_i}(\tau, x)\, d\tau + f(a(x), x)\frac{\partial a}{\partial x_i}(x) - f(b(x), x)\frac{\partial b}{\partial x_i}(x).$$

We can therefore use our non-convergent inclusion function to define an inclusion function for the first term of the above equation, and the natural interval extensions for the other two terms.[6] This yields an inclusion function for the partial derivatives of $F(x)$. The mean value form of Section 5.2.5 uses these partial derivatives

---

[6]That is, we can choose a finite N a priori to bound the derivatives of F, using the resulting bounds in a mean value form. Increasing N produces a tighter inclusion function, but any $N > 2$ generates a convergent mean value form.

to compute a convergent (in fact, order 2) inclusion function for the integration operator.

One snag in the analysis remains: the mean value form also requires a bound on the value of F at a point c in the interval domain. As we stated in the first paragraph, this bound is difficult to compute for integration, since greater accuracy in the bounds requires sampling the inclusion function for f at ever smaller intervals $[\tau_i, \tau_{i+1}]$. This problem highlights the main difficulty with interval analysis in that functions that must be evaluated numerically with iterative techniques are not good candidates for inclusion functions. Three approaches can be used to combat this problem:

1. Compute the integral bound using interval methods anyway. Depending on the accuracy required, we may still be able to bound $F(c)$ via

$$\sum_{i=1}^{N-1} \Box f([\tau_i, \tau_{i+1}], [c, c]).$$

2. Use symbolic integration to compute the parameterized indefinite integral of f, $G(x)$, so that

$$F(x) = G(a(x)) - G(b(x)).$$

   The natural interval extension or mean value form for G can then be used to define an inclusion function for F.

3. Bound $F(x)$ using standard numerical methods that return an error estimate, but don't guarantee the bound in the rigorous sense of interval analysis. While this is an unsatisfying approach because it degrades the robustness of the system, it can still yield good results if the user understands that errors can occur.

A similar technique, with similar problems, can be used to create an inclusion function for the ODE operator.

5.2.7   Inclusion Functions Based on Monotonicity

Given a differentiable function, $f: \mathbf{R}^n \to \mathbf{R}$, an inclusion function with very little excess width can be formed by noting where f is monotonic with respect to its input parameters, $x_1, x_2, \ldots, x_n$. Let Y be an interval in which to evaluate an inclusion function for f, given by

$$Y_i = [y_i^0, y_i^1].$$

Note that the behavior of f in the interval Y with respect to one of its input parameters x_i can be categorized in three ways:

$$\text{lb} \, \Box \frac{\partial f}{\partial x_i}(Y) \geq 0 \quad \Rightarrow \quad f \text{ is non-decreasing in the interval } Y$$

$$\text{ub} \, \Box \frac{\partial f}{\partial x_i}(Y) \leq 0 \quad \Rightarrow \quad f \text{ is non-increasing in the interval } Y$$

$$0 \in \Box \frac{\partial f}{\partial x_i}(Y) \quad \Rightarrow \quad \text{nothing can be concluded about } f.$$

If f is non-decreasing in an interval with respect to a parameter x_i, then the minimum value of f occurs at the minimum value of x_i in the interval. The maximum value of f occurs at the maximum value of x_i. Similarly, if f is non-increasing with respect to x_i, then its minimum value occurs at the maximum value of x_i, and its maximum value occurs at the minimum value of x_i.

We can thus form two intervals from Y, Y^- and Y^+, as follows:

$$Y_i^- = \begin{cases} [y_i^0, y_i^0], & \text{if lb} \, \Box \dfrac{\partial f}{\partial x_i}(Y) \geq 0 \\ [y_i^1, y_i^1], & \text{if ub} \, \Box \dfrac{\partial f}{\partial x_i}(Y) \leq 0 \\ [y_i^0, y_i^1], & \text{otherwise} \end{cases}$$

$$Y_i^+ = \begin{cases} [y_i^1, y_i^1], & \text{if lb} \, \Box \dfrac{\partial f}{\partial x_i}(Y) \geq 0 \\ [y_i^0, y_i^0], & \text{if ub} \, \Box \dfrac{\partial f}{\partial x_i}(Y) \leq 0 \\ [y_i^0, y_i^1], & \text{otherwise.} \end{cases}$$

Assume that an inclusion function exists for f, $\Box f$. For example, the natural interval extension for f can be used. A tighter inclusion function for f is then given by

$$\left[\text{lb} \, \Box f(Y^-), \text{ub} \, \Box f(Y^+) \right],$$

called the *monotonicity-test inclusion function*. This inclusion function is ideal if f is monotonic with respect to all its input parameters. If f is not a scalar function, then this technique can be used separately on each component of f.

Because an inclusion function based on monotonicity and the mean value form both evaluate inclusion functions for the partial derivatives of the function being bounded, it is reasonable to combine the two techniques and share these evaluations. This is easily accomplished since if $\Box_1 f, \Box_2 f, \dots, \Box_n f$ are all inclusion functions for f, then so is

$$\bigcap_{i=1}^{n} \Box_i f.$$

Thus the intersection of the bounds produced by the mean value form and the monotonicity-test inclusion function is also a valid inclusion function.

5.3   Constraint Solution Algorithm

A system of constraints can be represented as a function, $F: \mathbf{R}^n \to \mathbf{R}$, that returns a 1 if the constraints are satisfied and a 0 if they are not. Such a function can incorporate both equality and inequality constraints. It can be represented with the relational and logical operators discussed in Section 2.2.3. As discussed in Section 5.2.4, an inclusion function for F, $\Box F$, over a region $X \subset \mathbf{I}^n$ can take on three possible values:

$$\Box F(X) = [0,0] \quad \Rightarrow \quad X \text{ is an infeasible region}$$
$$\Box F(X) = [0,1] \quad \Rightarrow \quad X \text{ is an indeterminate region}$$
$$\Box F(X) = [1,1] \quad \Rightarrow \quad X \text{ is a feasible region}$$

An *infeasible region* is a region in which no point solves the constraint system. A *feasible region* is a region in which every point solves the constraint system. An *indeterminate region* is a region in which the constraint system may or may not have solutions.

The algorithm we will present also depends on an inclusion function, $\Box A$, called the *solution acceptance set constraint*, which determines when an indeterminate region should be accepted as a solution, as follows:

$$\Box A(X) = [0,0] \quad \Rightarrow \quad \text{subdivide } X$$
$$\Box A(X) = [0,1] \quad \Rightarrow \quad \text{subdivide } X$$
$$\Box A(X) = [1,1] \quad \Rightarrow \quad \text{accept } X \text{ as a solution}$$

The result $\Box A(X) = [0,0]$ is not expected since, for isotone inclusion functions, it implies that no region $Y \subset X$ will ever be accepted. We advocate keeping the functionality of rejection solely in the constraint inclusion function $\Box F$. On the other hand, some set constraints, like $w(X) < \delta$, are not isotone.[7] That is, a region Y for which $A(Y) = [0,0]$ may eventually be subdivided to generate a region Z for which $A(Z) = [1,1]$. It is therefore appropriate to subdivide a region even when its solution acceptance set constraint yields $[0,0]$.

Algorithm 5.1 finds a collection of intervals which are guaranteed to contain all solutions to the constraint system. In particular, by the property of inclusion

---

[7] In fact, such a set constraint is not even an inclusion function since it does not bound a function. Nevertheless, it is usefully applied as a solution acceptance set constraint in many situations. The solution acceptance set constraint, $\Box A$, is more appropriately seen as a mapping from intervals X to $\{0,1\}$, indicating whether X should be subdivided or accepted as a solution. Such a mapping is called a *set constraint* and is further explained in Section 5.3.4.1.

functions, if this algorithm finds no solutions, then the constraint system has no solutions, because a region Y is rejected only when $\Box F(Y)$ shows that it is infeasible. It can also be proved (Section C.2) that the constraint solution algorithm converges to the actual solution set if the inclusion functions used in the equality and inequality constraints are convergent.

Algorithm 5.1 (Constraint Solution Algorithm) We are given a constraint inclusion function $\Box F$, an initial region,[8] X, in which to find solutions $F(x) = 1$, and the solution acceptance set constraint $\Box A$.

---

place X on list L
while L is nonempty
      remove next region Y from L
      evaluate $\Box F$ on Y
      if $\Box F(Y) = [1, 1]$ add Y to solution
      else if $\Box F(Y) = [0, 0]$ discard Y
      else if $\Box A(Y) = [1, 1]$ add Y to solution
      else subdivide Y into regions Y_1 and Y_2 and insert into L
endwhile

5.3.1 The Problem of Indeterminacy

A computer implementation of the constraint solution algorithm can not iterate forever; it must terminate at some iteration n and accept the remaining regions as solutions. In particular, the algorithm may accept some indeterminate regions, which may contain zero, one, or more solutions. For example, consider solving a system of equations, $G(x) = 0$, for a function $G: \mathbf{R}^n \to \mathbf{R}^n$. Assume that the system has a finite, nonempty set of solutions for $x \in D \subset \mathbf{R}^n$. Any neighborhood of these solution points will also contain points, y, for which $G(y) \neq 0$. Hence an inclusion function for the system $G(x) = 0$ will always yield an indeterminate result in the neighborhood of a solution. The algorithm will accept such regions as solutions when they satisfy the solution acceptance set constraint. Of course, the algorithm may also accept an indeterminate region that contains no solutions; there is no way for the algorithm to make this distinction.

The problem that the constraint solution algorithm may yield regions that do not contain solutions, or regions that contain more than one solution, is mitigated by several factors. First, it may be enough to distinguish between the case that the constraint problem possibly has solutions (to some tolerance) and the case that

---

[8]The initial region X can be infinite if the technique of *infinite interval arithmetic* is used (see [RATS88]).

it has no solutions. For example, to compute interference detection between two parametric surfaces

$$S_1, S_2 \colon \mathbf{R}^2 \to \mathbf{R}^3,$$

a constraint system of three equations in four variables can be solved of the form

$$S_1(u_1, v_1) = S_2(u_2, v_2).$$

If we instead solve the relaxed constraint problem

$$\|S_1(u_1, v_1) - S_2(u_2, v_2)\| < \epsilon,$$

the algorithm can hope to produce feasible solution regions, for which the constraints are satisfied for every point in the region.[9] Such relaxed constraint problems are called ϵ-collisions in [VONH89]. If any feasible regions are found, the surfaces interfere to within the tolerance. If all regions are eventually found to be infeasible, the surfaces do not interfere within the tolerance, and in fact come no closer than ϵ. It is also possible that only indeterminate regions are accepted as solutions. In this case, we may consider the two surfaces to interfere to the extent that our limited floating point precision is able to ascertain.

Second, we may know a priori that the system has a single solution. This is not uncommon if the constraint solution problem is the result of a geometric modeling operation, such as computing the intersection of two curves. Let the solution acceptance set constraint have the simple form

$$\Box A(Y) \equiv (w(Y) < \epsilon).$$

If the inclusion functions bounding the constraint functionals are convergent, then such a solution approximation achieves any degree of accuracy as ϵ goes to 0. The algorithm can be run until a set of contiguous solution regions is accepted of small enough combined width. A point inside the set of regions can be used as an approximation to the solution contained within it. The technique of combining contiguous solution regions, called *solution aggregation*, will be discussed further in Section 5.3.3.

Third, we may be able to compute information about solutions to the constraint system as the algorithm progresses. For example, in solving the 1D system, $f(x) = 0$ for differentiable scalar function f, if we have that $f(x_0) < 0$ and $f(x_1) > 0$ and $\Box f'([x_0, x_1]) > 0$, then f is strictly increasing in the interval

---

[9]Note that the solution to the unrelaxed system is typically a curve of intersection between the two parametric surfaces. Any neighborhood of a point on this curve will also contain points for which the two surfaces do not intersect and hence do not solve the system of equations. The relaxed problem, on the other hand, has solutions for which a neighborhood of small enough size is completely contained within the solution space.

$[x_0, x_1]$ and hence has exactly one zero in this interval. This result can be generalized: Section 5.3.5 describes conditions computable with interval techniques guaranteeing that a region contains exactly one zero of a system of equations.

Finally, we can relax the constraints of a constraint system and/or accept indeterminate results of the algorithm. In practice, although we cannot guarantee the validity of such results, they are nevertheless useful. For example, if the constraint solution algorithm is used as part of a higher-level algorithm (e.g., an algorithm to approximate implicit curves, as will be presented in Section 6.2), then the global consistency of the result of the higher-level algorithm verifies to some extent the results of the constraint solution algorithm.

The next sections will discuss elements of the constraint solution algorithm in more detail.

5.3.2 Subdivision Methods

Subdivision in Algorithm 5.1 can proceed in two ways. First, each input space dimension can be cyclically subdivided at its midpoint. This is accomplished by storing the last subdivided dimension along with each region on the candidate solution list. Let n be the dimensionality of the input space, and let d be the last subdivided dimension of a region, $X = ([a_1, b_1], [a_2, b_2], \ldots, [a_n, b_n])$. The next dimension to subdivide, d', is computed as

$$d' = \begin{cases} d+1 & \text{if } d < n \\ 1 & \text{if } d = n. \end{cases}$$

The two child regions are then given by

$$
\begin{aligned}
Y_1 &= ([a_1, b_1], \ldots, [a_{(d'-1)}, b_{(d'-1)}], [a_{d'}, m], [a_{(d'+1)}, b_{(d'+1)}], \ldots, [a_n, b_n]) \\
Y_2 &= ([a_1, b_1], \ldots, [a_{(d'-1)}, b_{(d'-1)}], [m, b_{d'}], [a_{(d'+1)}, b_{(d'+1)}], \ldots, [a_n, b_n])
\end{aligned}
$$

where $m = (a_{d'} + b_{d'})/2$. The subdivided dimension, d', is stored along with the regions Y_1 and Y_2. This kind of subdivision, called *bisection* subdivision, is general, and simple to implement. Assuming that the list of Algorithm 5.1 is a LIFO, bisection subdivision guarantees that the width of all candidate regions shrink to 0 as the iteration level increases. It also produces sets of solution regions with special properties required by some of the geometric modeling algorithms, such as the implicit surface approximation algorithm of Section 6.6.

On the other hand, regions can be subdivided based on other criteria. By knowing properties of the constraint system whose solutions are sought, we can often deduce regions smaller than Y_1 and Y_2 where the constraints can be satisfied. For example, in the method of Hansen–Greenberg [RATS88] for finding zeroes of m nonlinear equations of m variables, gaps may be discovered in coordinate intervals of the region X where zeroes cannot exist. Hence, we can produce regions Y_1

and Y_2 that do not contain these infeasible points. Section 5.3.5 discusses another method for reducing the size of candidate intervals, known as the interval Newton method.

5.3.3   Solution Aggregation

Many times, we expect the solution set of a system of constraints to be a finite number of points. The constraint solution algorithm will typically return a collection of connected regions for each of the solution points, as shown in Figure 5.1. Using an argument similar to Theorem C.2, if a finite set of solutions exists, then Algorithm 5.1 will eventually produce candidate regions that can be organized into a collection of sets of connected regions, each set containing a single solution and disjoint from all other such sets. The technique of solution aggregation presumes that such an appropriate iteration level has been achieved, so that an approximate solution is given by a point inside each set, to any degree of accuracy as the iteration level is increased. The number of solutions to the constraint system is assumed to be the number of disjoint sets produced. This technique may be used heuristically, or in combination with the condition for existence of a unique zero presented in Section 5.3.6.

We now define a simple algorithm for solution aggregation. Given $A, B \in \mathbf{I}^n$, we define the *merge* operator, $A \vee B$, as

$$(A \vee B)_i \equiv [\min(\mathrm{lb}\, A_i, \mathrm{lb}\, B_i), \max(\mathrm{ub}\, A_i, \mathrm{ub}\, B_i)]$$

for each coordinate interval $i = 1, 2, \ldots, n$. Let S be a list of intervals, and X be an interval. We first define a function $\mathrm{add}(X, S)$ to add X onto the list S (with aggregation). We can then define a solution aggregation function, $\mathtt{aggregate}(Q)$, that takes a list of intervals, Q, and produces a new list of intervals, where all connected intervals are merged. The precise definitions of add and $\mathtt{aggregate}$ are shown in Figure 5.2.

5.3.4   Termination and Acceptance Criteria for Constraint Solution

Algorithm 5.1 can be applied to five specific problems:

1. Find a bound on the set of solutions

2. Determine whether or not a solution exists

3. Find one solution

4. Find all solutions

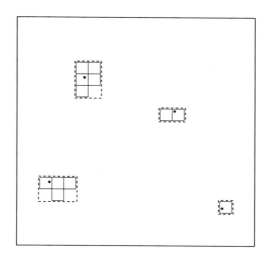

Figure 5.1: Solution aggregation. The solution regions returned by Algorithm 5.1 for an example problem with an input dimension of 2 are given by the collection of nondashed squares. The actual solutions are marked by dots. In this example, an adequate level of subdivision has been achieved so that sets of contiguous regions encompass each of the four solutions, and each contiguous region may be bounded in an interval (dashed boxes) that is disjoint from other such regions. □

---

add(X, S)

for each interval Y in S
   if $Y \cap X \neq \emptyset$ then
      $X = X \vee Y$
         delete Y from S
   endif
endfor
insert X into S
return S

---

aggregate(Q)

initialize aggregate list S to empty
for each interval X in Q
    $S = \text{add}(X, S)$
endfor
return S

Figure 5.2: Algorithms for solution aggregation. The function add adds a region X to the list of regions S, merging if necessary. The function aggregate then uses add to aggregate the regions of a list Q. □

5. Solve a "constrained partitioning problem"

Slight modifications to Algorithm 5.1 regarding when the algorithm is halted and when indeterminate regions are accepted as solutions can make it applicable to each of these specific subproblems. The following discussion analyzes the application of Algorithm 5.1 to these subproblems, making the distinction between *heuristic* approaches, in which the results are not guaranteed to be correct, and *robust* approaches, in which the results are guaranteed correct.

Algorithm 5.1 never rejects a region unless it contains no solutions to the constraint problem. Therefore, an unmodified Algorithm 5.1 can be used to robustly find a collection of regions which bound the set of solutions to the constraint system. As the solution acceptance set constraint, $\Box A$, is made stricter,[10] the bound on the solution set becomes tighter, at the expense of greater computation. Computing a bound on the set of solutions allows the definition of an inclusion function for the constraint solution operator. Solution set bounds are also useful in higher-level algorithms, such as the implicit curve and surface approximation algorithms of Chapter 6. Lastly, the solution bounds can also be visualized to obtain a rough idea of the nature of the solutions, even if the solutions form a multidimensional manifold rather than a finite set of points.

In using Algorithm 5.1 to determine whether or not the constraint system has solutions, two situations lead to a robust answer. If the algorithm terminates with an empty list of solutions, then the algorithm should terminate with the answer "no." If at any point the algorithm finds a feasible region, then the algorithm can immediately terminate with the answer "yes." If the algorithm can find only indeterminate regions, then nothing can be concluded with certainty. A heuristic solution to this problem is to return "yes" anyway. This heuristic approach can be made more robust through the choice of an appropriate solution acceptance set constraint. For example, in solving the system $f(x) = 0$ for a continuous function f, it is reasonable that a region Y, before being accepted as a solution, should satisfy

$$w(\Box f(Y)) < \delta$$

for some small δ. The algorithm should report an error when none of the indeterminate regions satisfies the acceptance criteria, before the machine precision limit is reached during subdivision. A robust solution to the problem can be achieved by testing indeterminate regions for the existence of solutions, using the test of Section 5.3.6.

To find any single solution to the constraint problem, Algorithm 5.1 may conclude that the entire starting region is infeasible, or find a feasible region. In the latter case, any point in the feasible region can be chosen as a representative solution, and the algorithm can be halted. Otherwise, a point on the first indeterminate

---

[10]Mathematically, one solution acceptance set constraint, $\Box A$, is *stricter* than another, $\Box B$, if, for every domain interval X, $\Box B(X) \subset \Box A(X)$. $\Box B$ therefore accepts regions earlier than $\Box A$.

region that satisfies the solution acceptance set constraint can be returned as a
(heuristic) solution. If a single solution exists, a more robust approach involves
analyzing the convergence of the solution superset as the algorithm iterates. Consider the sequence of summed widths, w_n, of candidate solutions on the list L

$$w_n = \sum_{i=1}^{s_n} w(U_n^i),$$

where U_n^i represents the i-th interval on the list L after iteration n, and s_n is the
number of such intervals. Iteration can be terminated when w_n becomes sufficiently small. A more robust solution to this subproblem can be achieved using a
robust test for the existence and uniqueness of a solution (see Section 5.3.6). This
test can be used to verify that an indeterminate region contains a solution. Any
point in such a region, such as its midpoint, can then be returned as a solution,
which is then within a bounded distance from the actual solution.

Algorithm 5.1 can also be applied to the problem of finding all solutions to a
constraint system when a finite set of solutions is expected. In this case, if the algorithm terminates with an empty solution list, there are no solutions. If a feasible
region is found, an infinitely many solutions exist. If only indeterminate regions
are found, then a useful heuristic approach is to use solution aggregation to obtain
a set of disjoint regions and pick a point inside each region as a solution. This
approach can be made more robust in the following ways:

- ensure each aggregated region is sufficiently small

- check convergence of the widths of each aggregated region

- use further acceptance criteria for each aggregated region

If the number of solutions is known beforehand, then the algorithm can be terminated with an error condition if the machine precision is reached in subdivision with a number of aggregated regions unequal to the number of solutions. Of
course, we note that although this approach almost always works correctly, it is
still heuristic, since, for example, one region may contain no solutions while another contains two. A robust approach to the subproblem of obtaining all solutions
to the constraint system is to use a robust test for solution existence in each aggregated region. In this case, reaching the machine precision limit during subdivision
without being able to verify solution existence should result in an error termination.

The next section defines the constrained partitioning problem and shows how
Algorithm 5.1 can be applied to it.

5.3.4.1   The Constrained Partitioning Problem

Related to the constraint solution problem is the *constrained partitioning problem*, which seeks to partition a domain D into a collection of hyper-rectangles, $\{R_i\}$, such that each partition satisfies a given *set constraint*. A set constraint is a mapping from a hyper-rectangle to $\{0, 1\}$.[11] Partitioning of the domain D means that

1. The union of all the partitions, R_i, is D.

2. The interiors of any two distinct partitions are disjoint.

For example, let $S \colon \mathbf{R}^2 \to \mathbf{R}^3$ be a parametric surface, and let $R \subset \mathbf{R}^2$. Define the distance function of the surface, $d(R)$, as the maximum distance between two surface points, mapped from R. The function $d(R)$ is given by[12]

$$d(R) \equiv \sup\{\|S(p_1) - S(p_2)\| \mid p_1, p_2 \in R\}.$$

A useful set constraint for the surface approximation problem, $G(R)$, is

$$G(R) \equiv (d(R) < \epsilon), \tag{5.3}$$

which requires that no two points on S mapped from R be farther apart than ϵ. By partitioning the domain of S so that each partition satisfies the set constraint, an approximation for S can be generated in each partition, with the knowledge that the surface mapped from any partition is bounded. Section 6.3 further describes how constrained partitioning can be applied to the surface approximation problem.

To solve a constrained partitioning problem, Algorithm 5.1 must be slightly modified so that it adds a region to the solution only when $\Box A$ is true, regardless of the value of $\Box F$. The constraint inclusion is therefore defined so that it returns true (i.e., the constant $[1, 1]$) for all regions. The solution acceptance set constraint then becomes the set constraint of the constrained partitioning problem.

A constrained partitioning problem can also be combined with a constraint problem in order to partition the constraint problem's solution set. In this case, an unmodified Algorithm 5.1 can be used, again with $\Box A$ specifying the partitioning problem's set constraint. Algorithm 5.1 will be applied in this way to compute an initial set of regions bounding implicit curves (in Section 6.2) and implicit surfaces (in Section 6.6).

---

[11] Note that a set constraint is naturally represented using an inclusion function for a relational/logical expression, $\Box R$, where the results $[0, 0]$ and $[0, 1]$ are both mapped to 0 (constraint not satisfied), and $[1, 1]$ is mapped to 1 (constraint is satisfied).

[12] sup denotes supremum, the least upper bound of a set.

5.3.5 Interval Newton Methods

When the constraint system of Algorithm 5.1 contains equality constraints, interval Newton methods can be used to improve the bounds on the set of solutions to the constraint problem. Interval Newton methods are robust methods for finding bounds on the set of zeroes of a system of n equations of n variables. They are the interval analogs of multidimensional Newton iteration for the simultaneous solution of nonlinear equations.

Consider the problem of finding all zeroes of a differentiable function $f: \mathbf{R}^n \to \mathbf{R}^n$ over an interval $X \in \mathbf{I}^n$. Let the coordinates of f be given by $x_1, x_2, \ldots, x_n$. By the Mean Value Theorem, given a $c \in X$, for each $x \in X$, there exist n points, $\xi_1, \xi_2, \ldots, \xi_n$ such that

$$f(x) = f(c) + J(\xi_1, \ldots, \xi_n)(x - c),$$

where the matrix J is given by

$$J_{ij} = \frac{\partial f_i}{\partial x_j}(\xi_i)$$

and where each ξ_i is a point within the smallest hyper-rectangle containing x and c. Because X is an interval, and $x, c \in X$, each ξ_i is a member of X. Let $\Box f'$ be an inclusion function for Jacobian matrix of f, i.e.,

$$\Box f'(Y) = \left\{ J \mid J_{ij} \in \Box \frac{\partial f_i}{\partial x_j}(Y) \right\} \qquad \text{for all } Y \in I(X).$$

If x is a zero of f, then there exsist $J \in \Box f'(X)$ such that

$$f(x) = 0 = f(c) + J(x - c).$$

Therefore, if Q is the set of solutions

$$Q = \{ x \mid \exists J \in \Box f'(X) \text{ such that } f(c) + J(x - c) = 0 \},$$

then Q contains all zeroes of f in X.

This leads to the following iterative algorithm for finding the zeroes of f, called an *interval Newton method*. The initial interval X_0 is set to X. The next interval X_{n+1} is computed from the interval X_n as follows:

---

choose c in X_n
find an interval Z that bounds the set of solutions

$$\{ x \mid \exists J \in \Box f'(X_n) \text{ such that } 0 = f(c) + J(x - c) \}$$

if Z is empty, no zeroes of f exist in X
otherwise set $X_{n+1} = Z \cap X_n$

By the argument of the previous paragraph, no zero is ever lost by this iterative procedure. Remarkably, if at any stage of the iteration $Z \subset X_n$, then f has a unique zero in X_n, a result that is further discussed in Section 5.3.6.

Interval Newton methods are typically combined with an exhaustive subdivision algorithm such as Algorithm 5.1. That is, when interval Newton iteration is effective at reducing the size of the set of possible zeroes, its use is continued. Otherwise, bisection subdivision is performed. Interval Newton methods are also effective in concert with local methods, such as standard Newton or quasi-Newton iteration. This is because the interval Newton procedure is most effective when the point c is as close as possible to a zero of f. The Hansen–Greenberg algorithm for finding zeroes of f [RATS88] uses exhaustive subdivision, interval Newton methods, and local Newton methods.

The crux of the interval Newton algorithm is to find an interval Z that bounds Q, the solution set of the linear interval equation. If the interval determinant of the matrix $\Box f'(X)$ is not zero, then the interval analog of LU decomposition or matrix inversion can be used to bound Q (for a concise description of LU decomposition, see [PRES86, pages 31–38]).

For example, let $f: \mathbf{R}^2 \to \mathbf{R}^2$, so that $\Box f'(X)$ is a 2×2 interval matrix of the form

$$\begin{bmatrix} A & B \\ C & D \end{bmatrix}$$

with $A, B, C, D \in \mathbf{I}$. Let $-f(c)$ be bounded by the vector-valued interval

$$\begin{pmatrix} b_1 \\ b_2 \end{pmatrix}$$

where $b_1, b_2 \in \mathbf{I}$. We must solve a linear interval equation of the form

$$\begin{bmatrix} A & B \\ C & D \end{bmatrix} \begin{pmatrix} x_1 \\ x_2 \end{pmatrix} = \begin{pmatrix} b_1 \\ b_2 \end{pmatrix}$$

where the solution, $\begin{pmatrix} x_1 \\ x_2 \end{pmatrix}$, is a bound on $x - c$ for all solutions x. Assuming $0 \notin A$, a bound on the solution set of the linear interval equation can be computed using the interval arithmetic analog of LU decomposition:

$$x_2 = \frac{b_2 - \dfrac{C}{A} b_1}{D - \dfrac{CB}{A}}$$

$$x_1 = \frac{b_1 - B x_2}{A}.$$

That is, the LU decomposition algorithm is applied with all floating point operations replaced by their interval arithmetic counterparts. We then have

$$Q \subset \begin{pmatrix} x_1 \\ x_2 \end{pmatrix} + \left(\begin{bmatrix} [c_1, c_1] \\ [c_2, c_2] \end{bmatrix} \right)$$

where

$$c = \begin{pmatrix} c_1 \\ c_2 \end{pmatrix}.$$

If the interval determinant does contain zero, then the interval analog of Gauss–Sidel iteration, described in the next section, can be effective. Neither of these methods results in a tight bound for the solution set, which can be computed using linear optimization (see Section 5.3.5.2).

5.3.5.1 Implementing Interval Newton with Matrix Iteration

In the previous section, we showed that the interval Newton method requires computation of a bound on the set

$$\{x \mid \exists \, J \in \Box f'(X) \text{ such that } 0 = f(c) + J(x - c)\}.$$

To compute this, let $y = x - c$, and let Z' be an interval bound on the set

$$\{y \mid \exists \, J \in \Box f'(X) \text{ such that } Jy = -f(c)\}.$$

Then the interval Z, defined by

$$Z = Z' +_\Box [c, c],$$

is an interval bound on the original set. Thus, computing the interval Newton bound Z can be accomplished by solving a linear interval equation of the form

$$Mx = b$$

where M is a given $n \times n$ interval matrix, and b is a given interval vector. We require a bound on the set of solutions of this equation for x, given any matrix in M and vector in b, that is, on the set

$$Q(M, b) \equiv \{x \mid \exists \mathcal{M} \in M, \beta \in b \text{ such that } \mathcal{M}x = \beta\}.$$

To solve this problem, we first assume we have an initial bound on the interval x.[13] This poses no problem for interval Newton iteration, since interval Newton starts with such an initial bound. A simple method for computing an improved bound on x involves the following steps:

---

[13] That is, we seek a bound on the set $Q(M, b) \cap X_0$ where X_0 is an initial bound on the set of solutions.

1. Compute the inverse of the matrix midpoint of M, M_{mid}^{-1}:

$$M_{\text{mid}}^{-1} \equiv (\text{mid}(M))^{-1}.$$

   Here we assume that the midpoint of M is invertible. If not, some other matrix in M must be chosen.

2. Using interval arithmetic, multiply both sides of the equation $Mx = b$ by M_{mid}^{-1}. We thus seek a bound on the set $Q(M', b')$ where

$$
\begin{aligned}
M' &= M_{\text{mid}}^{-1} M \\
b' &= M_{\text{mid}}^{-1} b.
\end{aligned}
$$

   Note that this does not eliminate any solutions, since $Q(M, b) = Q(M', b')$. Presumably though, the matrix M' is closer to the identity matrix than M.

3. Using interval arithmetic, for each component i compute the interval x_i'

$$x_i' = \frac{b_i' - \sum_{k \neq i} M_{ik}' x_k}{M_{ii}'}.$$

   The interval division above may be avoided if $0 \in M_{ii}'$ (so that no improvement in the interval x_i results), or may be computed using infinite interval division, discussed in the next section.

4. Intersect the old interval x_i and the new interval x_i':

$$x_i \leftarrow x_i \bigcap x_i'.$$

We note that when implementing this algorithm on real computers, M_{mid}^{-1} becomes an interval matrix so that $Q(M, b) \subset Q(M', b')$.

A similar algorithm, which computes a tighter bound on $Q(M, b)$ at the expense of greater computation, is the following:

```
repeat
    loop through rows of M (i = 1, 2, ..., n)
        loop through columns of M (j = 1, 2, ..., n)
            if 0 ∉ M_ij then
                compute x̃_j = (b_i − Σ_{k≠j} M_ik x_k)/M_ij
                x_j ← x̃_j ∩ x_j
                if x_j = ∅ return no solution
            endif
        endloop
    endloop
until there is insufficient improvement in x
```

5.3.5.2   Implementing Interval Newton with Linear Optimization

Linear optimization is a technique for optimizing a linear function of n variables, subject to a set of linear constraints. Let $x_1, x_2, \ldots, x_n$ be a set of n variables. More precisely, the *linear optimization problem* is to minimize a function

$$a_1 x_1 + a_2 x_2 + \cdots + a_n x_n$$

subject to N_u inequality constraints of the form

$$b_{i1} x_1 + b_{i2} x_2 + \cdots + b_{in} x_n \leq u_i,$$

N_l inequality constraints of the form

$$c_{j1} x_1 + c_{j2} x_2 + \cdots + c_{jn} x_n \geq l_j,$$

and N_e equality constraints of the form

$$d_{k1} x_1 + d_{k2} x_2 + \cdots + d_{kn} x_n = e_k.$$

See, for example, [PRES86, pages 312-326] for more information about the linear optimization problem, and an algorithm for solution called the simplex method.

Naively, the problem of finding a bound on the set of solutions to the linear interval equation

$$Mx = b$$

is not amenable to linear optimization algorithms because variables in M and x are multiplied together. However, it is possible to transform the problem so that it is posed as a linear optimization problem. We represent x as the difference of two vectors, y and z, where each component of y and z is nonnegative:

$$x_i = y_i - z_i \qquad y_i, z_i \geq 0.$$

Let the matrix M be given by the component intervals

$$M_{ij} = [c_{ij}, d_{ij}]$$

and let b be represented by the component intervals

$$b_i = [p_i, q_i].$$

Let $m_{ij} \in M_{ij}$. We then get n constraints of the form

$$m_{i1} y_1 - m_{i1} z_1 + \cdots + m_{in} y_n - m_{in} z_n \in [p_i, q_i] \qquad (5.4)$$

where $y_j, z_j \geq 0$. If we let all the variables y_j and z_j be 0 except for one, say y_k, then we can find an interval in y_k that solves (5.4). This interval is called the y_k *interval intercept* of (5.4), and written $\widetilde{Y}_k$ ($\widetilde{Z}_k$ for variable z_k). The interval intercepts can be computed using the technique of infinite interval division, whose rules are given by

$$[a,b]/_\square[c,d] =$$
$$\begin{cases} \begin{array}{l} [\min(a/c, a/d, b/c, b/d) , \\ \max(a/c, a/d, b/c, b/d)] \end{array} & \text{if } 0 \notin [c,d] \\ [b/c, +\infty] & \text{if } b \leq 0 \text{ and } d = 0 \\ [-\infty, b/d] \cup [b/c, +\infty] & \text{if } b \leq 0, c < 0, \text{ and } d > 0 \\ [-\infty, b/d] & \text{if } b \leq 0 \text{ and } c = 0 \\ [-\infty, a/c] & \text{if } a \geq 0 \text{ and } d = 0 \\ [-\infty, a/c] \cup [a/d, +\infty] & \text{if } a > 0, c < 0, \text{ and } d > 0 \\ [a/d, +\infty] & \text{if } a \geq 0 \text{ and } c = 0 \\ [-\infty, +\infty] & \text{if } a < 0, b > 0 \text{ and } 0 \in [c,d] \\ [-\infty, +\infty] & \text{if } c = d = 0. \end{cases}$$

The appropriate y_k and z_k interval intercepts are therefore given by

$$\widetilde{Y}_k = [p_i, q_i] /_\square [c_{ik}, d_{ik}]$$
$$\widetilde{Z}_k = [-q_i, -p_i] /_\square [c_{ik}, d_{ik}] .$$

Solutions to (5.4) are limited to points on the set of hyperplanes whose intercepts with each of the $2n$ variables y_j and z_j lie in the appropriate interval intercept $\widetilde{Y}_k$ and $\widetilde{Z}_k$. According to the rules for infinite interval division, there are five cases for the structure of an interval intercept:

1. Finite interval $[e, f]$

2. Negative semi-infinite interval $[-\infty, f]$

3. Positive semi-infinite interval $[e, \infty]$

4. Pair of semi-infinite intervals $[-\infty, f] \cup [e, \infty]$

5. Infinite interval $[-\infty, \infty]$

In cases 4 and 5, and in case 1 when $0 \in [e, f]$, the interval intercept must be considered as two separate intervals, termed *splitting* the problem. The two intervals that must be considered for each of the splittable cases are

$$\begin{array}{lll} \text{Case 1.} & [e, f] & \rightarrow & [e, 0] \text{ and } [0, f] \\ \text{Case 4.} & [-\infty, f] \cup [e, \infty] & \rightarrow & [-\infty, f] \text{ and } [e, \infty] \\ \text{Case 5.} & [-\infty, \infty] & \rightarrow & [-\infty, 0] \text{ and } [0, \infty] \end{array}$$

I. Finite intervals: **II. Finite and semi-infinite:**

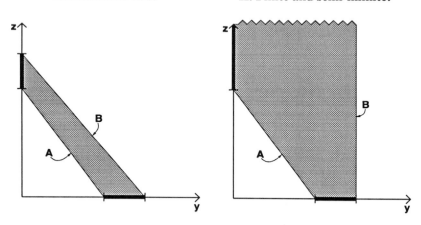

III. Semi-infinite intervals:

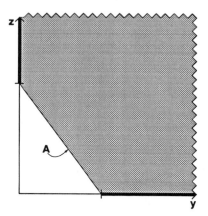

Figure 5.3: Solution set of the interval linear equation depending on the interval intercepts. All three examples are for the simple case of one y and one z variable. Case I shows two finite interval intercepts. The solutions are points between the lines A and B, where A connects the two lower bounds, and B the two upper bounds of the interval intercepts. Cases II and III show the solution regions when one or both of the interval intercepts are semi-infinite. □

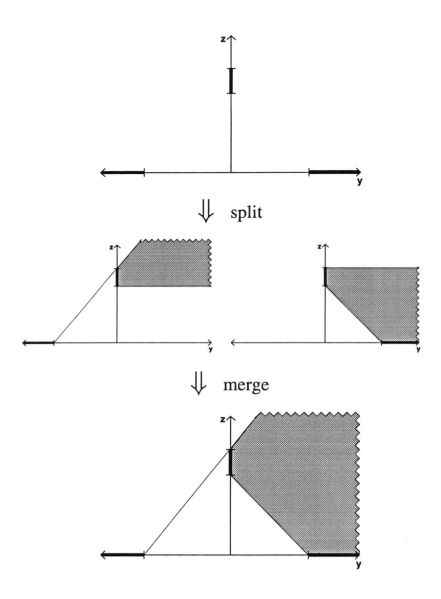

Figure 5.4: Splitting the linear optimization problem. When the interval intercept of one of the y or z variables is a pair of semi-infinite intervals, the problem is split into two, one for each semi-infinite interval. The resulting problems are solved separately, and the resulting solution regions later merged. □

Color Plates

Plate 1: Scenes from the computer animation "Going Bananas." All the objects in the rooms: teapots, chairs, tables, and fruit, were modeled using an early version of GENMOD. Rendering was accomplished by ray tracing a polygonal approximation to each object, as described in [SNYD87].

Plate 2: Teddy bear with and without fur. The teddy bear "skin" was modeled using the GENMOD code given in Appendix B.4. The direction of the teddy bear fur was modeled as a vector field over the bear skin, as described in Section 3.3.3. (Reprinted with permission from James T. Kajiya, Timothy L. Kay, and the ACM, from the article "Rendering Fur with Three-Dimensional Textures," *Computer Graphics*, 20(4), page 280, 1989.)

Plate 3: Animated creature "Waldo." This dragon-like creature was modeled as a set of time-varying surfaces in GENMOD. For example, Waldo's flapping wing was specified with a time-varying damped sinusoid curve of constant arclength, as described in Section 3.3.2.

Plate 4: Bottle. The technique of parameterizing cross sections used in constructing this bottle surface is described in Section 3.2.4. The GENMOD code defining the bottle is given in Section B.3.

Plate 5: Simple gravitational simulation using the ODE operator. The path of a particle in the gravitational field of three masses is represented using the ODE operator, resulting in a complicated 3D curve.

Plate 6: Rendering methods for surfaces. The figure compares the results of four rendering methods on a bumpy spherical shape. The rendering methods are (clockwise from upper left) line drawing, z-buffering, ray tracing with soft shadows, and ray tracing with hard shadows. Note how much the diffuse shadows enhance shape perception.

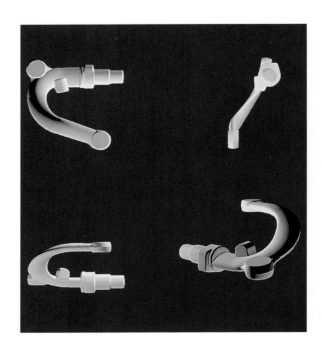

Plate 7: Steering arm. A steering arm of a car was modeled in GENMOD from actual engineering drawings in [JENS66]. This model sweeps a cross section along a 3D wire curve, while interpolating this cross section between circular, elliptical, and flared shapes.

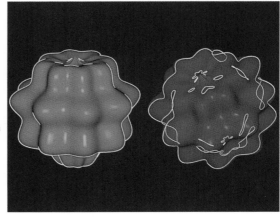

Plate 8: Silhouette curve of a bumpy sphere. This silhouette curve was computed using the algorithm for implicit curve approximation in Section 6.2. On the left, the silhouette curve is viewed using the same viewing parameters used to define the silhouette. On the right, it is viewed from a different angle.

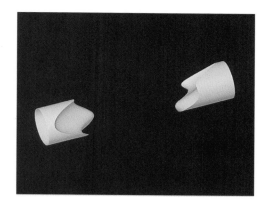

Plate 9: CSG-like operations. A cylinder is subtracted from a bumpy sphere at top, and below it, the bumpy sphere is subtracted from the cylinder. Both were computed using the algorithm described in Section 6.4. Note the accuracy of the result at the interface between the intersecting surfaces.

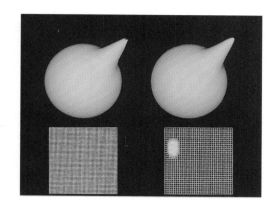

Plate 10: Uniform vs. adaptive sampling. On the left, a sphere with a sharp projection is approximated using a uniform grid of samples. On the right, using the same number of samples, the shape is much better approximated with adaptive sampling that limits the variation of normal vectors across the surface.

Plate 11: Implicit surface polygonalization. Both the jade plant surface and the "torus" were computed using the implicit surface approximation algorithm of Section 6.6. The jade plant is an isosurface of a parametric function which smoothly interpolates through 3D data. The data was obtained from a magnetic resonance (MR) machine. The "torus" is an isosurface of a simple function specified procedurally in GENMOD.

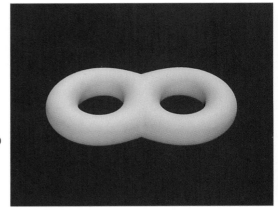

By splitting the interval intercepts that straddle 0, we can consider interval intercepts of the form

$$\widetilde{Y}_k = [e_k, f_k]$$
$$\widetilde{Z}_k = [g_k, h_k]$$

where none of the interval intercepts straddles 0; that is, $e_k, f_k \geq 0$ or $e_k, f_k \leq 0$ (and similarly for g_k and h_k).

The part of the set of hyperplanes with these interval intercepts that also satisfies $y_k, z_k \geq 0$ lies between two boundary hyperplanes in $\mathbf{R}^{2n}$. One hyperplane intersects each variable's axis at the lower bound of the interval intercept (e_k or g_k); the other intersects each variable's axis at the upper bound of the variable's intercept (f_k or h_k). Figure 5.3 illustrates how the character of the solution set changes for finite and semi-infinite interval intercepts. Figure 5.4 illustrates how the linear optimization problem is split when an interval intercept is a pair of semi-infinite intervals.

We note that a hyperplane in $\mathbf{R}^m$ that intersects each coordinate axis x_i at the point $a_i \neq 0$, $i = 1, \ldots, m$ is given by the equation

$$x_1/a_1 + x_2/a_2 + \cdots + x_m/a_m = 1.$$

The minimum and maximum boundary hyperplanes bounding the solution to (5.4) yield the following inequalities

$$y_1/e_1 + z_1/g_1 + \cdots + y_n/e_n + z_n/g_n \;\geq\; 1 \tag{5.5}$$
$$y_1/f_1 + z_1/h_1 + \cdots + y_n/f_n + z_n/h_n \;\leq\; 1. \tag{5.6}$$

A pair of such inequalities results for each value of i in (5.4), for a total of $2n$ inequalities. Inequality (5.5) yields the inequality for the lower bound hyperplane; inequality (5.6) yields the inequality for the upper bound hyperplane.

In each inequality, if any of the e_i, f_i, g_i or h_i is 0, the constraint is eliminated. This is appropriate since, for example, if $e_i = 0$, then $f_i \geq 0$, so that

$$\lim_{e_i \to 0+} y_i/e_i = \infty > 1,$$

reducing (5.5) to a tautology. Similarly, if $f_i = 0$, then $e_i \leq 0$, so that

$$\lim_{f_i \to 0-} y_i/f_i = -\infty < 1,$$

which reduces (5.6) to a tautology.

If either e_i or g_i is $-\infty$, the corresponding y_i or z_i variable is eliminated from inequality (5.5), since

$$\lim_{e_i \to -\infty} y_i/e_i = 0.$$

Similarly, if either f_i or h_i is ∞, the corresponding y_i or z_i variable is eliminated from inequality (5.6). If all the variables are eliminated in this way, the entire constraint is eliminated for an inequality from (5.6), or the entire subproblem has no solutions for an inequality from (5.5). We also note that if

$$e_i, g_i < 0 \ \forall i$$

then the entire subproblem has no solutions, since inequality (5.5) is false for all $y_i, z_i \geq 0$.

For each subproblem (where a subproblem is one obtained by considering each half of a split interval intercept separately), we have a system of linear constraints where the constants e_i, f_i, g_i and h_i are given, and the y_j and z_j are variables. To find bounds on the solutions to this subproblem, we must solve $2n$ linear optimization problems to minimize and maximize the quantities

$$x_i = y_i - z_i$$

subject to the $2n$ constraints from inequalities (5.5) and (5.6).[14] If m variable intercepts are split, then 2^m subproblems must be solved, for each combination of split variable intercepts. Bounds on each of the subproblems are computed using linear optimization and then merged, using the simple merge operation of Section 5.3.3. This method is clearly impractical for all but very small linear systems. Further study is required to make it computationally useful.

5.3.6   Existence of Solutions

An interesting and useful result can be proved that guarantees the existence of a unique solution of $f(x) = 0$ for a differentiable function $f : \mathbf{R}^n \rightarrow \mathbf{R}^n$ in an interval domain X. As we have stated previously, the test implied by this result is extremely useful

1. To verify solution existence without actually finding a solution. This allows us to robustly determine whether or not a constraint solution problem has solutions (subproblem 2 of Section 5.3.4). As we will see in Section 5.4, ensuring a region contains a feasible point is also useful in the constrained minimization algorithm to allow updating of the progressively refined upper bound.

2. To ensure a region contains a unique solution when finding a single representative solution, or all solutions to a constraint problem (subproblems 3

---

[14]Note that a feasible point for the constraints need be computed once and can be shared in each of the $2n$ linear optimization problems. If no feasible point exists, there is no solution to the subproblem.

or 4 of Section 5.3.4). Although this test itself provides no information pin-pointing the actual location of the solution, it guarantees its existence in a bounded interval, a fact used in, for example, the implicit curve and surface algorithms of Chapter 6.

The result states that if the set of solutions to the linear interval equation

$$Q = \{x \mid \exists\, J \in \Box f'(X) \text{ such that } f(c) + J(x - c) = 0\}$$

is non-empty and a subset of the domain interval X, then f has a unique zero in X. The techniques of Section 5.3.5.1 and 5.3.5.2 are therefore useful in implementing a test for solution existence and uniqueness. Section C.4 contains a formal state-ment and proof of this result. We note the conditions for existence and uniqueness can only be verified when the determinant of the Jacobian of f is nonzero in some neighborhood of the solution.

5.3.7 A Constraint Evaluation Enhancement

Typically, the constraint function F in Algorithm 5.1 is composed of a logical combination of relational operators on constraint functionals. For example, in the analysis of the convergence of the algorithm in Section C.2, a constraint involving the logical conjunction of $r + s$ relational subconstraints was used, of the form

$$
\begin{aligned}
g_i(x) &= 0 & i = 1, \ldots, r \\
h_j(x) &\le 0 & j = 1, \ldots, s.
\end{aligned}
$$

For a relational inclusion function, $\Box r(X)$ (e.g., an inclusion function for the **equal to** operator), we have

$$Y \subset X \Rightarrow \overset{\text{idl}}{\Box} r(Y) \subset \overset{\text{idl}}{\Box} r(X) \subset \Box r(X)$$

by the property of inclusion functions and ideal inclusion functions. In particular, this means that if the subconstraint is true (yields $[1, 1]$) in a region X, it is true for any interval subset of X. Similarly, if the subconstraint is false (yields $[0, 0]$) in a region X, it is false for any interval subset of X.

Algorithm 5.1 thus wastes computation whenever a subconstraint becomes ex-actly true or false (rather than indeterminate, i.e., yielding the interval $[0, 1]$) in some region Y that is not discarded or accepted. This is because the region Y will later be subdivided, and the same subconstraint evaluated over the child regions, with a result identical to the parent's.

It is therefore reasonable to associate with each candidate region an array of tags, one for each subconstraint, noting whether the subconstraint is true, false, or indeterminate in the candidate region. Whenever a region is subdivided, only those subconstraints that are indeterminate need be reevaluated; the rest are simply copied from the parent. The constraint function F is evaluated from this array of tags using the ternary logic introduced in Section 5.2.4.

5.4   Constrained Minimization Algorithm

A constrained minimization problem involves finding the global minimum (or global minimizers) of a function $f: \mathbf{R}^n \rightarrow \mathbf{R}$, called the *objective function*, for all points that satisfy a constraint function $F: \mathbf{R}^n \rightarrow \{0, 1\}$. This constraint function is defined exactly as in Section 5.3. Algorithm 5.2 finds solutions to such problems.

Algorithm 5.2 (Constrained Minimization Algorithm) We are given a constraint inclusion function, $\Box F$, a solution acceptance set constraint, $\Box A$, an inclusion function for the objective function, $\Box f$, and an initial region, X. The variable u is a progressively refined least upper bound for the value of the objective function f evaluated at a feasible point. Regions are inserted into the priority queue L so that regions with a smaller lower bound on the objective function f have priority.

place X on priority queue L
initialize upper bound u to $+\infty$
while L is nonempty
 get next region Y from L
 if $\Box A(Y) = [1, 1]$ add Y to solution
 else
  subdivide Y into regions Y_1 and Y_2
  evaluate $\Box F$ on Y_1 and Y_2
  if $\Box F(Y_i) = [0, 0]$ discard Y_i
  evaluate $\Box f$ on Y_1 and Y_2
  if lb $\Box f(Y_i) > u$ discard Y_i
  insert Y_i into L according to lb $\Box f(Y_i)$
  if Y_i contains an identified feasible point q
   $u = \min(u, f(q))$
  else if Y_i contains an unidentified feasible point
   $u = \min(u, \text{ub } \Box f(Y_i))$
  endif
 endif
endwhile

Algorithm 5.2 uses a progressively refined least upper bound of the value of the objective function, the variable u. Regions encountered by the algorithm affect u in one of three ways:

1. If a feasible point q can be found in the region, then $f(q)$ can be used as an upper bound for f's global minimum. Thus, u may be updated by

$$u = \min(u, f(q)).$$

   In particular, if Y is a feasible region, then any point $q \in Y$ may be used.

2. If a feasible point is not explicitly identified, but it is known that one exists in the region Y, then ub $\Box f(Y)$ is an upper bound for f's global minimum in the region Y. Therefore, the update

$$u = \min(u, \text{ub}\,\Box f(Y))$$

   is appropriate. In particular, if Y is a feasible region, then every point in Y satisfies the constraints, so that u may be updated in this way.

3. If the region is indeterminate, and it cannot be verified that the region contains at least one feasible point, then u cannot be decreased.

Let the region U_n^i be the i-th region on the priority queue L after n while loop iterations of the algorithm. Let u_n be the value of u at iteration n, and let l_n be given by

$$l_n \equiv \text{lb}\,\Box f(U_n^1).$$

The interval U_n^1 is called the *leading candidate interval*. Let f^* be the minimum value of the objective function subject to the constraints. We note that if a region X contains feasible points for the constraint function F, then f^* exists. Given existence of a feasible point, an important property of Algorithm 5.2 is

$$l_n \le f^* \le u_n \quad \forall n.$$

This property holds because no feasible regions that can possibly contain global minima to the constrained minimization problem are discarded by the algorithm. Because L is organized as a priority queue, the leading candidate interval has the smallest lower bound for f. Obviously, u_n is an upper bound for f^* by its construction. If the inclusion functions $\Box F$ and $\Box f$ are isotone, a further property of the algorithm is that the sequences $\{l_n\}$ and $\{u_n\}$ are monotonic in n. In fact, it can be proved that

$$l_n \to f^* \quad \text{as} \quad n \to \infty$$

assuming that the set of feasible points of F is nonempty, and that the inclusion functions used for the constraint functionals and objective function are convergent. A proof of this convergence result can be found in Section C.3.

Algorithm 5.2 is similar to Algorithm 5.1, except that candidate regions are ordered with respect to the objective function. The algorithm also suffers the same problems that Algorithm 5.1 does. Specifically, an indeterminate region (i.e., a region Y for which $\Box F(Y) = [0, 1]$) may or may not include feasible points of the system of constraints. This implies that the algorithm may accept indeterminate regions as solutions that are, in fact, infeasible. Moreover, if the constraints are not satisfied exactly (e.g., they are represented using equality constraints), then all candidate regions are indeterminate, so that u is never updated. In this case, the algorithm is unable to reject any of the candidate regions on the basis of the objective function bound and accepts all indeterminate regions as solutions.

A robust solution to this problem is to use an existence test such as the one presented in Section 5.3.6 to verify that a region contains at least one feasible point. A heuristic approach is to consider indeterminate regions of small enough width as if they contained a feasible point. These indeterminate regions may also be subjected to further acceptance tests that provide more confidence that the region contains a feasible point.

It should be noted that Algorithm 5.2 can be enhanced with a great many techniques, both local and global. Most of these techniques involve, first, finding a feasible point in a given interval so that a better upper bound can be found for the minimum function value, or, second, improving the upper bound by finding another feasible point with a smaller value of the objective function. [RATS88] discusses such enhancements in detail. Section 5.4.2 will discuss a further enhancement that rejects regions based on a monotonicity test.

5.4.1   Termination and Acceptance Criteria for Constrained Minimization

A constrained minimization problem can be "solved" in three ways:

1. Find the minimum value of the objective function

2. Find one feasible point that minimizes the objective function

3. Find all feasible points that minimize the objective function

Slight modifications to Algorithm 5.2 regarding when the algorithm is halted and when indeterminate regions are accepted as solutions can make it applicable to each of these specific subproblems.

To find the minimum value of the objective function, f^*, Algorithm 5.2 should be terminated when a leading candidate interval, U_n^1, is encountered with $w(\Box f(U_n^1))$ sufficiently small, given that U_n^1 contains at least one feasible point.[15]

---

[15]If all candidate intervals are rejected, then no feasible points exist in the original region, so f^* does not exist.

In this case, the value $f(q)$ should be returned for some $q \in U_n^1$. This approach is justified because if U_n^1 contains a feasible point, then

$$\text{lb} \, \Box f(U_n^1) \le f^* \le \text{ub} \, \Box f(U_n^1).$$

This approach assumes that we can verify the presence of a feasible point in an indeterminate region before the machine precision is reached in subdivision. Lack of this verification should result in some form of error termination. A heuristic approach is to accept indeterminate regions of small enough width (and, possibly, satisfying other criteria) as though they contained a feasible point.

Finding one or all minimizers of the objective function is a difficult problem that is currently not amenable to completely robust solution. Under certain conditions,[16] Algorithm 5.2 converges, in a theoretical sense, to the set of global minimizers of the minimization problem. In practice, however, we obtain a set of intervals that bound the set of global minimizers after a finite number of iterations. Although techniques exist to verify whether a given interval in this superset contains a local minimizer of the minimization problem, we will not know, in general, if these local minimizers are also global minimizers.

If we know a priori that a single global minimizer exists, then the technique of solution aggregation (Section 5.3.3) can be used to collect candidate solutions into a single interval. We can then verify that the width of this aggregated interval sufficiently decreases as the algorithm iterates. If we expect a finite set of global minimizers, then a reasonable heuristic approach is to aggregate solutions and pick a point in each aggregated region as a global minimizer. Such an aggregated region should be small enough in width and satisfy other acceptance criteria that increase confidence that it contains a global minimizer.

5.4.2   Monotonicity Test

Consider the case that a candidate interval, Y, in Algorithm 5.2 is feasible, and the objective function, f, is monotonic with respect to any of the minimization problem's input variables $x_1, \ldots, x_n$. If Y is a subset of the interior of the problem's starting domain, X, then Y cannot contain a global minimum. On the other hand, if $Y \cap \partial X \ne \emptyset$,[17] then Y cannot be completely eliminated because points on $\partial X \cap Y$ may still be global minimizers. We can, however, replace Y with $Y' \cap \partial X$ where Y' is the interval Y with the monotonic coordinate interval replaced by a constant.

Precisely, if f is monotonic in the interval Y with respect to x_j and

$$Y_i = \left[y_i^0, y_i^1 \right]$$

---

[16] A sufficient condition is the existence of a sequence of points in the interior of the feasible domain that converges to a global minimizer; see [RATS88].

[17] The notation ∂X denotes the boundary of the set X.

then Y' is given by

$$Y'_i = \begin{cases} [y_i^0, y_i^1], & \text{if } i \neq j \\ [y_i^0, y_i^0], & \text{if } i = j \text{ and } f \text{ is monotonically increasing in } Y \\ [y_i^1, y_i^1], & \text{if } i = j \text{ and } f \text{ is monotonically decreasing in } Y. \end{cases}$$

This enhancement is called the *monotonicity test*. Note that the region Y must be feasible (i.e., every point in Y satisfies the constraints) for the monotonicity test to be valid.

If f is a differentiable function, then f is monotonic with respect to any input variable x_i in a region Y if

$$0 \notin \square \frac{\partial f}{\partial x_i}(Y).$$

We can therefore add the following test to Algorithm 5.2:

```
if F(Y) = [1, 1] then
    if 0 ∉ □ ∂f/∂xᵢ (Y) for some i then
        if Y ∩ ∂X = ∅ then reject Y
        else replace Y with Y' ∩ ∂X
    endif
endif
```

Chapter 6

Applying Interval Methods to Geometric Modeling

This chapter discusses applications of Algorithms 5.1 and 5.2 to the following problems:

- computing non-intersecting boundaries of offset curves and surfaces

- approximating implicitly defined curves

- approximating parametric shapes using arbitrary adaptive sampling criteria

- approximating trimmed surfaces and boundaries of CSG operations on solids bounded by generative surfaces

- approximating implicitly defined surfaces

6.1   Offset Operations

An *offset* of an object is an enlarged or reduced version of the object. The concept of a planar curve offset was introduced in Section 3.2.2.2. This offset was defined as the locus of centers of circles of a given radius tangent to the curve. Such a definition suffers from the following problems:

- The offset curve can self-intersect.

- Parameterization of the offset is easily accomplished only if the curve to be offset has a nonvanishing tangent vector.

- Points where the original curve is not differentiable create discontinuities in the resulting offset.

Requicha and Rossignac [ROSS86a] have defined a more robust offset operation, called an *s-offset* (for *solid offset*), that addresses these problems. They define the positive s-offset of radius r of an object S, written $S \uparrow r$, as the union of S and the set of points exterior to S within a distance r from the boundary of S. Mathematically,

$$S \uparrow r \equiv \{p \mid \|p - q\| \leq r \text{ for some } q \in S\}.$$

Similarly, the negative s-offset of radius r of an object S, written $S \downarrow r$, subtracts from S all points within a distance r from its boundary. Mathematically, the negative s-offset can be defined as the complement of the positive offset of the complement of S, i.e.,

$$S \downarrow r \equiv \neg((\neg S) \uparrow r).$$

[ROSS86a] applies this definition to regular[1] solids in 3D space. S-offsets may also be applied to other objects, including objects of different dimension (e.g., 2D planar areas), and to non-regular objects (e.g., curves and surfaces in 3D space).

The s-offset operation is an extremely useful one in geometric modeling. [ROSS86a] cites many applications, such as design rule checking for VLSI, generation of NC milling tool paths, tolerance analysis for solid modeling, and collision detection and obstacle avoidance. In addition, sequences of s-offset operations can be used as a blending operation. A positive followed by a negative s-offset results in an operation called *filleting*, which rounds concave corners and edges of an object. A negative followed by a positive s-offset results in an operation called *rounding*, which rounds convex corners and edges of an object.

Computing the boundary of an s-offset is an important operation. [ROSS86a] describes a technique that computes a superset of the s-offset boundary, given a boundary representation of the solid to be offset. This technique categorizes points on the boundary of the solid into three parts: faces, singular curves, and singular points. Faces are the smooth surfaces that form the boundary of the solid. Singular curves are space curves that form the non-smooth edge where faces are joined. Similarly, singular points are vertices that form the non-smooth corners where singular curves are joined. The resulting offset superset is formed by the union of the following:

1. Normal offsets of the faces — each point on the face is transformed to a new point a distance r along the face normal. The resulting face is called a normal offset.

---

[1] A *regular* set is a set S for which $S = \overline{S^0}$; i.e., the closure of the interior of S equals S.

2. Canal surfaces around singular curves — each point on the singular curve gives rise to a circle of radius r normal to the tangent vector to the singular curve. The resulting surface is called a canal surface.

3. Spheres around singular points.

We will term this offset superset the *singularity categorization offset.*

The next section discusses a more convenient and tighter representation for the boundary of an s-offset than the singularity categorization offset. Objects that may be offset are generative models (i.e., the image of a parametric function evaluated over a rectilinear domain). Such a class of primitive objects is more powerful than the set of simple solids: rectangular prisms, spheres, cylinders, cones, and tori, included in a prototype system in [ROSS86a]. The representation is convenient because it does not require a priori identification of singular points and curves on the parametric object. Approximation and bounding of the s-offset boundary are amenable to the interval analysis techniques previously discussed.

6.1.1 The B-Offset: A Tighter Representation for the S-Offset Boundary

Let S be a parametric object (e.g., curve, surface, etc)

$$S: D_S \rightarrow R_S, \quad D_S \in \mathbf{I}^m, \quad R_S \subset \mathbf{R}^n$$

with parameters $x = (x_1, x_2, \ldots, x_m) \in D_S$. Let $Y \in \mathbf{I}^n$ include all points at a distance r from R_S. We define the *b-offset* (for *boundary offset*) of S of radius r, written $S\partial r$, as the set of points whose minimum distance to the parametric object R_S is r. Mathematically,

$$S\partial r \equiv \left\{ y \in Y \mid \min_{s \in R_S} \|y - s\| = r \right\}$$
$$\equiv \left\{ y \in Y \mid \min_{x \in D_S} \|y - S(x)\| = r \right\}.$$

Thus, the b-offset is described implicitly as a set of points solving a constraint problem whose constraint involves unconstrained minimization.[2]

We note that the b-offset of an object is a superset of the boundary of its positive s-offset, i.e.,

$$\partial(S \uparrow r) \subset S\partial r.$$

---

[2] *Unconstrained minimization* is minimization where the constraint function F in Algorithm 5.2 is a constant 1. Thus, every candidate interval is feasible, and the algorithm must only find the minimum value of the objective function over the entire starting region. Unconstrained minimization is appropriate here because the only constraint on x in the minimization is that $x \in D_S$, where $D_S \in \mathbf{I}^m$. This constraint is addressed simply by using D_S as the starting interval.

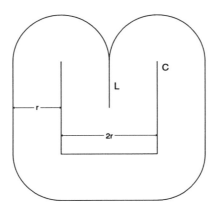

Figure 6.1: The b-offset is a superset of the s-offset boundary. C is a planar curve consisting of three line segments. The b-offset of radius r is shown surrounding it. This b-offset contains the segment L, which is not part of the boundary of the positive s-offset of C. A point on L is at a distance r from C, but is in the interior of the positive s-offset. A similar situation can arise when a surface is s-offset, yielding a surface (rather than a curve like L) in the b-offset that is not on the positive s-offset boundary. For example, if the curve C is extruded normal to the page, then the surface formed by the extrusion of the segment L is in the b-offset of the surface, but not on the s-offset boundary. □

Typically, the subset relation in the above can be replaced with set equality, although pathological cases, such as in Figure 6.1, do exist. Figure 6.2 compares the singularity categorization offset with the b-offset, for the case of a nonsmooth planar curve. It is easy to see that the b-offset produces a smaller superset of the boundary of the positive s-offset (in fact, it produces the exact boundary) and requires no identification of singularities on the curve.

6.1.2   A Constraint-Based Approach for Computing B-Offsets

Consider the use of the constraint solution algorithm (Algorithm 5.1) to find a superset of the b-offset of some parametric object. That is, we wish to compute a subset of Y that bounds the b-offset. The constraint solution algorithm works by subdividing Y into smaller intervals, using an inclusion function to see whether the constraint is satisfied in each interval. In the case of a b-offset, the constraint is that the minimum distance of a point in the interval to the set R_S must be equal to r. Let $Z \in \mathbf{I}(Y)$ be an arbitrary interval processed by the constraint algorithm.

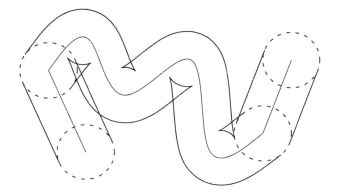

singularity categorization offset

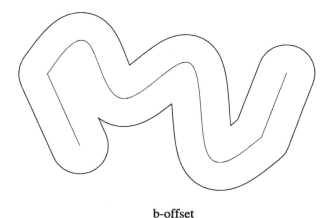

b-offset

Figure 6.2: Singularity categorization offset and b-offset. The top figure shows a 2D planar curve and its singularity categorization offset boundary. The curve has a derivative
discontinuity at two points, where two straight segments are joined to the middle bumpy
curve. These two points and the two curve endpoints are the singular points, each of which
contributes a circle to the offset superset. Note that the offset curves to the middle bumpy
curve self-intersect and contain points that are not on the offset's boundary. The b-offset in
the bottom figure, in contrast, gives the exact boundary of the offset. □

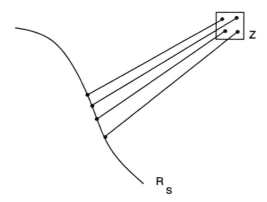

Figure 6.3: Example minimization problem in offset computation. In this case the object being offset is a planar curve (parametric range R_S). We require a bound on the minimum distance of a point in the interval Z to the set R_S. Four points in Z are illustrated as examples, connected by lines to their closest point in the set R_S. The required bound involves considering all such points in Z, finding their closest neighbor in R_S, and finding the maximum and minimum line lengths so obtained (i.e., $f^-(Z)$ and $f^+(Z)$). In this example, the interval Z is fairly large and close to the planar curve R_S. Therefore, the range of minimum distances that need to be bounded is fairly large. □

To compute whether Z can satisfy the constraint, an unconstrained minimization subproblem can be solved, as shown in Figure 6.3. More precisely, let f be the function

$$f(x; z) = \|z - S(x)\|,$$

where $z \in Z$ and $x \in D_S$. We require a bound on the minimum distance of a point in Z to the set R_S. That is, given an interval Z, we must find $f^-(Z)$ and $f^+(Z)$ given by

$$f^-(Z) = \min_{z \in Z} \left(\min_{x \in D_S} \|z - S(x)\| \right)$$

$$f^+(Z) = \max_{z \in Z} \left(\min_{x \in D_S} \|z - S(x)\| \right).$$

Once this bound is obtained, it is tested in the constraint solution algorithm to see whether the minimum and maximum distances straddle r, i.e.,

$$f^-(Z) \le r \le f^+(Z).$$

The constrained minimization algorithm (Algorithm 5.2) can be used to obtain an interval containing $f^-(Z)$ and $f^+(Z)$. To do this, an inclusion function, $\Box f$, can be formed for f. Algorithm 5.2 then works with $\Box f(X, Z)$ as the objective function inclusion, where Z stays fixed during the unconstrained minimization, while X is subdivided. At the start of the algorithm, $X_0 = D_S$. We assume, for the sake of simplicity, that the solution acceptance set constraint of the algorithm is given by

$$w(X) < \epsilon.$$

For any ϵ, the algorithm will produce a bound on $[f^-(Z), f^+(Z)]$, which becomes tighter as ϵ is decreased. Algorithm 5.2 is terminated at the first leading interval, $P \in \mathbf{I}(D_S)$, whose width is less than ϵ, since for any leading interval P we have

$$\text{lb}\,\Box f(P, Z) \le f^-(Z) \le f^+(Z) \le \text{ub}\,\Box f(p, Z) \le \text{ub}\,\Box f(P, Z),$$

where p is any element of P. We note that a termination condition such as

$$w(\Box f(P, Z)) < \delta$$

is not appropriate in these circumstances since $f^+(Z) - f^-(Z) > 0$, in general.

Of course, it does not make sense to use a small ϵ in the minimization subproblems when Z is a big interval. The larger $w(Z)$, the larger one would expect $f^+(Z) - f^-(Z)$. Another way of looking at this is that

$$f^+(Z) - f^-(Z) \to 0 \quad \text{as} \quad w(Z) \to 0.$$

There is also some excess width in the inclusion function $\Box f$ with respect to the fixed interval Z, which remains no matter how small ϵ is chosen. This is because ϵ only affects subdivision of intervals in D_S, not in Z. This excess width is again related to the width of the interval Z. Because of these two factors, ϵ in the minimization algorithm should be related to the width of Z, so that ϵ shrinks as $w(Z)$ shrinks. Empirically, dramatic performance improvements result when ϵ is linearly related to $w(Z)$, rather than made a fixed, small constant for every minimization subproblem.

In summary, because the b-offset is defined in terms of the solution of a constraint involving minimization, it can be computed using the tools for solving global problems already discussed. An inclusion function is defined in terms of variables used in both the constraint problem and the minimization subproblem, i.e., the function $f(x; z) = \|z - S(x)\|$, where the z variable is manipulated in the "outer" constraint solution algorithm and the x variable is manipulated in the "inner" minimization algorithm. For each interval Z processed in the constraint solution algorithm, a new inclusion function $\Box f(X, Z)$ is defined. The constrained minimization algorithm uses this inclusion function, looking for minima of $\Box f$ in

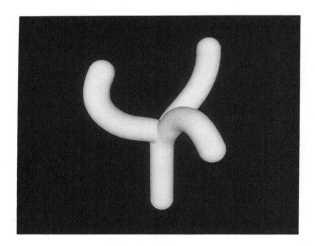

Figure 6.4: Branching surface defined with a b-offset. This three-way branching surface is represented as the b-offset of a collection of three space curves, which form a "skeleton" within each of the surface's arms. That is, the surface is the set of points whose minimum distance to any of these three curves equals a given constant. The implicit surface approximation algorithm of Section 6.6 was used to create the polygonal approximation shown.
□

terms of X, while Z stays fixed. Dramatic performance improvement results when the ϵ used in the minimization subproblems is related to the width of the interval Z.

This technique can also be used to find offsets of non-parametric objects (e.g., offsets of offsets to do blending operations). For example, $(S\partial r_1)\partial r_2$ can be computed by

$$(S\partial r_1)\partial r_2 \;=\; \underset{z_2 \in Z_2}{\text{solve}} \left(\|z_2 - \underset{z_1 \in Z_1}{\text{solve}} \left(\underset{x \in D_S}{\min} \|z_1 - S(x)\| = r_1 \right) \| = r_2 \right)$$

$$=\; \underset{z_2 \in Z_2, z_1 \in Z_1}{\text{solve}} \left(\|z_2 - z_1\| = r_2 \text{ and } \underset{x \in D_S}{\min} \|z_1 - S(x)\| = r_1 \right),$$

where Z_1 and Z_2 are chosen large enough to bound $S\partial r_1$ and $(S\partial r_1)\partial r_2$, respectively. The key to computing these operations is to use the constrained minimization algorithm to compute a bound on the minimum value of the objective function, some of whose variables remain fixed from the outer constraint problem.

Finally, we can use this technique not only to bound the b-offset in a convergent set of intervals, but also to approximate the b-offset, using techniques for approximating implicitly defined curves and surfaces. These techniques will be treated in following sections. Figure 6.4 illustrates an example of a surface defined using the b-offset, approximated using the implicit surface algorithm of Section 6.6.

6.2 Approximating Implicit Curves

An *implicit curve* is the solution to a constraint system $F(x) = 1$, $x \in X \subset \mathbf{R}^n$, such that the solution forms a 1D manifold, except at a zero-dimensional collection of singularities.[3] Implicit curves are extremely useful in geometric modeling. They can represent, for example, the intersection of two parametric surfaces in $\mathbf{R}^3$, the b-offset of a planar curve (see Section 6.1.1), or the silhouette edges of a parametric surface in $\mathbf{R}^3$ with respect to a given view. Typically, the constraint system is represented as a system of $n - 1$ equations in n parameters. However, it is often useful to define other constraint systems. For example, the union of two implicitly defined curves may be defined by

$$F_1(x) = 1 \text{ or } F_2(x) = 1,$$

where $F_1(x) = 1$ and $F_2(x) = 1$ are constraint systems representing the curves to be unioned. Also, inequality constraints (e.g., **less than** and **not equal to**) are often useful in excluding unwanted parts of the implicit curve.

This section discusses an algorithm for approximating implicit curves that solves a constraint system represented using the symbolic operators of Chapter 2. An implicit curve rarely has a global analytic parameterization and must be approximated when points on the curve are required in geometric operations. For example, rendering a shape defined as a CSG operation on two solids bounded by generative surfaces may require approximation of the intersection curve between the two surfaces. Implicit curve approximation involves producing a sequence of points on the curve (possibly with curve tangent vectors or other information) and information about how these points are linked.

Many forms of interpolation exist with different characteristics of accuracy, speed of computation, degree of curve smoothness, etc. The simplest example of a continuous interpolation scheme is linear interpolation, where the implicit curve between each pair of solution points is approximated by a straight line in the parameter space of the constraint system. Higher order interpolation methods use additional information, such as the tangent vector of the implicit curve at each solution point, to obtain a smoother approximation. Interpolation can also take place in a space other than the constraint system's parameter space. For example, in approximating the curve of intersection between two parametric surfaces in $\mathbf{R}^3$, the approximation may be computed in $\mathbf{R}^3$, the output space of the parametric

---

[3] A singularity is a point where the solution self-intersects or is isolated, i.e., for which a neighborhood exists containing no other solutions.

surfaces. Whatever the interpolation scheme, the same basic information is always required: a sequence of parameter space points that lie on the solution curve and a graph specifying how these solution points are linked (called the *local topology graph*).

Implicit curve approximation also involves a choice of an *approximation quality metric* — a measure of how well the approximation corresponds to the actual solution. Such a metric gives rise to acceptance criteria for the set of points used to approximate the curve: if the metric is satisfactory, the set of points is accepted; otherwise, more points must be computed. Perhaps the simplest example of an approximation quality metric is the maximum distance of the approximation from the solution curve. Many other metrics can be devised that are appropriate in special circumstances. For example, we may wish to approximate areas of high curvature on the implicit curve with more points by weighting the solution-to-approximation distance metric with some function of the curvature.

The implicit curve approximation algorithm presented in the next section uses the constraint solution algorithm to find points on the implicit curve. It produces a sequence of points with linkage information to which different interpolation schemes can be applied. It also allows a diverse set of approximation quality metrics.

The robustness of this algorithm is superior to methods such as the one developed by Timmer [TIMM77, MORT85] and other such local methods [BAJA88]. Timmer's method separates implicit curve approximation into a hunting phase, where intersections of the implicit curve with a preselected grid are computed, and a tracing phase, where the curve inside each grid cell is traced to determine how to connect the intersections. The robustness of the algorithm proposed here is the result of two factors:

- Computing points on the implicit curve is done with a global, robust technique (Algorithm 5.1) that guarantees a bound on the result. This method is superior to local methods, such as Newton iteration, which are not guaranteed to converge.

- Finding disjoint components of the curve is done robustly, rather than in an ad hoc manner. Timmer's method fails to find a disjoint segment of the curve if it "falls within the cracks" of the sampling grid used in the hunting phase (i.e., it lies completely within one grid cell). The proposed algorithm uses a global parameterizability criterion that subdivides parameter space until no curve segment can be lost.

Furthermore, the algorithm described here can be applied to many types of implicit curves, not just to those defined by a single equation in two variables, or two equations in three variables.

6.2.1   An Implicit Curve Approximation Algorithm

The following are inputs to the approximation algorithm:

1. An interval $X \in \mathbf{I}^n$, called the *interval of consideration*, in which to approximate the implicit curve

2. An inclusion function $\Box F(Y)$, $Y \in \mathbf{I}(X)$ for the constraint system defining the implicit curve

3. An inclusion function $\Box G(Y)$, $Y \in \mathbf{I}(X)$, called the approximation acceptance inclusion function. This inclusion function tells when an interval Y is small enough that the segment of the implicit curve it contains can be approximated by a single interpolation segment between a pair of solution points.[4] The approximation acceptance inclusion function thus encodes the approximation quality metric discussed previously.

The algorithm subdivides the region X into subregions that contain the implicit curve, satisfy the approximation acceptance inclusion function, and allow simple computation of the local topology of the curve. Such a subregion is called a *proximate interval*. Generating the proximate intervals is precisely the constrained partitioning problem described in Section 5.3.4.1.

The algorithm makes the following assumptions:

1. The solution to the constraint system $F(x) = 1$ is a continuous, 1D manifold. This implies that the solution contains no self-intersections, isolated singularities, or solution regions of dimensionality greater than 1. It further implies that each disjoint curve segment of the solution is either closed or has endpoints at the boundary of the region X (i.e., a curve segment does not terminate in the interior of the interval of consideration).

2. The intersection of the solution curve with a proximate interval's boundaries is either empty or a finite collection of points (not a 1D manifold).

Under these assumptions, the local topology graph of the approximation becomes a simple linked list, where each solution point is linked to two neighbors, or possibly a single neighbor if the point is on the boundary of X. Figure 6.5 illustrates this kind of local topology, and contrasts it with a more complicated local topology graph which is disallowed by the algorithm's assumptions. Relaxation of these assumptions will be treated in Section 6.2.4.

The output of the approximation algorithm is a list of "curves," where each curve is a linked list of points on a single, disjoint segment of the implicit curve, as shown in Figure 6.6.

---

[4]This is not to say that Y contains only a single curve segment. Rather, Y is acceptable if *each* curve segment it contains can be approximated by one interpolation segment between two solution points.

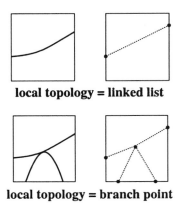

Figure 6.5: Local topology graph. The behavior of an implicit curve inside a single prox-imate interval is illustrated. On the top, a single curve passes through the interval; the two intersections of the curve with the interval's boundary can simply be connected. On the bottom, the implicit curve is composed of two curves which are tangent to each other. In this case, the point of tangency must be found, generating a more complicated local topol-ogy graph. This kind of local topology is prohibited by the algorithm described here, but is addressed in Section 6.2.4. □

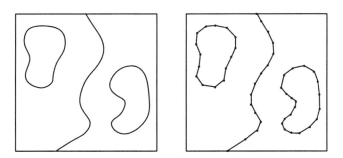

Figure 6.6: Implicit curve approximation. The figure on the left shows an implicit curve satisfying the algorithm's assumptions. This implicit curve is defined over a 2D parameter space and might be obtained by a constraint system such as $f(x,y) = 0$. The implicit curve consists of three segments: two closed segments, and one segment intersecting the boundary of the interval of consideration. The figure on the right shows an approximation of the implicit curve that might be computed by the approximation algorithm. In this case, the algorithm produces three linked lists of points on the implicit curve as output, one for each segment of the implicit curve. The linked list is shown by lines connecting the solution points. □

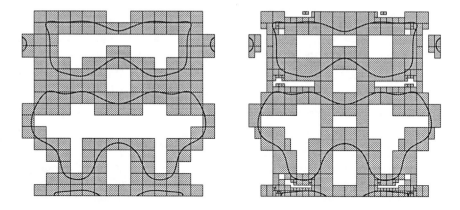

Figure 6.7: Collection of proximate intervals bounding an implicit curve. In these examples, the constraint system is given by the equation $f(x, y) = 0$ where

$$f(x, y) = x^2 + y^2 + \cos(2\pi x) + \sin(2\pi y) + \sin(2\pi x^2)\cos(2\pi y^2) - 1.$$

The interval of consideration is $X = [-1.1, 1.1] \times [-1.1, 1.1]$. The approximation acceptance inclusion function for the left example simply requires that the width of the parameter space interval should be less than 0.2, while that on the right guarantees the global parameterizability of the solution in each interval. $\square$

Algorithm 6.1 (Implicit Curve Approximation Algorithm)

1. **Subdivide X into a collection of proximate intervals bounding the implicit curve and satisfying the approximation acceptance inclusion function.** This can be accomplished using Algorithm 5.1, where $\square F$ is the constraint inclusion function and $\square G$ is the solution acceptance set constraint. Figure 6.7 shows an example of a collection of proximate intervals.

2. **Check each proximate interval for global parameterizability.** The implicit curve contained in a proximate interval Y is called *globally parameterizable in a parameter i* if there is at most one point in Y on the curve for any value of the i-th parameter. Figure 6.8 illustrates the concept of global parameterizability. The global parameterizability of the implicit curve (together with Assumption 1) implies that the curve has a simple local topology. In particular, we can find the points of intersection of the implicit curve with each of Y's boundaries and sort these boundary intersections in increasing order of their i-th parameter. *The global parameterizability of the implicit curve means that only boundary intersections adjacent in this sorted list can possibly be connected by a segment of the implicit curve.* However,

they may not be connected. A simple test verifies whether a pair of points is connected: we merely test whether the i-th hyperplane between these two points intersects the implicit curve. Figure 6.9 illustrates how global parameterizability is related to the connection of boundary intersections.

If the implicit curve is not globally parameterizable in Y for any parameter, then Y is recursively subdivided and tested again.

3. **Find the intersections of the implicit curve with the boundaries of each proximate interval, using Algorithm 5.1.** We assume (Assumption 2) that this intersection will be empty or a finite collection of points.

4. **Ensure that the boundary intersections are disjoint in the global parameterizability parameter.** The previous step produces bounds for the points of intersection of the implicit curve with each proximate interval's boundary. Let i be the global parameterizability parameter for a proximate interval Y, computed from Step 2. This step checks that the intersections of the implicit curve with Y's boundary are non-overlapping in coordinate i, as shown in Figure 6.10. Disjointness in coordinate i implies that the boundary intersections can be unambiguously sorted in increasing order of coordinate i, necessary for connection testing in the next step.

If Y's boundary intersections are not disjoint in parameter i, Y is recursively subdivided and retested.

5. **Compute the connection of boundary intersections in each proximate interval.** If an interval Y contains no boundary intersections, it can be discarded. This is because the solution cannot be a closed curve entirely contained in Y, because of the global parameterizability condition. Nor can the solution be a curve segment that does not intersect Y's boundary, by Assumption 1. Hence, Y contains no part of the implicit curve.

If Y contains a single boundary intersection, then the solution is either tangent to a boundary of Y or passes through a corner or edge of Y. In either case, the solution does not intersect the interior of Y, so Y can be discarded.

If Y contains more than one boundary intersection, the boundary intersections are sorted in order of the global parameterizability parameter i. For each pair of boundary intersections adjacent in parameter i, Algorithm 5.1 is used to see if the solution curve intersects the i-th parameter hyperplane midway between the two boundary intersections. If so, the boundary intersections are connected in the local curve topology linked list.

6. **Find the set of disjoint curve segments comprising the implicit curve. Ensure a consistent ordering of points in each segment.** This step requires straightforward processing on the connected list of boundary intersection points.

I. Globally Parameterizable in x

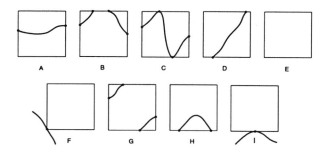

II. Not Globally Parameterizable in x

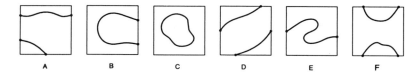

III. Not Allowed by Assumptions

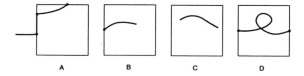

Figure 6.8: Global parameterizability. The figure illustrates some of the possible behaviors of an implicit curve in an interval. In this case, the parameter space is 2D with the x parameter on the horizontal axis of the page. Case I shows intervals in which the implicit curve is globally parameterizable in x. This includes situations in which the interval contains a single segment (A,C,D,H), two segments (B,G), or no segments (E,F,I). Case II shows intervals in which the implicit curve is not globally parameterizable in x. In each case, there is a vertical line that intersects the solution in more than one point. Finally, Case III shows intervals in which the implicit curve exhibits behaviors not allowed by the assumptions of the algorithm. Example A shows a segment of the implicit curve contained entirely on the interval boundary. Examples B and C have curve endpoints that are not on the boundary of the interval of consideration. Example D self-intersects. □

I. Boundary Intersections of an Implicit Curve

II. Eight Cases of Implicit Curve Behavior

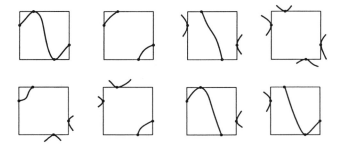

III. Not Allowed by Global Parameterizability

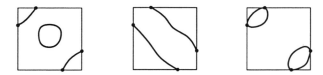

Figure 6.9: Global parameterizability and the linking of boundary intersections. In this figure, we assume an implicit curve defined in $\mathbf{R}^2$ is globally parameterizable in x in an interval. The implicit curve has four intersections with the interval's boundary, as shown in I. Because of global parameterizability and the curve approximation algorithm's assumptions, there are only eight possible ways the implicit curve can connect the boundary intersections, as shown in II. The possibilities shown in III are not globally parameterizable in x, and are therefore excluded. To disambiguate between these eight cases, we need only see if the implicit curve intersects the x hyperplane (dashed vertical line in I) between each pair of adjacent boundary intersections. If the implicit curve intersects the hyperplane, we connect the pair of points; otherwise, we do not. □

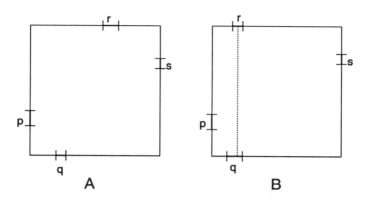

Figure 6.10: Boundary intersection sortability. Figure A illustrates a 2D interval containing four boundary intersections that are disjoint in the x parameter (horizontal axis). They can therefore be sorted in x, yielding the ordering p, q, r, s. In figure B, boundary intersections q and r are not disjoint in x (the dashed line shows a common x coordinate). □

Step 1 of the algorithm combines the constraint inclusion with the approximation acceptance inclusion to create an initial collection of proximate intervals bounding the implicit curve. Consider approximating the intersection of two parametric surfaces, $S(u_1, v_1): \mathbf{R}^2 \rightarrow \mathbf{R}^3$, and $T(u_2, v_2): \mathbf{R}^2 \rightarrow \mathbf{R}^3$. An appropriate constraint function, $F(u_1, v_1, u_2, v_2)$, is given by a system of three equations in four parameters

$$
\begin{aligned}
S_1(u_1, v_1) &= T_1(u_2, v_2) \\
S_2(u_1, v_1) &= T_2(u_2, v_2) \\
S_3(u_1, v_1) &= T_3(u_2, v_2).
\end{aligned}
$$

Let a particular interval of Step 1 be given by $Y = (U_1, V_1, U_2, V_2)$, where $U_1, V_1, U_2, V_2 \in \mathbf{I}$. A reasonable choice for the approximation acceptance inclusion function, $\Box G(Y)$, is

$$
w\left(\Box S(U_1, V_1) \bigcap \Box T(U_2, V_2)\right) < \delta.
$$

This implies that each segment of the approximate intersection curve (mapped into the output space of the parametric functions, $\mathbf{R}^3$) lies in a cube in $\mathbf{R}^3$ of width no larger than δ. In particular, this implies that the maximum distance of the approximation from the implicit curve is less than $\delta\sqrt{3}$. Of course, many other choices for $\Box G(Y)$ are possible.

Step 2 of the algorithm ensures that each proximate interval satisfies a global parameterizability criterion that allows simple computation of the local topology of the curve inside the interval. Intervals not satisfying this criterion are subdivided until each of their subregions does satisfy it. How can the algorithm know when the solution contained in a given interval is globally parameterizable? Section 6.2.2 presents a theorem identifying robust conditions for global parameterizability, computable with interval techniques already discussed. This theorem pertains to the special case of a system of $n - 1$ continuously differentiable equality constraints in n parameters. We have also developed a more general but heuristic test for global parameterizability, discussed in Section 6.2.3.

Step 3 of the algorithm computes the intersections of the implicit curve with the boundary of each proximate interval. Algorithm 5.1 is used with the original constraint inclusion, $\square F(Y)$, and an initial region formed by one of the $2n$ $(n - 1)$-dimensional hyperplanes bounding the proximate interval. A hyperplane is formed by holding one variable fixed at either the upper or lower bound of a component interval of the proximate interval, while the rest of the variables vary. For each boundary hyperplane, Algorithm 5.1 searches for all the constraint system's solutions (see Section 5.3.4 for an explanation of the use of Algorithm 5.1 to find all solutions to a constraint system when the solutions form a finite set). Note that Algorithm 5.1 does not compute the precise solution points, but instead produces a set of intervals bounding them, called *boundary intersection intervals*.

Since neighboring proximate intervals share boundaries, boundary intersection intervals are shared between proximate intervals. When a proximate interval is processed, all neighboring intervals are first searched. Boundary intersection intervals in neighboring intervals that also lie on the interval's boundary are reused. This saves computation since Algorithm 5.1 need not be invoked for boundary hyperplanes that have already been computed in a contiguous, previously visited interval (or a combination of such intervals). Sharing of boundary intersection intervals also allows the approximation linked list to be "grown" locally, as shown in Figure 6.11. Boundary intersection intervals on "corners" of the proximate interval (i.e., on the $(n - 2)$-dimensional boundary of a boundary hyperplane) require special treatment. When the implicit curve intersects the proximate interval's boundary at or near such a corner, boundary intersection intervals may be computed for more than one boundary hyperplane, as shown in Figure 6.12. Such corner boundary intersections must be merged to eliminate multiple copies of the same boundary intersection. Merging involves computing the merge operation on the intervals (see Section 5.3.2) and combining all neighbor pointers.

Steps 4 and 5 link boundary intersection intervals that are connected by the same segment of the implicit curve. Boundary intersection intervals are sorted in the global parameterizability parameter, and each pair of adjacent intersections is tested. The test uses Algorithm 5.1 to discover whether the implicit curve intersects a hyperplane midway between the pair of intersections. This application of

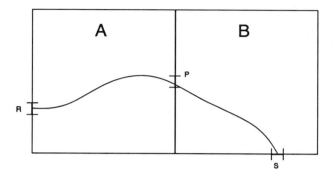

Figure 6.11: Boundary intersection sharing. Two contiguous proximate intervals, A and B, share a boundary intersection interval, P. Each boundary intersection interval stores a pointer to two neighbors. After processing interval A, boundary intersection P is connected to R, so that P points to R. When interval B is processed, boundary intersections on the shared face from A are searched to find P, which is reused. P is then connected to S, so that P's two pointers point to R and S, respectively. This effectively attaches two curve segments together. Before Step 6, the two neighbor pointers are not usefully ordered, but are accumulated as the algorithm processes the proximate intervals in Step 5. Boundary intersections are traversed in Step 6 to reorder the first and second neighbor pointers so that the first pointer points to the "next" intersection on the implicit curve, and the second pointer points to the "previous" intersection. □

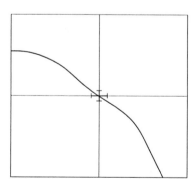

Figure 6.12: Corner boundary intersections. An implicit curve passes very close to the corner of four proximate intervals. In this case, two boundary hyperplanes in each of the four intervals will contain a boundary intersection interval. Boundary intersection intervals at the corners should be merged to reflect the fact that they contain only a single intersection point. □

the constraint algorithm need only ascertain whether a solution exists; the location of the intersection point is not required. On the other hand, the intersection point can be used to better approximate the implicit curve's behavior between the boundary intersections, at little extra computational cost.

Finally, Step 6 associates each of the boundary intersection intervals with a disjoint segment of the implicit curve. Step 6 also ensures a consistent ordering of intersections from beginning to end of each segment (e.g., the intersection's first pointer always points to the previous intersection on the curve, the second pointer always points to the next intersection). The following simple algorithm performs these tasks:

> let S be the set of boundary intersections
> while S is nonempty
>   remove an intersection point P from S
>   find and remove all points P' in S that are
>   (indirectly) connected to P by following neighbor pointers
>   associate P and the set of P' with a new curve
> endwhile

We note that in accumulating the set of points on a particular curve using this algorithm, if a point P' is eventually found such that $P = P'$ then the curve is closed. Otherwise, the curve has two endpoints on the boundary of X by Assumption 1.

A point inside each of the boundary intersection intervals should be chosen to represent the actual point of intersection of the proximate interval's boundary with the implicit curve. This point can be chosen arbitrarily (e.g., midpoint of the interval) or computed using a local iterative technique such as Newton's method.

Figure 6.13 and Plate 8 show examples of the results of this algorithm for the problem of finding the silhouette curve of a surface with respect to a given orthographic view.

6.2.2   A Robust Test for Global Parameterizability

Section C.5 proves a result called the Interval Implicit Function theorem, which gives conditions for the global parameterizability of an r-dimensional manifold defined as the solution of

$$f(x^1, x^2, \ldots, x^n) = 0$$

for a differentiable function $f: \mathbf{R}^n \rightarrow \mathbf{R}^{n-r}$. Global parameterizability for arbitrary-dimensional manifolds means that r input parameters of f can be found, $\{x_{k_1}, x_{k_2}, \ldots, x_{k_r}\}$, such that there is at most one zero of f for any value of these parameters in a given domain.

In the case of approximation of a 1D solution manifold, $r = 1$; that is, we are solving a system of $n - 1$ equations in n variables. The theorem guarantees that if,

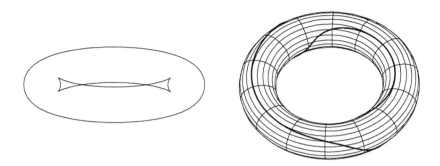

Figure 6.13: Silhouette curve approximation. The silhouette curve of a parametric surface, $S(u, v)$, with respect to a given orthographic view can be found with the implicit curve approximation algorithm. The silhouette is given by the solution of a single constraint in the variables u and v that specifies that the dot product of the surface's normal and the view direction, E, is 0, i.e., $E \cdot (\frac{\partial S}{\partial u} \times \frac{\partial S}{\partial v}) = 0$. The illustration shows the torus and its silhouette, viewed from direction E on the left, and from another viewing direction on the right. $\square$

in an interval X, we can find a parameter index k such that the determinant of the $n - 1 \times n - 1$ interval Jacobian submatrix is nonzero, then the solution manifold is globally parameterizable in X over the parameter x_k.

The notation $\square J_{\{k\}}(X)$ refers to the interval Jacobian submatrix. It is formed by deleting the k-th column from the interval Jacobian matrix. That is,

$$\square J_{\{k\}}(X) = \left[\square \frac{\partial f_i}{\partial x_j} \right]_{j \neq k}.$$

We can verify that $\det \square J_{\{k\}}(X) \neq 0$ by forming an inclusion function for the determinant of the interval Jacobian submatrix. The determinant inclusion function, $\det_\square$, can be constructed for any interval matrix using the interval arithmetic presented in Section 5.2.2. If, for any of the n interval Jacobian submatrices, we have

$$0 \notin \det_\square \square J_{\{k\}}(X),$$

then the implicit curve is globally parameterizable in parameter x_k over the interval X.

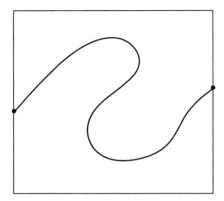

Figure 6.14: Step 5 connectability vs. global parameterizability. An implicit curve defined in a 2D parameter space has two intersections with the boundary of an interval. The implicit curve is not globally parameterizable in x or y, yet it is step 5 connectable. Step 5 of the approximation algorithm will link the two boundary intersections after determining that an x or y hyperplane between the two boundary intersections intersects the implicit curve. □

6.2.3   A Heuristic Test for Global Parameterizability

This section discusses a heuristic test for global parameterizability in an interval Y. The test is useful because the implicit curve to be approximated may be represented with a constraint system that does not satisfy the hypothesis of Theorem C.5 (i.e., not a system of $n-1$ equations in n parameters, equating continuously differentiable functions to 0). Also, we may wish to avoid computation at the expense of robustness. The heuristic test eliminates computation of interval Jacobian determinants and often allows earlier acceptance of intervals. Early acceptance of intervals is significant because larger intervals require fewer implicit curve/boundary intersection computations.

In fact, the heuristic test discussed in this section is related to "connectability" of boundary intersections rather than to global parameterizability. That is, the test ensures that boundary intersections linked in step 5 of the approximation algorithm are *connected* in Y: on the same segment of the implicit curve that is contained entirely in Y. This condition, which we will call *step 5 connectability*, is guaranteed by global parameterizability. Global parameterizability is, however, a much stronger condition, as Figure 6.14 shows. Unfortunately, the heuristic test is not robust in checking for this weaker condition of step 5 connectability. It assumes that the solution does not form a closed curve entirely contained in Y, termed the *nonperiodicity assumption* in the following text.

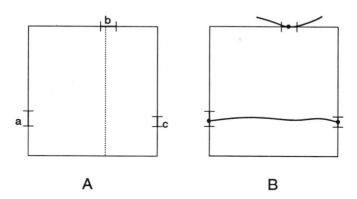

Figure 6.15: Boundary univalence test. In Figure A, three boundary intersections are disjoint in the x parameter, yielding the intersection ordering a, b, c. The boundary univalence test checks whether the implicit curve intersects the x hyperplane at b, shown by the dashed line. If there is only a single intersection between the implicit curve and this hyperplane (i.e., the same intersection contained in b), then the implicit curve cannot connect the boundary intersections a and c, as in Figure B, which would yield two implicit curve/hyperplane intersections. $\square$

The test first finds all intersections of the solution curve with the boundaries of Y, yielding a set of intervals, each containing a boundary intersection. This is the same computation that occurs in step 3. The test checks that these intervals are disjoint in some parameter i, just as in step 4. If the boundary intersection intervals are not disjoint in any parameter, the test fails, and Y must be subdivided. Otherwise, the boundary intersections can be unambiguously sorted in parameter i. The test then checks that the solution curve has only a single intersection with the i-th coordinate hyperplane of each of the boundary intersections, as shown in Figure 6.15. This check is called the *boundary univalence test*.

More precisely, let the intervals $X^1, X^2, \ldots, X^m \in \mathbf{I}^n$ be a sequence of intervals each bounding an intersection of the implicit curve and the boundary of $Y \in \mathbf{I}^n$. Let Y be given by

$$Y = [a_1, b_1] \times \ldots \times [a_n, b_n].$$

Assume that the boundary intersection sequence is sorted by parameter i, i.e.,

$$\text{ub } X_i^k < \text{lb } X_i^{k+1} \quad k = 1, 2, \ldots, m - 1,$$

where X_i^k represents the i-th coordinate interval of X^k. The i-th coordinate hyperplane of a boundary intersection X_k is an interval subset of X^k whose i-th

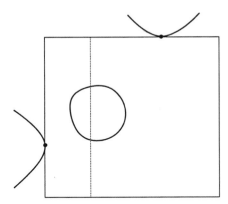

Figure 6.16: Necessity of the nonperiodicity assumption in the heuristic test. In this example, an implicit curve intersects the boundary of a region in $\mathbf{R}^2$ at two points. The implicit curve does not connect these two boundary points, but is tangent to the boundary there. Nevertheless, step 5 of the approximation algorithm will decide that the two points should be connected. This is because the x-coordinate hyperplane shown by the dashed line has a nonempty intersection with a closed segment of the implicit curve. □

coordinate is a constant:

$$
\begin{array}{ll}
X_j^k & j \neq i \\
[x, x] \quad x \in X_i^k & j = i.
\end{array}
$$

The boundary univalence test is based on the observation that if an i-th coordinate hyperplane of a boundary intersection interval X^k contains only a single intersection with the implicit curve, then no boundary intersections $X^p, p < k$ can be connected to boundary intersections $X^q, q > k$. If the boundary univalence test succeeds on each of the boundary intervals X^k, then the implicit curve can only connect boundary intersections adjacent in parameter i, i.e., X^k and X^{k+1}. Assuming there are no closed segments of the implicit curve contained entirely within Y (nonperiodicity assumption), step 5 of the approximation algorithm then correctly determines whether adjacent boundary intersections should be connected. Figure 6.16 illustrates why the nonperiodicity assumption is necessary.[5] If the boundary univalence test fails for any boundary intersection, the whole heuristic test fails, and Y must be subdivided.

---

[5]Fortunately, when the nonperiodicity assumption is violated, the approximation algorithm can easily detect when boundary intersections have been incorrectly connected. Incorrect connection, such as would occur in Figure 6.16, will lead to the linking of a boundary intersection that already has two distinct linked list neighbors.

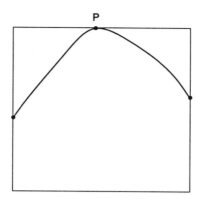

Figure 6.17: Pathological case for naive subdivision. The implicit curve has three intersections with the boundary of the interval. At the intersection labeled P, the implicit curve
is exactly tangent to the interval's boundary. No matter how the interval is subdivided,
any child interval containing P will also have three implicit curve/boundary intersections,
unless the boundary interval containing P is split during subdivision in x. Depending on
the size of the interval containing P, the original interval may have to be subdivided many
times for this to happen. $\square$

The boundary univalence test need be performed only if there are more than
two boundary intersections. Given the nonperiodicity assumption, if there are two
boundary intersections, then either the implicit curve does not intersect the interior of Y, or it connects the two boundary intersections. These two possibilities
are correctly distinguished by step 5 of the approximation algorithm. In practice,
the great majority of intervals Y contain no boundary intersections or a single
pair. Thus, the heuristic test performs very little computation most of the time,
compared with the robust test.

Furthermore, the boundary univalence test need be performed only on boundary intersections that do not lie on the i-th coordinate boundaries of Y. That is, if
the first interval X^1 has $X_i^1 = [a_i, a_i]$, or the last interval X^m has $X_i^m = [b_i, b_i]$,
then the boundary univalence test on these intervals is not required. This is because
the univalence of such intervals is already guaranteed by the sortability condition.

One might reasonably ask why the boundary univalence test is required at all.
Why not instead subdivide until each interval Y contains at most two boundary
intersections with the implicit curve? The reason is that this scheme will lead to an
inordinate amount of subdivision, in rarely occurring circumstances. Figure 6.17
illustrates one such pathological case.

6.2.4   Relaxing the Approximation Algorithm's Restrictions

Algorithm 6.1 assumes that the implicit curve to be approximated satisfies two assumptions. In this section, we examine these assumptions in more detail and show how the algorithm can be enhanced to handle more general implicit curves.

Assumption 1a — No Self-Intersections or Isolated Singularities

Algorithm 6.1 assumes that the implicit curve has no self-intersections or isolated singularities. One approach to handling curves that do contain such singularities is to distinguish proximate intervals in which the implicit curve is well behaved from proximate intervals in which the implicit curve may have singularities. For example, for an implicit curve described by a system of $n-1$ continuously differentiable functions of n parameters equated to 0, the robust test for global parameterizability (i.e., the Interval Implicit Function Theorem of Section 6.2.2) guarantees that the implicit curve will not contain singularities. This is true because of the Implicit Function Theorem, whose conditions are sufficiently satisfied by those of the Interval Implicit Function Theorem. Since we expect the set of singularities to be zero-dimensional, it should be possible to subdivide the ill-behaved proximate intervals until their child intervals are either well behaved or are small enough.

We can then process the well-behaved proximate intervals in the same way as before. What should be done with the remaining (small) ill-behaved intervals? A reasonable course is to connect all their boundary intersections in a star-like graph. More precisely, the midpoint of the ill-behaved interval is connected to each of the interval's boundary intersections. Essentially, we assume that an ill-behaved interval represents a possibly multibranching self-intersection of the implicit curve to some tolerance. This tolerance is the largest width of an ill-behaved proximate interval. Thus, such ill-behaved intervals create a local topology graph with more complexity than a simple linked list.

Assumption 1b — No Abrupt Endings

We may also wish to handle implicit curves that violate the continuity part of Assumption 1; that is, curves that end abruptly in the interior of the region of consideration. An approach to relaxing this assumption is similar to the technique for relaxing the lack of singularities assumption of the previous section — proximate intervals in which the implicit curve may abruptly end are distinguished from intervals in which the curve satisfies Assumption 1. For example, an implicit curve may be described by the following constraint system:

$$f_i(x) = 0 \quad i = 1, 2, \ldots, n - 1$$
$$g_j(x) \geq 0 \quad j = 1, 2, \ldots, m$$

where $x \in \mathbf{R}^n$, and f_i and g_j are continuous functions $f_i, g_j \colon \mathbf{R}^n \to \mathbf{R}$. Even if the equality constraints f_i determine a solution that is a continuous, 1D manifold, this solution can still have abrupt endings in the interior of an interval whenever the inequality constraints reject parts of that solution curve. If for some proximate interval Y we have

$$0 \notin \Box g_j(Y) \quad \text{for any } j \in \{1, 2, \ldots, m\}, \tag{6.1}$$

and again assuming the solution determined by the equality constraints is a 1D manifold, then Y can contain no abrupt endings. We can therefore subdivide intervals until they satisfy the criterion in Equation 6.1, or are very small. Regions satisfying the criterion can be processed using steps 2, 3, 4, and 5 of Algorithm 6.1.

The remaining small regions may contain abrupt endings. In general, the behavior of the implicit curve in these regions cannot be easily analyzed because the inequality constraint may or may not cause breaks in the implicit curve that solves the system without the inequality constraint. It may be sufficient, however, to allow the curve's local topology to be uncertain within these small intervals. On the other hand, we may do better in many circumstances. For example, in the above constraint system, we can find solutions to the $n \times n$ system

$$f_i(x) = 0 \quad i = 1, 2, \ldots, n - 1$$
$$g_j(x) = 0 \quad j \in \{1, 2, \ldots, m\}$$

using Algorithm 5.1. That is, we can find the points of intersection between the implicit curve satisfying the equality constraints and each of the m manifolds where $g_j(x) = 0$. Assuming the solution to the constraint system $f_i(x) = 0$ is globally parameterizable in the small region, the combined set of boundary intersections and solutions to the m $n \times n$ systems can be processed using steps 4 and 5 of Algorithm 6.1.

Assumption 2 — No Segments along Proximate Interval Boundaries

Algorithm 6.1 assumes that the implicit curve has no segments that run along the boundary of a proximate interval. During step 3, Algorithm 5.1 can detect violations of this assumption by detecting when the constraint system solutions fail to converge to a set of finite points. For example, we can check whether the number of candidate solution intervals continues to grow as the iteration proceeds.

If this checking determines that Assumption 2 is violated, then the parameter space of the constraint system should be transformed. That is, given a constraint system $F(x) = 1$ and an invertible transformation $T(x): \mathbf{R}^n \to \mathbf{R}^n$, then solving the system $F(T(x)) = 1$ transforms the implicit curve by T^{-1}. Thus, we can use Algorithm 6.1 on the transformed constraint system and transform each of the resulting points by T^{-1} to yield an approximation of the implicit curve that solves the original constraint system. T should be chosen so that the segment of the implicit curve no longer lies along the boundary of a proximate interval in the transformed parameter space. For example, a simple translation transformation,

$$T(x) = x + a$$

where a is chosen to translate the offending segment to the interior of the proximate interval, is sufficient.

6.3 Approximating Parametric Shapes Using Adaptive Criteria

In Section 6.2, an algorithm was presented to approximate implicit curves. The first part of this algorithm involved constructing a collection of intervals bounding the implicit curve and satisfying an approximation acceptance inclusion function. A similar technique can be applied to the problem of generating an approximation of a parametric shape that satisfies user-specified criteria.

Let $F: \mathbf{R}^n \to \mathbf{R}^m$ be a parametric shape, and let $D \in \mathbf{I}^n$ be the domain of F. F can be approximated in three steps:

1. Subdivide the domain D into a collection of subregions that satisfy some criteria. This problem is the *constrained partitioning problem* discussed in Section 5.3.4.1.

2. Choose a small number of points from each subregion (typically on the subregion's boundary) and evaluate F at each point.

3. Construct an approximation of the shape in each subregion, using the samples from step 2. These approximations should fit together without cracks at the subregion boundaries.

The criteria of step 1 are represented using an inclusion function

$$\Box G: \mathbf{I}(D) \to \mathbf{I}.$$

$\Box G$ takes a subregion X and produces the following results:

$$[1, 1] \qquad \text{accept the region } X$$
$$[0, 1] \text{ or } [0, 0] \quad \text{continue subdividing the region } X$$

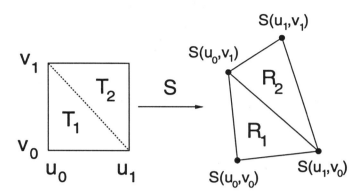

Figure 6.18: Pair of triangles approximating a surface. The four corners of the (u, v) parametric rectangle are mapped to the object space of S to form two triangles, R_1 and R_2. We wish to bound the distance of these two triangles from the surface mapped from the two parametric rectangles T_1 and T_2. $\square$

An example of a useful subregion acceptance inclusion function is

$$\Box G(X) \equiv (w(\Box F(X)) < \delta).$$

This inclusion function guarantees that each subregion is small enough that the output of the parametric function can be bounded in an interval of width at most δ.

As another example, we can use an inclusion function to more directly bound the approximation error. Consider a surface in $\mathbf{R}^3$, $S(u, v)$, which is to be approximated as a collection of triangles. We may wish to subdivide the (u, v) parameter space of S until each (u, v) rectangle,

$$[u_0, u_1] \times [v_0, v_1]$$

determines two triangles in $\mathbf{R}^3$ such that the distance from the actual surface to its triangular approximation is bounded. Figure 6.18 shows how these triangles are formed.

Let the corners of the (u, v) rectangle be given by

$$\begin{aligned}
P_0 &= (u_0, v_0) \\
P_1 &= (u_1, v_0) \\
P_2 &= (u_0, v_1) \\
P_3 &= (u_1, v_1).
\end{aligned}$$

The corresponding mapped values of S at these points are

$$
\begin{aligned}
S_0 &= S(P_0) = S(u_0, v_0) \\
S_1 &= S(P_1) = S(u_1, v_0) \\
S_2 &= S(P_2) = S(u_0, v_1) \\
S_3 &= S(P_3) = S(u_1, v_1).
\end{aligned}
$$

We first consider the triangle formed by mapping the vertices P_0, P_1, and P_2. Let $T_1(r, s)$ be a parameterization of this triangle

$$
T_1 \colon [0, 1] \times [0, 1] \to [u_0, u_1] \times [v_0, v_1]
$$

given by

$$
T_1(r, s) = rs(P_0 - P_1) + s(P_2 - P_0) + r(P_1 - P_0) + P_0.
$$

For $r, s \in [0, 1]$, the function T_1 is thus onto the triangle in (u, v) parameter space whose vertices are P_0, P_1, and P_2. A similar parametric triangle, $T_2(r, s)$, can be formed for the second parametric triangle with vertices P_1, P_2, and P_3.

We also define a parametric triangle in the object space of S,

$$
R_1 \colon [0, 1] \times [0, 1] \to \mathbf{R}^3,
$$

with vertices S_0, S_1, and S_2. Such a triangle is given by

$$
R_1(r, s) = rs(S_0 - S_1) + s(S_2 - S_0) + r(S_1 - S_0) + S_0.
$$

A second parametric triangle, $R_2(r, s)$, whose vertices are S_1, S_2, and S_3, is defined similarly.

A function relevant to the approximation error is then

$$
F_1(r, s) = \| S(T_1(r, s)) - R_1(r, s) \|.
$$

The maximum value of $F_1(r, s)$ for $r, s \in [0, 1]$ is a pessimistic bound for the the maximum distance of a point on the surface mapped from the first parametric triangle, T_1, to the triangle approximating the surface, R_1. This bound is pessimistic since we really wish to bound the distance of the surface from its corresponding **closest** point on the approximation, namely the function

$$
G_1(r, s) = \min_{\hat{r}, \hat{s} \in [0, 1]} \left(\| S(T_1(r, s)) - R_1(\hat{r}, \hat{s}) \| \right).
$$

Corresponding F_2 and G_2 functions can be defined similarly to bound the distance of the surface from the second triangle.

We can use inclusion functions for $F_1(r, s)$ and $F_2(r, s)$ in a solution acceptance set constraint for the surface approximation problem via

$$
\max(\mathrm{ub}\,\square F_1, \mathrm{ub}\,\square F_2) < \epsilon.
$$

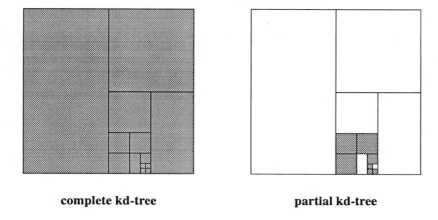

complete kd-tree   **partial kd-tree**

Figure 6.19: The kd-tree data structure. The figure illustrates two 2D kd-trees. The left kd-tree is complete: its leaf nodes form the complete partition of the original 2D region. The right kd-tree is partial: some of its the leaf nodes have been deleted. □

This set constraint guarantees that the distance of a point on the surface mapped from either parametric triangle and a point on its corresponding triangular approximation does not exceed ϵ.

An even better error function is

$$G(u,v) = \min_{\hat{r},\hat{s}\in[0,1]} \left(\min(\|S(u,v) - R_1(\hat{r},\hat{s})\|, \|S(u,v) - R_2(\hat{r},\hat{s})\|)\right)$$

whose maximum over $(u,v) \in [u_0, u_1] \times [v_0, v_1]$ is precisely a bound on the maximum distance of the surface from its approximation by two triangles. We note that while $G(u,v)$ can be computed using the minimization operator, its use is very computationally expensive compared to the bound defined with F_1 and F_2.

6.3.1   Kd-Trees

A convenient data structure for organizing the collection of subregions is a *kd-tree*, for *k-dimensional tree* (also called *bintrees* in [TAMM84]). A kd-tree represents a binary subdivision of multidimensional space, one dimension at a time. Each node stores a left and right subtree and an index representing the subdivided dimension. Let *(left,right,d)* represent a kd-tree node, where *left* is the left subtree, *right* is the right subtree, and *d* is the subdivided dimension. The special value NIL represents an empty kd-tree. For example, a leaf node is represented by the kd-tree (NIL,NIL,0), since both its child nodes are empty. Kd nodes can even have one child empty and another nonempty to represent spatial subdivisions that do not occupy all of the original space. Such kd-trees are called *partial kd-trees*. Although such trees are not important in the current discussion, since we wish to sample the whole parameter space of F, they will be used in Section 6.4. Figure 6.19 illustrates two examples of 2D kd-trees.

If we represent the collection of subregions in the approximation by a kd-tree, an algorithm for step 1 may be defined using the following recursive function.

```
subdivide(X,□G,d)
      evaluate Y = □G(X)
      if Y = [1, 1] then
            return (NIL,NIL,0)
      else
            subdivide X in parametric dimension d into X₁ and X₂
            let d' be the next dimension to subdivide
            return (subdivide(X₁,□G,d'),subdivide(X₂,□G,d'),d)
      endif
```

Subdivision takes place along the midpoint of the parametric coordinate d. Step 1 is accomplished using the invocation subdivide($D, \Box G, 1$).

Once an appropriate collection of subregions has been computed, a set of points must be chosen in each leaf of the kd-tree, and the points must be interpolated in some manner. The next section discusses this process for the case when F is a parametric surface, and the approximating network is a triangular mesh.

6.3.2   Generating a Triangular Mesh

Given a 2D kd-tree, a triangular mesh approximating the surface can be generated. The parametric function is first evaluated at the corners of each kd-tree leaf, as shown in Figure 6.20. The corner samples are then used to construct a collection of triangles. Note that the evaluation of corner samples should be shared among leaves to avoid needless evaluation of the parametric function. Triangularization such as that shown in Figure 6.20 is easily accomplished using the algorithm in Figure 6.22. An example 2D kd-tree and the resulting collection of triangles generated using this algorithm is shown on the right side of Figure 4.3.

Alternatively, an additional point can be sampled at the midpoint of each 2D region, and triangles formed that connect this midpoint to each of the boundary points. Figure 6.21 shows this kind of triangle generation.

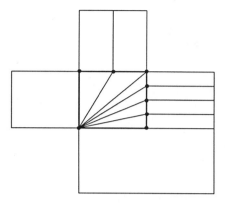

Figure 6.20: Approximating a surface as a triangular mesh. The center rectangle is a kd-tree leaf, surrounded by its neighbors. The parametric function is evaluated at each point on the boundary of the leaf that is a corner of the leaf or of its neighbor. A collection of triangles is then generated so that each boundary point is a vertex of at least two triangles, thus guaranteeing that there will be no cracks in the surface approximation. □

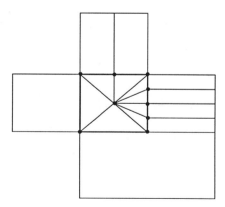

Figure 6.21: Approximating a surface as a triangular mesh. In this case, the location of the surface at the center of the leaf node is sampled. Triangles are then generated with one vertex at this point and the other two at the boundary points. □

```
triangularize(vlist)

ncorners ← 4
i ← head(vlist)
j ← next(i)
k ← tail(vlist)
while (j ≠ k and j ≠ NIL)
        if (ncorners = 3 and corner(j) and
            corner(k) and next(j) ≠ NIL) then
                k ← i
                i ← j
                j ← next(j)
        endif
        triangle(i,j,k)
        ncorners ← ncorners-1
        if (not corner(j)) then
                corner(j) = 1
                ncorners ← ncorners+1
        endif
        if (not corner(k)) then
                corner(k) = 1
                ncorners ← ncorners+1
        endif
        i ← j
        j ← next(j)
endwhile
```

Figure 6.22: Triangularization algorithm. The function `triangularize` takes a list of vertices, `vlist`, on the boundary of a 2D rectangular region, and produces a set of triangles partitioning this region whose vertices are all in `vlist`. For a vertex i, the function `next(i)` returns the next vertex in `vlist`. The function `corner(i)` returns 0 or 1 depending on whether this vertex is a "corner." Initially, only the four vertices at the corners of the 2D rectangle have this corner flag set. `triangularize` sets this flag for each vertex when it is no longer between two other, active vertices, all three of which are on the same line. An active vertex is one which is on the boundary of the remaining polygon still to be split into triangles (i.e., it does not include vertices, i, processed in earlier loop iterations). The first if test after the while loop is necessary to reorder the vertices when connecting the segment from j to k would pass over other, collinear vertices between j and k. The algorithm assumes that the list starts at a corner (i.e., `corner(head(vlist))` is 1). The symbol NIL marks the end of the list, so that `next(tail(vlist))` is NIL. □

6.4   CSG-Like Operations with Trimmed Surfaces

A *trimmed surface* is the image of a parametric surface over a domain specified with a collection of curves called *trimming curves*. The trimming curves form the boundary of a region over which the trimmed surface is evaluated. Figure 6.23 shows an example of a trimmed parametric surface. Trimmed surfaces are a useful modeling tool. For example, by letting the trimming curve be the curve of intersection of one surface with another, simple CSG operations can be represented.

Let $S(u, v)$ and $T(s, t)$ be two non-self-intersecting, continuous, closed, and bounded parametric surfaces in $\mathbf{R}^3$. Let the sets S° and T° be the regions in $\mathbf{R}^3$ bounded by S and T, respectively. A trimmed surface can be used to represent the part of S that lies outside T°. This is accomplished by computing the curve of intersection of S and T in (u, v, s, t) space, and projecting it to the (u, v) parameter space of S. The projected intersection curve is then used as the trimming curve for a trimmed version of S. Similarly, another trimmed surface can be used to represent the part of T that lies inside S°. The union of the two resulting trimmed surfaces forms the boundary of the region $R = S^\circ - T^\circ$, where the $-$ operator denotes set subtraction.

Similar operations that compute Boolean set subtractions, unions, and intersections will be termed *CSG-like operations*. CSG-like operations are distinguished from fully general CSG on parametric surfaces in that CSG-like operations prohibit the intersection of trimming curves. The result of a CSG-like operation cannot therefore be used as an input to another CSG-like operation. However, CSG-like operations are extremely useful and can be developed into a more sophisticated technique to implement full CSG, as we will see in Section 6.5.

A difficult problem in geometric modeling has been to approximate the boundary of the result of CSG-like operations, such as R, so that the trimmed surfaces resulting from $S - T^\circ$ mesh together without artifact with the trimmed surfaces resulting from $T - \neg(S^\circ)$.[6] In this section, an algorithm that solves this problem is presented. This algorithm uses the implicit curve approximation algorithm discussed in a previous section to compute the curve of intersection between the two parametric surfaces.

6.4.1   An Algorithm for Approximating CSG-like Operations

The ideas of Sections 6.2 and 6.3 can be combined to produce an algorithm that approximates the results of CSG-like operations. This algorithm ensures that the

---

[6]The $\neg$ operator denotes set complement.

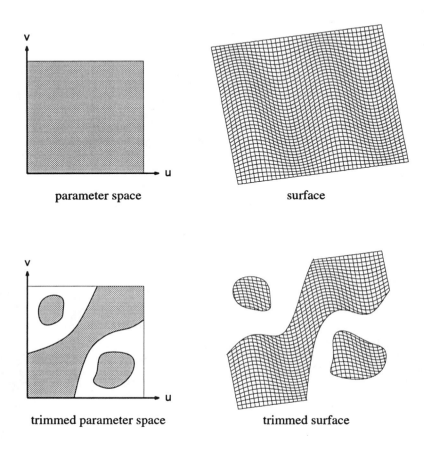

parameter space   surface

trimmed parameter space   trimmed surface

Figure 6.23: Trimmed parametric surface. The top of the figure shows a parametric surface $S(u, v)$ evaluated over a square region of (u, v) parameter space. The bottom shows a trimmed parametric surface. Four trimming curves have been used to define a new domain for S. □

trimmed surfaces mesh together by guaranteeing that all samples on the curve of intersection between the two parametric surfaces are shared.

To continue the example of the previous section, let $S(u, v)$ and $T(s, t)$ be parametric surfaces. The following algorithm approximates the boundary of $S^\diamond \star T^\diamond$ where $\star$ represents a binary set operation such as union, intersection, or subtraction. The algorithm assumes that the curve of intersection between S

and T satisfies the assumptions of Algorithm 6.1 (e.g., that the intersection curve does not self-intersect).

Algorithm 6.2 (CSG-like Operation Approximation Algorithm)

1. **Find the curve of intersection of S and T in (u, v, s, t) space.** Algorithm 6.1 is used to compute a set of linked points approximating the intersection curve. It also generates a kd-tree in (u, v, s, t) space whose terminal nodes are the proximate intervals bounding the intersection curve. Each terminal node stores the intersection points on or within its boundary.

2. **Project the (u, v, s, t) intersection kd-tree into (u, v) and (s, t) space.** The two resulting 2D kd-trees will be referred to as *projected intersection kd-trees*.

3. **Join curve segments that intersect periodic parameter space boundaries.** For example, if a curve segment in (u, v) space does not end on the u, v parameter rectangle, it must have been artificially stopped by hitting a periodic s or t boundary. It should therefore be joined with another curve segment that continues from the opposite side of that boundary.

4. **Order the projected intersection curves based on $\star$ so that the appropriate interior of the trimmed parameter space lies to the left of the trimming curves.**

5. **Generate sampling kd-trees for S and T, using the algorithm of Section 6.2.** The sampling kd-trees represent an approximation of the entire surface S or T, not considering the intersection. The two kd-trees will be referred to as *surface sampling kd-trees*. They are generated using the algorithm presented in Section 6.3.

6. **Merge the projected intersection kd-tree from step 2 with the surface sampling kd-tree from step 5 for both S and T.** The merging operation produces a kd-tree whose terminal nodes are the union of the terminal nodes from the two kd-tree inputs, which will be referred to as a *merged kd-tree*. The merging must be done so that *no terminal kd node in the projected intersection kd-tree is further subdivided.* This is essential because subdivision of the projected intersection kd-tree will require additional sampling of the intersection curve to determine where it intersects the new subdivision boundary. It is then possible that intersection curve samples will be computed for S but not T (or vice versa) so that the intersection curve is no longer shared by the trimmed surfaces.

7. **Generate triangles for each trimmed surface.**

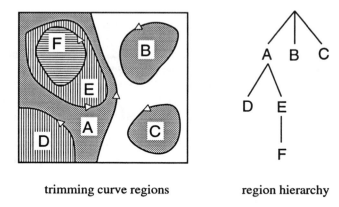

trimming curve regions   region hierarchy

Figure 6.24: Trimming region hierarchy. The parameter space shown contains five regions bounded by trimming curves: A, B, C, D, E, and F. The trimming curve boundary of each region is traversed so that the region's interior lies to the left. A hierarchy of regions, shown on the right, is generated where a child region is directly inside its parent. □

Steps 4 and 7 of this algorithm deserve more explanation. In step 4, the curve segments are initially processed so that each closed curve segment is traversed in a counterclockwise manner (interior to the left). Curve segments intersecting the parameter space rectangle are traversed to form closed regions with a counterclockwise traversal of any included boundaries of the parameter rectangle. A hierarchy of projected intersection curve segments is then constructed according to an inside/outside relationship, as shown in Figure 6.24.

For example, the curve of intersection projected into (u, v) space may have two segments, A and B. Three relationships are possible: the two segments are disjoint, A is inside B, or B is inside A (intersection is not allowed by the assumption of the algorithm). The inside/outside relationship of two curve segments can be easily computed by performing two point-in-polygon tests as shown in Figure 6.25.

Once this hierarchy is constructed, the ordering of each segment must be made opposite to its immediate ancestor in the hierarchy. Finally, a single bit of information remains unspecified since two valid regions can be constructed. That is, we can switch the ordering of every curve segment and create a new region that is the subtraction of the old region from the parameter space rectangle, as shown in Figure 6.26. This single bit of information can be determined by testing whether a single point in parameter space is in the desired set $S^{\diamond} \star T^{\diamond}$, using the technique of point-set classification (see the section starting on page 42).

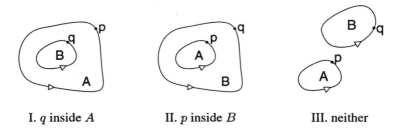

I. q inside A II. p inside B III. neither

Figure 6.25: Relationship between two trimmed regions. To determine the relationship between two trimmed regions, A and B, a point p on A and q on B is selected. Three cases are possible: q inside A (Case I), p inside B (Case II), or neither of these (Case III). Cases in which the trimming curves intersect each other are prohibited. Thus, Case I implies B is inside A, Case II implies A is inside B and Case III implies that the two regions are disjoint. □

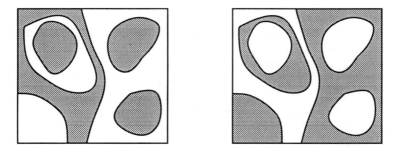

Figure 6.26: Two possible trimmed regions. The two possible trimmed regions resulting from the hierarchy of Figure 6.24 are shown. A choice between them is made by testing a single point in the interior of any trimmed region to see whether it is inside the desired solid. □

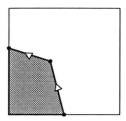 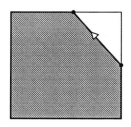 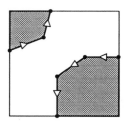

Figure 6.27: Typical behavior of a trimmed surface in a projected kd-tree node. Three typical cases of the approximate trimmed region are illustrated. Note that many kd-nodes originally bounding the curve of intersection of the two parametric surfaces in the 4D (u, v, s, t) space may be merged into a common ancestor during the projection operation. Thus, each kd-tree node in the (u, v) parameter space can have an arbitrary number of samples on the intersection curve, shown by dots. These intersection points are linked so that the trimming region is to the left of the trimming boundary segments. The resulting polygonal regions must then be triangularized. □

Step 6 can be accomplished by applying the following neighbor-finding algorithm to each of the trimmed surfaces independently:

```
initialize the stack L with one node containing the intersection curve
while L is nonempty
        pop node X off the list L
        find all neighbors of X that haven't been visited yet
        if X has intersections
                generate triangles inside X
                label nodes sharing included boundaries as INSIDE
                label nodes sharing excluded boundaries as OUTSIDE
                leave nodes neighboring pierced boundaries unspecified
        else
                if X is INSIDE generate triangles
                label all of X's neighbors as same as X (INSIDE or OUTSIDE)
        endif
        push unvisited X neighbors onto list
        mark X as visited
endwhile
```

Note that the generation of triangles inside a kd-node completely within the trimmed interior is done in the same manner as was discussed in Section 6.3.2. Generation of triangles for nodes containing the intersection curve is shown in Figure 6.27. In this case, we require an algorithm for splitting an arbitrary, non-

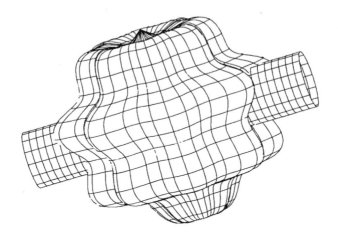

Figure 6.28: Hole drilling with trimmed surfaces (part 1). A hole is to be drilled in the bumpy sphere shape by subtracting a cylinder from the shape. The bumpy sphere is a profile product of two curves, cross section $c(u)$ and profile $p(v)$ where

$$c(u) = \begin{pmatrix} \cos(2\pi u) \\ \sin(2\pi u) \end{pmatrix} (1 + 0.1 \sin(16\pi u))$$

$$p(v) = \begin{pmatrix} \cos(\pi(2v - 1)/2) \\ \sin(\pi(2v - 1)/2) \end{pmatrix} (1 + 0.1 \sin(8\pi v)).$$

The cylinder $T(s, t)$ is aligned with the x axis, extending from $x = -1.5$ to $x = 1.5$, with radius 0.3. The domain of u, v, s, and t is the interval $[0, 1]$. $\square$

self-intersecting polygon into triangles (see [PREP85] for a discussion of such an algorithm).

6.4.2 Example Application of the CSG-Like Operation Algorithm

We now present an example of how Algorithm 6.2 works. Figure 6.28 shows two surfaces, $S(u, v)$ and $T(s, t)$, on which a CSG-like operation is to be performed. Specifically, the region bounded by T is to be subtracted from the region bounded by S, simulating a hole-drilling operation. Figure 6.29 illustrates the steps of Algorithm 6.2 on the hole-drilling example. Note that both of the parametric surfaces are periodic in one parameter, $S(u, v)$ in u and $T(s, t)$ in s. During

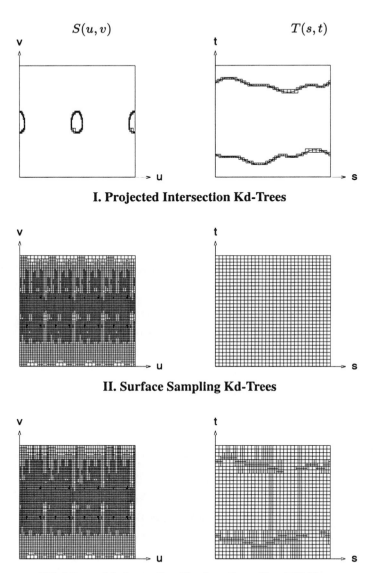

Figure 6.29: Hole drilling with trimmed surfaces (part 2). The results of Steps 2, 5, and 6 of Algorithm 6.2 are displayed. The (u, v) and (s, t) projection of the curve of intersection is also drawn within the projected intersection kd-trees. $\square$

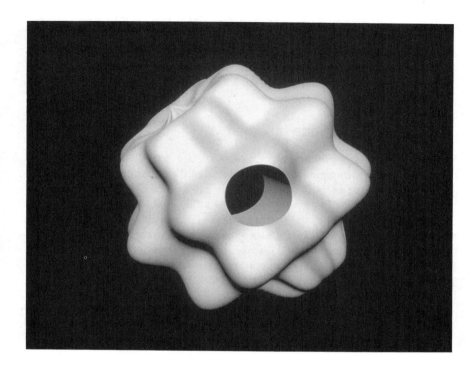

Figure 6.30: Hole drilling with trimmed surfaces (part 3). The result of the hole drilling operation is illustrated. Note that the curve of intersection between the bumpy sphere and cylinder is approximated without visual artifacts. □

step 3, one of the projected curve segments in (s, t) parameter space is artificially broken because its corresponding (u, v) projection hits the periodic u boundary. These two curve segments must be joined in order to complete the curve ordering of step 4. The results of the CSG-like approximation are shown in Figure 6.30. Plate 9 shows solid shaded images of the results of this CSG-like operation.

The key element of Algorithm 6.2 is the use of a kd-tree to encompass the intersection curve between two parametric surfaces. This kd-tree is projected into the parameter spaces of the two parametric surfaces in such a way that no extra subdivisions (and thus no extra sample points on the curve) are produced. Prohibiting such subdivision thus guarantees that the approximated intersection curve intersects each of the terminal kd-nodes in the parameter spaces of both surfaces in samples that have already been computed. The same approximated curve of intersection (with the same samples) thus forms the boundary where the two trimmed surfaces meet.

6.4.3   Kd-Tree Algorithms for CSG-like Operations

Algorithm 6.2 requires two algorithms that operate on kd-trees: one to project a 4D kd-tree to a 2D kd-tree, and another that merges two kd-trees. This section describes the simple algorithms required for these tasks.

6.4.3.1   Kd-Tree Node Insertion

We first define two primary algorithms that are used as tools in the kd-tree projection and merging.   These two algorithms, insert_addonly and insert_nosubdivide, both insert a kd node into a given kd-tree. The kd node to be inserted is described by its *kd-address*. The kd-address is an array of sequences of bits, one sequence for each dimension of the kd-tree. Each bit in the sequence represents whether the left or right side of the kd-tree must be traversed in the particular dimension in order to find the node, starting from the root of the kd-tree. For example, consider a 1D kd-tree representing a subdivision of the interval $[0, 1]$. The following are examples of kd-address/interval correspondences:

$$
\begin{array}{ccl}
00 & \rightarrow & [0, 0.25] \\
01 & \rightarrow & [0.25, 0.5] \\
10 & \rightarrow & [0.5, 0.75] \\
11 & \rightarrow & [0.5, 1.0] \\
0010 & \rightarrow & [0.125, 0.0.1875]
\end{array}
$$

Next consider a 2D kd-tree representing a subdivision of the interval $[0, 1] \times [0, 1]$. The following are examples of kd-address/interval correspondences:

$$
\begin{array}{ccl}
00, 00 & \rightarrow & [0, 0.25] \times [0, 0.25] \\
01, 10 & \rightarrow & [0.25, 0.5] \times [0.5, 0.75] \\
0010, 1100 & \rightarrow & [0.125, 0.0.1875] \times [0.75, 0.8125]
\end{array}
$$

Here, the comma separates the bit address of the first dimension from the second. We will use the term *kd-address component* for a single dimension of a node's kd-address (i.e., one bit sequence in the above comma separated list).

The two primary algorithms differ only slightly. insert_addonly adds a node to a given kd-tree such that no existing leaf node in the kd-tree is subdivided. insert_nosubdivide adds a node to a given kd-tree such that no existing leaf node in the kd-tree is subdivided and any nodes in the kd-tree that represent subdivisions of the node to be inserted are eliminated. Both algorithms take two parameters: a kd-tree, T, and the address of a kd node to insert, A. Figure 6.31 presents sketches of the two algorithms.

```
insert_addonly(T,A)

let X be the node represented by address A

find farthest-from-root node Y in T that is ancestor to X
        by finding node whose address matches an initial
        substring of A in each kd dimension

let A' be the address of X left over after deleting
        the initial matching

if Y lacks the child that is ancestor to X
        lead_add(Y,A')
else if Y is a leaf node
        leaf_add(Y,A')
else
        create left or right child of Y if it doesn't exist
        insert_addonly(Y.left,A')
        insert_addonly(Y.right,A')
endif
```

```
insert_nosubdivide(T,A)

let X be the node represented by address A

find farthest-from-root node Y in T that is ancestor to X
        by finding node whose address matches an initial
        substring of A in each kd dimension

let A' be the address of X left over after deleting
        the initial matching

if Y lacks the child that is ancestor to X
        leaf_add(Y,A')
else if Y is not a leaf node
        delete all of Y's children
endif
```

Figure 6.31: Basic kd-tree algorithms. The function `insert_addonly` adds a node, represented by its address A, to a kd-tree T such that T is only affected by the addition of new kd-nodes; none of T's nodes is subdivided. The function `insert_nosubdivide` is similar, except that T's nodes are not subdivided and any of T's nodes that represent subdivisions of the node represented by kd-address A are eliminated (i.e., a subtree of T whose root is the farthest-from-root ancestor of A is replaced by a single terminal node). Insertion of a node into a leaf node of the kd-tree is accomplished using `leaf_add`. □

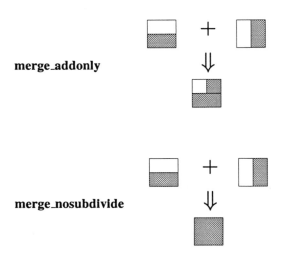

Figure 6.32: Kd-tree merging operations. The output of merge_addonly and merge_nosubdivide is compared for the case of the merging of a pair of 2D kd-trees, one containing the interval $[0, 1] \times [0, 0.5]$, and the other containing the interval $[0.5, 1] \times [0, 1]$. merge_addonly produces a kd-tree with two leaf nodes, so that the leaf node of the first kd-tree is not subdivided. merge_nosubdivide produces a kd-tree with a single leaf node, which is the ancestor to the leaf nodes of both input kd-trees. This is done because neither leaf node can be subdivided. □

6.4.3.2   Kd-Tree Merging

The insert primitives can be used to define two analogous merge algorithms: merge_addonly and merge_nosubdivide. merge_addonly takes two kd-trees as parameters, T_1 and T_2, and produces a single kd-tree by adding the leaf nodes of T_2 to T_1. The algorithm for merge_addonly is given by

merge_addonly(T_1,T_2)

for each leaf node X of T_2
    find kd-address of X
    insert_addonly(T_1,X)
endfor

The merge_nosubdivide algorithm is similar, except that it uses insert_nosubdivide in place of insert_addonly. Figure 6.32 illustrates the difference between these two algorithms.

The merge_addonly algorithm is used to perform the merge operation be-

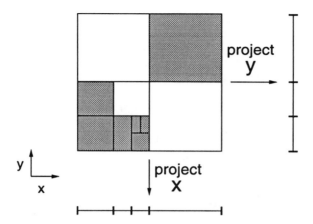

Figure 6.33: Kd-tree projection. A partial 2D kd-tree with dimensions labeled x and y is projected into two 1D kd-trees. Existing leaf nodes in the 2D kd-tree are dark. On the bottom, the result of projecting the x dimension is shown; on the right is shown the result of projecting the y dimension. Note that the 1D projection does not necessarily contain as highly subdivided nodes as the corresponding projection of the smallest leaf nodes in the original kd-tree, because no leaf node projection is ever subdivided. □

tween the projected intersection kd-tree and the surface sampling kd-tree. It is appropriate because it ensures that no node in the projected intersection kd-tree is subdivided. The `merge_nosubdivide` algorithm is used in a higher-level algorithm that projects the 4D intersection kd-tree into the parameter space of each surface. This algorithm is discussed in the next section.

6.4.3.3 Kd-Tree Projection

The *projection* of a kd-tree is the generation of a smaller-dimensional version of the kd-tree containing subdivisions only in a selected set of dimensions. CSG-like operations, for example, require the projection of a 4D kd-tree into the 2D parameter spaces of two parametric surfaces. This projection can be accomplished by visiting each leaf node of the original kd-tree, computing its kd-address, a, and inserting a new node into the projected kd-tree using a subset of a's kd-address components. Note, however, that in computing this simple projection, we may insert a node into the projected kd-tree and later attempt to insert its more highly subdivided child (or vice versa). This is because different nodes in the original kd-tree, with different numbers of children, have the same projection. The algorithm we present solves this problem by inserting only the largest projected leaf nodes,

```
project(N,W)

if N is NIL return NIL
else if N is leaf return (NIL,NIL,0)
else
        L ← project(N.left,W)
        R ← project(N.right,W)
        if N.d is in W
              return (L,R,N.d)
        else if L ≠ NIL and R = NIL
              return L
        else if L = NIL and R ≠ NIL
              return R
        else
              merge_nosubdivide(L,R)
              delete R
              return L
        endif
endif
```

Figure 6.34: Kd-tree projection algorithm. The projection function, project, takes a kd-tree N, and a set of indices W, and returns a new kd-tree which is the projection of N using only the dimensions in W. The new kd-tree has dimension equal to the cardinality of the set W. project uses merge_nosubdivide to combine the kd-trees formed by projecting the left and right subtrees. This ensures that no extra subdivisions will occur that were not already present in the unprojected 4D kd-tree. □

by inserting with insert_nosubdivide. Figure 6.33 illustrates this kind of kd-tree projection. This technique ensures that no new subdivisions are introduced into the parameter space bounding rectangles of either surface's trimming curves.

The project algorithm, presented in Figure 6.34, performs kd-tree projection. It takes as input a kd-tree (parameter N) and a set of indices representing the kd dimensions to project (parameter W), and returns a kd-tree whose leaf nodes are the appropriate projections of the leaf nodes of N. For example, consider a kd-tree N bounding the curve of intersection of surfaces $S(u,v)$ and $T(s,t)$. Assume that the kd dimensions in N are mapped so that dimension 1 is u, dimension 2 is v, dimension 3 is s, and dimension 4 is t. The invocation project$(N, \{1, 2\})$ then returns a 2D kd-tree representing the projection of N into (u, v) space.

6.5 Constructive Solid Geometry with Trimmed Surfaces

CSG-like operations can be used to implement full CSG on solid regions bounded by parametric surfaces. Full CSG operations differ from CSG-like operations in that the results of full CSG operations can be used in further CSG operations. To compute full CSG operations, we must therefore handle trimming curves that intersect.

For example, consider the CSG operation $(A^\circ - B^\circ) - C^\circ$, for three regions A°, B°, and C° bounded by three parametric surfaces A, B, and C. The CSG-like approximation algorithm described previously can compute an approximation of the boundary of $A^\circ - B^\circ$, yielding two trimmed surfaces (i.e., trimmed versions of the surfaces A and B). Algorithm 6.2 cannot be applied to these trimmed surfaces to subtract C, since, for example, the projection of the intersection curve of A and C into the parameter space of A may intersect the projected intersection curve of A and B. A simple modification of the algorithm, however, suffices. Figure 6.35 shows how the CSG operation $(A^\circ - B^\circ) - C^\circ$ can be computed, by computing Boolean operations on 2D parametric regions. Such 2D Boolean operations were called CPG operations in Section 3.2.3.

For each parametric surface in the Boolean expression, the modified algorithm stores the appropriate trimming curves, which are consistently ordered so that the interior of the trimming region lies to the left of the trimming curve. The trimming curves are bounded in a 2D kd-tree in the surface's parameter space. Let S^1 be a trimmed parametric surface resulting from a series of CSG operations, and let S be the corresponding untrimmed parametric surface. Let T° be a closed region in $\mathbf{R}^3$ bounded by an untrimmed parametric surface T. A completely general CSG algorithm results from a description of how a CSG operation is performed on S^1 and T (e.g., $S^1 - T^\circ$). A CSG operation like $(A^\circ - B^\circ) - C^\circ$ can then be performed by a series of these operations. That is, the surface A is first trimmed by subtracting B°. The resulting trimmed version of A is then further trimmed by subtracting C°. Similar sequences of operations are performed on B and C to yield the complete boundary of the nested subtraction.

The following algorithm outlines how to perform such a CSG operation on a trimmed surface S^1 and untrimmed surface T, resulting in a trimmed surface S'. Although this algorithm has not actually been implemented in the GENMOD prototype system, all of the tools it uses have already been implemented and presented in this book.

1. Apply Algorithm 6.2 (steps 1–4) to the untrimmed surfaces S and T, resulting in a trimmed surface S^2.

2. Compute the intersection points between the 2D trimming curves from S^1

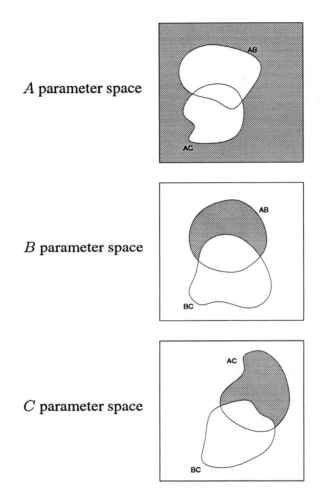

A parameter space

B parameter space

C parameter space

Figure 6.35: CSG operation on parametric surfaces. The boundary of the region $(A^\circ - B^\circ) - C^\circ$ can be represented using trimmed parametric surfaces. The boundary surface is given by a combination of trimmed versions of the parametric surfaces A, B, and C, bounding A°, B°, and C°, respectively. The intersection curves projected into the parameter space of each of the three surfaces are displayed. These intersection curves form a superset of the boundaries of the appropriate trimming regions, which are displayed in a darker shade. For example, the trimmed version of A must exclude the parts of A in either B° or C°. This can be done by finding the parametric regions of A corresponding to $A - B^\circ$ and $A - C^\circ$ and computing their 2D intersection. $\square$

and S^2. Note that the constraint solution algorithm can be used to robustly compute these points. The computed intersection points should be added to the trimming curves of S and to all other parametric surfaces that share the intersection curve to which the points have been added.

3. Perform a CPG operation on the trimmed parameter spaces of S^1 and S^2, resulting in a new trimming region for S'. This operation discards parts of the trimming curves (and their bounding kd-trees) that are excluded by the Boolean operation. The kd-tree surrounding the trimming curves of S' must be constructed so that no nodes from either original kd-tree are subdivided. This is easily accomplished by choosing the closest containing ancestor node, rather than splitting.

After a trimmed surface, such as S^1, has been processed with respect to all parametric surfaces in the CSG operation, steps 5–7 of Algorithm 6.2 are computed. A surface sampling kd-tree is generated for S and merged with the final trimmed version of S^1. Triangles are then generated just as in Algorithm 6.2.

This approach processes all pairs of parametric surfaces. That is, to compute the approximation of a CSG operation involving n parametric surfaces, $\binom{n}{2}$ invocations of Algorithm 6.2 must take place, along with $(n-1)(n-2)$ CPG operations on trimmed regions. Typically, many of these operations can be eliminated by hierarchically organizing the collection of parametric surfaces, so that nonintersecting surface pairs are immediately recognized.

6.6 Approximating Implicit Surfaces

As a final application of interval analysis techniques to geometric modeling, we examine an algorithm to approximate implicit surfaces. For example, given a continuous function $f(x, y, z): \mathbf{R}^3 \rightarrow \mathbf{R}$, the equation

$$f(x, y, z) = 0$$

describes an implicit surface. Similarly, any system of $n - 2$ equations in n variables can be used to describe an implicit surface. The algorithm described in this section differs from others (such as [BLOO88]) in that the approximation is robust. That is, global information about the implicit surface's behavior is used to guarantee that no part of the surface is missed.

An algorithm very similar to Algorithm 6.1 for implicit curve approximation can be applied to implicit surface approximation. This algorithm restricts the kinds of surfaces it can approximate in a manner analogous to the restrictions of Algorithm 6.1. It requires that the surface not self-intersect, that it not stop abruptly in the interior of the interval of consideration,[7] and that it intersect the edges of each proximate interval in a finite set of points.

In broad outline, this algorithm performs the same basic tasks as does Algorithm 6.1, namely

1. Compute proximate intervals bounding the implicit surface

2. Test each proximate interval for global parameterizability

3. Find edge points

4. Connect edge points along faces

5. Process completed network

In order to explain these steps, several definitions are appropriate. The *face* of a proximate interval is the interval formed by holding one of the input variables at one endpoint and letting the rest vary over their original intervals. Similarly, an *edge* of a proximate interval is the interval formed by holding two of the input variables at one endpoint and letting the rest vary over their original intervals. A proximate interval in $\mathbf{R}^n$ thus has $2n$ faces and $4 \begin{pmatrix} n \\ 2 \end{pmatrix}$ edges. A *proper face of a proximate interval* is a face that borders at most one neighbor and that is a subset of the bordering neighbor's face. A neighbor refers to another adjacent proximate interval in the bounding collection. A *face curve* is the intersection of the implicit surface with a proximate interval's face. An *edge point* is the intersection of the implicit surface with a proximate interval's edge.

Step 1 computes a collection of intervals bounding the implicit surface and satisfying a user-defined approximation acceptance inclusion function. This processing is exactly the same for curve or surface approximation. Step 2 tests each of the proximate intervals for global parameterizability. For surface approximation, unlike curve approximation, two global parameterizability criteria must be satisfied:

1. The surface must be globally parameterizable in the proximate interval as a 2D manifold (see Section 6.2.2 for a definition of global parameterizability for 2D manifolds). This prevents cases where a closed surface exists entirely within a proximate interval.

2. Each of the face curves must be globally parameterizable (as 1D manifolds). This allows robust connection of edge points.

---

[7]More precisely, the implicit surface must be a 2D manifold in the interior of the region of consideration.

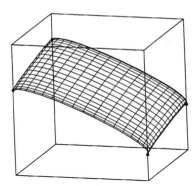

Figure 6.36: Behavior of an implicit surface in a proximate interval. The figure illustrates an implicit surface inside a proximate interval. The surface intersects the edges of the interval at four edge points, drawn with circles. The surface also intersects the faces of the proximate interval in four face curves. Each of the edge points is shared by two face curves. If neighboring proximate intervals are included, then edge points can be shared by up to four face curves. □

Step 3 computes intersections of the implicit surface with each edge of each proximate interval. This yields solutions that should be zero-dimensional and can be computed using the constraint solution algorithm.[8] Steps 4 and 5 are performed exactly as in Algorithm 6.1, except that the processing must take place for each face of the proximate interval. That is, each face curve is approximated independently.

The local topology graph for surface approximation differs from curve approximation. For surface approximation, each edge point has a pointer to four neighboring intersections, rather than two. This is because each proximate interval edge is shared by four faces. As shown in Figure 6.36, an edge point is typically included in four face curves, and thus may connect to four neighboring edge points.

6.6.1   An Implicit Surface Approximation Algorithm

The five steps can be simply combined to produce an algorithm for implicit surface approximation.

Algorithm 6.3 (Implicit Surface Approximation Algorithm)

1. **Compute an initial collection of proximate intervals bounding the implicit surface.** An approximation acceptance inclusion function is used to

---

[8]The curve approximation algorithm intersects the implicit curve with each face of a proximate interval while the surface approximation algorithm intersects the implicit surface with each edge. The respective approximation algorithms assume that this intersection will result in a finite set of points.

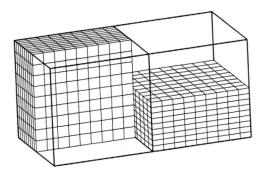

Figure 6.37: Disallowed bordering of proximate intervals. The figure illustrates the the case where a proximate interval contains a face that is not allowed. Two neighboring intervals are shown, one on the left (at the back of an enclosing cube) and one on the right (at the bottom of an enclosing cube). The face to the left of the right interval is not proper, nor is it a superset of the face of its neighbor, the left interval. □

determine whether a region is acceptable or should be subdivided.

2. **Subdivide the initial collection until it satisfies the two global parameterizability criteria.** As discussed previously, the implicit surface and each of its face curves should be globally parameterizable.

3. **Compute the edge points in each proximate interval using Algorithm 5.1.**

4. **For each proper face, compute the connections between edge points.** Because each face curve is globally parameterizable, this can be done with the techniques already discussed for Algorithm 6.1. Since edge points are shared between faces, all connections to a given edge point along any face should be collected.

   After all proper faces have been processed, faces that are not proper are handled by simply aggregating the results for all neighboring proper faces. The algorithm assumes *that each proximate interval face is proper or is a superset of the set of contiguous faces of all its neighbors.* Situations such as that shown in Figure 6.37 are therefore excluded. The cyclic bisection technique described in Section 5.3.2 never produces such situations.

5. **For each improper face, copy edge point and approximate face curve information from contiguous proper faces.** The edge points of each proximate interval can now be organized into one or more closed loops, using the connections along faces computed in step 4.

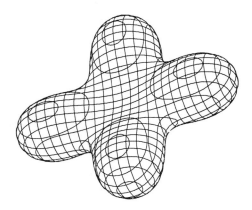

Figure 6.38: Approximation of a blobby implicit surface. The results of the implicit surface approximation algorithm are shown for a blobby surface, described by the implicit equation

$$f(p) = \sum_i \alpha_i \exp^{-\beta_i \|p - q_i\|} = 0.$$

In this case, a sum of four such terms was used. □

6. **For each closed loop of linked edge points in each proximate interval, ensure that there exists a 2D projection forming a valid, non-intersecting polygon.** Here, a 2D projection is a choice of 2 of the n input cordinates, which forms a 2D point from each n-dimensional edge point. The 2D projection of a closed loop of edge points thus forms a 2D polygon. If, for any closed loop, there is no 2D projection (i.e., no choice of a pair of input parameters) that produces a valid polygon, then the proximate interval containing this closed loop should be subdivided and retested. This criterion is important because it allows each closed loop to determine a collection of triangles that approximate the surface inside the proximate interval, using a simple algorithm to subdivide a polygon into triangles.

7. **Generate triangles from the finished network.** In each proximate interval, each closed loop of connected edge points determines a 2D polygon which can be split into triangles.

Figure 6.38 illustrates the results of Algorithm 6.3 to generate a polygonal approximation to an implicitly defined "blobby" surface [BLIN82]. Plate 11 shows two further results of Algorithm 6.3.

Chapter 7

Conclusion

An approach to shape design may be broken down into three parts: representation, interface, and tools. The representation defines what a shape is. The interface allows shapes to be specified. The tools determine what can be done with shapes. This book has focused on a new representation, interface, and set of tools, called generative modeling, that solve some of the problems of geometric modeling systems studied in the past.

Generative modeling represents a shape as the image of a parametric function over a rectilinear subset of $\mathbf{R}^n$. Parametric functions are built using a set of symbolic operators, such as the arithmetic operators. Associated with each operator is a set of methods, which perform all the primitive shape computations needed by the tools. The tools described in this book require only the following methods:

- evaluate the parametric function at a point

- evaluate the parametric function on a uniform rectilinear lattice

- evaluate an inclusion function for the parametric function

- take a symbolic partial derivative of the parametric function

- determine whether the parametric function is differentiable over a specified domain

What is the advantage of such a representation? First, the representation is sufficient for shapes of different dimensionality. It can represent both curves and surfaces, shapes parameterized by time or other variables, and shapes embedded in space of any number of dimensions. Second, the representation is high-level. Shapes can be defined using sophisticated operators such as integration, differentiation, and constraint solution. Unlike simple representations such as polyhedra and NURBS, the representation can be matched to a high-level interface without conversions and approximation error. Third, the representation is extensible. Extension is accomplished by adding new primitive operators, with a few attendant methods.

The interface advocated here is an interpreted language. This language is essentially a textual specification of the operators used in the representation. With a language interface, a modeler can construct meta-shapes — parameterized shapes such as the profile product of Chapter 3. In our research, meta-shapes have proved to be an extremely powerful specification tool. The user can build libraries of meta-shapes, using combinations of the primitive operators. These meta-shapes, in turn, can be used in building higher-level and more convenient meta-shapes. Augmented with such meta-shape libraries, the interface provided for the user can be quite complex and powerful, while the basic implementation of the modeling system (i.e., the primitive operators and methods) remains simple.

Certainly, such an interface is not suitable for all users. It requires a fairly sophisticated mathematical background and a substantial training investment. On the other hand, the specification is well suited for two groups: customizers and researchers. Customizers produce sets of meta-shapes appropriate for their targeted users. For example, a customizer may represent a limited family of parts, so that engineers can edit, assemble, and simulate them. The customizer hides unimportant details and provides an interface with parameters familiar to his or her users. Researchers can use the power of an interpreted language to test new ideas easily. More study is needed to design a less-demanding user interface that still retains the power of the representation.

The tools discussed in this book fall into three categories: rendering tools, synthesis tools, and analysis tools. Rendering tools produce images of shapes; synthesis tools allow simple shapes to be combined into more complex shapes, and analysis tools allow computation of physical and geometric properties of shapes.

Most rendering methods appropriate for generative models involve approximating the shape as a collection of simple pieces. This book has presented two techniques to do this; one suitable for "quick and dirty" interactive rendering and another allowing robust control of approximation error. Approximated shapes can easily be converted into a form suitable for interactive rendering using z-buffer hardware, or expensive, realistic rendering using ray tracing. Because shapes are represented as the image of parametric functions, approximation can often be accomplished with very little computation.

Tools for rendering, synthesis, and analysis presented in this book have been built using the technique of interval analysis. Interval analysis allows computation of global properties of the shape, using inclusion functions. This book presents algorithms for solution of two very hard problems: finding solutions to nonlinear constraints, and finding global minima of a nonlinear function subject to nonlinear constraints. By restricting the class of functions that can express constraints and objective functions to those that are formed by recursive composition of primitive operators, these problems are solvable. The two algorithms are useful in themselves and for a host of other, more advanced geometric computations, such as approximating curves of intersection between shapes. Interval analysis enables the algorithms to control errors robustly even when the computation is done using imprecise floating point hardware.

Appendix A

The GENMOD Language

Parametric functions form the backbone of the generative modeling representation. This appendix discusses a language for representing parametric functions that was developed for a prototype modeling system called GENMOD. This language is patterned after the mathematical language of vector calculus and differential geometry.

The GENMOD language was written using a C language substrate. To achieve a more natural syntax, the C language used was extended to allow overloading of the C operators. Several additional operators have also been added. GENMOD contains an interpreter for this extended C language that allows models to be built, edited, analyzed, and displayed interactively. The GENMOD system is extensible. Language primitives can be combined using C functions to produce higher-level meta-shapes. Libraries of such meta-shapes can be constructed and extended by the user.

A.1 Language Extensions

This section describes some new features that were added to the C language in developing the GENMOD system.

A.1.1 New Operators

The C language was extended with the addition of several new operators. These operators all begin with the @ character.

An exponentiation operator @^ was added which has precedence greater than multiplication and division, but less than a cast. This allows the exponentiation operator to be used in the same way as in the FORTRAN language. Note that overloading another operator, such as ^, would have allowed exponentiation but with an operator of inappropriate precedence.

Three array creation operators, @{}, @[], and @(), were also added. These operators take a list of arguments separated by commas, perform appropriate type casting, and create an array of the converted arguments. For example, the C expression @{1,2,3} creates an object of type array of size 3 of int. If the operator arguments are of mixed type, then each argument is converted to the most "general" type. For example, a mixture of int and double types will be converted to double. Similarly, a mixture of double and MAN types is converted to type MAN (see Section A.2 for a definition of the MAN type).

The type of the array element may also be directly specified by placing a type cast after the @. For example, @(double){1,2,3} will produce an object of type array of size 3 of type double, with elements 1.0, 2.0, and 3.0, respectively.

A.1.2   Overloaded Operators

The following C language operators were overloaded:

- the binary arithmetic operators +, -, *, and /

- the unary negation operator -

- the comparison operators >, >=, <, <=, ==, and !=

- the logical operators !, &&, and ||

- the index operator []

- the cast operator for type MAN

- the new exponentiation operator @^

- the new array creation operators @() and @[]

The meanings of these overloaded operators will be precisely defined in Section A.3.

A.2   Language Types

Type	Description
MAN	parametric function
MAN_ARRAY	array of parametric functions
MAN_MATRIX	parametric function representing a matrix
INT_ARRAY	array of integers

The GENMOD language uses the standard types defined in the C language. In addition, it defines several new types, shown in the previous table. The type MAN is the basic type of a parametric function. Many of the C language operators have been overloaded for the MAN type. For example, the C language's + operator has been overloaded to perform addition of parametric functions.

The MAN type is actually a C structure that keeps track of several characteristics of the parametric function:

- input and output dimension of the function

- specific parametric coordinates used in the function

- methods used by the function for evaluation and analysis

The C language definition of the MAN type is

```
typedef struct mantyp {

    int             outputs;                /* output dimension */
    int             inputs;                 /* input dimension */
    int             input_set[MAXINPUTS];   /* set of coords */
    int             input_list[MAXINPUTS];  /* list of coords */
    void            *prms;                  /* internal parms  */
    void            (*free)();              /* clean up method */
    struct mantyp   *(*derivative)();       /* derivative method */
    int             (*point)();             /* evaluation method */
    int             (*inclusion)();         /* inclusion method */

    /* ... */
} *MAN;
```

The C cast operator, (MAN), has been overloaded to convert numeric arguments to type MAN. This conversion results in a constant parametric function.

The MAN_ARRAY type is an array of type MAN that also keeps track of the size of the array. Its C language definition is

```
typedef struct {
    MAN *ptr
    int n;
} MAN_ARRAY;
```

The @[] operator has been overloaded to produce the MAN_ARRAY type. For example, if f, g, and h are of type MAN, the C expression @[f,g,h] produces an object of type MAN_ARRAY. The ptr field points to an array containing f, g, and h in succession. The n field has the value 3.

The MAN_MATRIX type contains a parametric function that represents the components of the matrix (of type MAN), but also keeps track of the number of rows and columns in the matrix. Its C language definition is

```
typedef struct {
    MAN m;
    int r,c;
} MAN_MATRIX;
```

It can be used anywhere the type MAN is used as well as in several special circumstances, such as arguments for the matrix multiply operator.

A.3   Language Primitive Operators

The GENMOD language specifies parametric functions through a set of primitive operators that take lower-level parametric functions (and possibly other parameters) as arguments and create a higher-level parametric function. For example, if two parametric functions f and g exist, then the sum of f and g can be represented using the addition operator on the arguments f and g.

A.3.1   Constants and Parametric Coordinates

Function	Operator	GENMOD example	Explanation
parametric coordinate	MAN m_x(int)	MAN F = m_x(i);	$F = x_i$
constant	double	MAN F = 3.3;	$F = 3.3$

Two of the primitive operators in the GENMOD language do not take lower-level MAN arguments. These are the operators that specify a constant or parametric coordinate, shown in the the table above. Parametric coordinates are numbered starting at 0 and are referred to using the variables $x_0, x_1, \ldots$ in the following text.

A.3.2   Arithmetic Operators

Function	Operator	GENMOD example	Explanation
addition	+	MAN F = f + g;	$F = f + g$
subtraction	−	MAN F = f - g;	$F = f - g$
multiplication	*	MAN F = f * g;	$F = f * g$
division	/	MAN F = f / g;	$F = f/g$
exponentiation	@^	MAN F = f @^ g;	$F = f^g$
negation	−	MAN F = -f;	$F = -f$

Arithmetic operators in the GENMOD language include the binary addition, subtraction, multiplication, and division operators, and the unary negation operator. The exponentiation operator, while more fittingly included in the elementary operators of the next section (not the arithmetic operators), is included here because of its similarity with the other binary operators. The binary operators, including exponentiation, can be used in two modes.

In the first mode, if the two parametric function arguments have the same output dimension, then the operator is performed separately for each component on the corresponding components of the two arguments. The result has the same output dimension. For example, if the parametric functions f and g both have output dimension 2, then $f * g$ denotes a parametric function of output dimension 2 whose first coordinate is the product of the first components of f and g, and whose second component is the product of the second components of f and g. Note that the addition operator thus denotes ordinary addition in $\mathbf{R}^n$.

In the second mode, if the output dimension of one argument is 1, and the output dimension of the other argument is greater than 1, then the operator is performed on each component of the multicomponent argument. The result has the output dimension of the multicomponent argument. For example, if f has output dimension 2, $1/f$ takes the reciprocal of each component of f. Similarly, $f * 2$ scales each component of f by 2.

The unary negation operator negates each component of its argument.

A.3.3 Elementary Operators

Function	Operator	GENMOD example	Explanation
sine	MAN m_sin(MAN)	MAN F = m_sin(f);	$F = \sin(f)$
cosine	MAN m_cos(MAN)	MAN F = m_cos(f);	$F = \cos(f)$
tangent	MAN m_tan(MAN)	MAN F = m_tan(f);	$F = \tan(f)$
inverse sine	MAN m_asin(MAN)	MAN F = m_asin(f);	$F = \sin^{-1}(f)$
inverse cosine	MAN m_acos(MAN)	MAN F = m_acos(f);	$F = \cos^{-1}(f)$
inverse tangent	MAN m_atan(MAN)	MAN F = m_atan(f);	$F = \tan^{-1}(f)$
inverse tangent	MAN m_atan2(MAN,MAN)	MAN F = m_atan2(f,g);	$F = \tan^{-1}(f/g)$
exponential	MAN m_exp(MAN)	MAN F = m_exp(f);	$F = \exp(f)$
logarithm	MAN m_log(MAN)	MAN F = m_log(f);	$F = \log(f)$
absolute value	MAN m_fabs(MAN)	MAN F = m_fabs(f);	$F = |f|$
integer floor	MAN m_floor(MAN)	MAN F = m_floor(f);	$F = \lfloor f \rfloor$
integer ceiling	MAN m_ceil(MAN)	MAN F = m_ceil(f);	$F = \lceil f \rceil$

The elementary operators work on scalar arguments; that is, the output dimension of the argument or arguments must be 1. The output dimension of the result is also 1.

A.3.4   Vector Operators

Function	Operator	GENMOD example	Explanation
cartesian product	`@()`	`MAN F = @(f,g,h);`	$F(X) = (f, g, h)$
projection	`[]`	`MAN F = f[i];`	$F(X) = f_i$
length	`MAN m_length(MAN)`	`MAN F = m_length(f);`	$F(X) = \|f\|$
dot product	`MAN m_dot(MAN,MAN)`	`MAN F = m_dot(f,g);`	$F(X) = f \cdot g$
cross product	`MAN m_cross(MAN,MAN)`	`MAN F = m_cross(f,g);`	$F(X) = f \times g$
normalize	`MAN m_normalize(MAN)`	`MAN F = m_normalize(f);`	$F(X) = f / \|f\|$

The cartesian product operator has two forms. In the first, a list of MAN objects, separated by commas, is combined using cartesian product. There is also a second form, where the MAN objects are specified using an array. Its functional prototype is

```
MAN m_cartesian(MAN_ARRAY funs)
```

The second form is mainly used to specify a cartesian product of an array built programmatically.

The projection operator takes a parametric function argument of arbitrary output dimension and produces a given component of this function. The result is of output dimension 1. The dot product operator works on arguments that have the same output dimension. The cross product operator can only be used on arguments whose output dimension is 3.

A.3.5   Matrix Operators

Matrices can be created using the `m_matrix` function, which takes a parametric function as its first argument, and number of rows and columns of the matrix as its second and third arguments. Its functional prototype is given by

```
MAN_MATRIX m_matrix(MAN components,int r,int c)
```

The product of rows and columns must equal the output dimension of the first argument. Transpose, inverse, and determinant operators exist, with the following functional prototypes:

```
MAN_MATRIX m_transpose(MAN_MATRIX m)
MAN_MATRIX m_matrix_inverse(MAN_MATRIX m)
MAN        m_determinant(MAN_MATRIX m)
```

The inverse and determinant functions both expect a square matrix argument.

For example, assuming m is a parametric function of output dimension 9, a 3 by 3 matrix and its transpose, inverse and determinant can be created using

```
MAN M = m_matrix(m,3,3);
MAN Mt = m_transpose(M);
MAN Minv = m_matrix_inverse(M);
MAN det = m_determinant(M);
```

Arithmetic operations on matrices, shown in the next table, are also available.

Function	Operator	GENMOD example	Explanation
addition	+	MAN_MATRIX F = A + B;	$F = A + B$
subtraction	-	MAN_MATRIX F = A - B;	$F = A - B$
negation	-	MAN_MATRIX F = -M;	$F = -M$
multiplication	*	MAN_MATRIX F = A*B;	$F = AB$
row projection	[]	MAN F = M[1];	F is second row of M

The addition and subtraction operators both check that the matrices added or subtracted have the same size. Similarly, the multiplication operator requires its operands to be of suitable size for multiplication (i.e., number of columns of first operand equals number of rows of second). The row projection operator produces a result of type MAN representing the specified row of the matrix. The output dimension of the result is the number of columns in the matrix.

A.3.6 Integral and Derivative Operators

The derivative operator takes partial derivatives of its first argument with respect to any parametric coordinate whose index is specified as the second coordinate. Its functional prototype is

```
MAN m_derivative(MAN in,int parameter)
```

For example, the function

```
m_derivative(f,i)
```

returns the parametric function $\frac{\partial f}{\partial x_i}$.

GENMOD includes two forms of the integration operator: a 1D integration operator and a multidimensional integration operator. The 1D integration operator integrates functions numerically using Romberg integration (see [PRES86]). The function being integrated, as well as the upper and lower bounds of integration, are specified as arguments and may depend on any number of parameters. The integrand parametric function must be of output dimension 1 (i.e., a scalar function). Its functional prototype is

```
MAN m_integrate(MAN integrand,MAN lower,MAN upper,
                int parameter)
```

For example, the function

```
m_integrate(f,b,a,i)
```

returns the parametric function

$$\int_b^a f \, dx_i.$$

The multidimensional integration operator is based on a NAG routine and has the following functional prototype:

```
MAN m_integrate_multi(MAN integrand,MAN lower,MAN upper,
           INT_ARRAY parms,double abserr,double relerr)
```

In this case, the integrand parametric function (integrand) can have arbitrary output dimension. Let $f(x_1, x_2, x_3)$ be a parametric function, and a and b be parametric functions of output dimension 3. The function

```
m_integrate_multi(f,b,a,@[1,2,3],1e-6,1e-4);
```

returns the parametric function

$$\int_{b_1}^{a_1} \int_{b_2}^{a_2} \int_{b_3}^{a_3} f(x_1, x_2, x_3) \, dx_1 \, dx_2 \, dx_3.$$

A.3.7   Curves and Tables

The curve operator has the functional prototype

```
MAN m_crv(char *curve_file,MAN in)
```

The m_crv function takes the name of a file, produced using a curve editor program, and creates a parametric curve that is evaluated over the parametric function in. For example, the function

```
m_crv("cross.crv",m_x(0))
```

produces a parametric curve parameterized by x_0, whose shape is specified in the file cross.crv.

The table operator produces a function that linearly interpolates a multidimensional data set. Its functional prototype is

```
MAN m_table(double *samples,INT_ARRAY dimen,MAN in)
```

The samples argument contains the samples to be interpolated. The dimen argument is an array of dimensions, specifying the organization of the samples. Assume dimen contains $s + 1$ entries $n_0, n_1, \ldots, n_s$. The samples are arranged as a multidimensional rectilinear table of points, each having n_0 coordinates. The table has s dimensions of size $n_1, n_2, \ldots, n_s$, respectively. Samples are stored in a linear fashion, with the dimension whose size has the lowest index varying the most rapidly. The in parameter specifies a table input to be interpolated. It should be of output dimension s, with each coordinate varying between 0 and 1. The resulting parametric function is of output dimension n_0.

A.3.8 Relational Operators

Function	Operator	GENMOD example	Explanation
greater	>	MAN F = f > g;	$F = \begin{cases} 1 & \text{if } f > g \\ 0 & \text{otherwise} \end{cases}$
greater or equal	>=	MAN F = f >= g;	$F = \begin{cases} 1 & \text{if } f \geq g \\ 0 & \text{otherwise} \end{cases}$
less	<	MAN F = f < g;	$F = \begin{cases} 1 & \text{if } f < g \\ 0 & \text{otherwise} \end{cases}$
less or equal	<=	MAN F = f <= g;	$F = \begin{cases} 1 & \text{if } f \leq g \\ 0 & \text{otherwise} \end{cases}$
equal	==	MAN F = f == g;	$F = \begin{cases} 1 & \text{if } f = g \\ 0 & \text{otherwise} \end{cases}$
not equal	!=	MAN F = f != g;	$F = \begin{cases} 1 & \text{if } f \neq g \\ 0 & \text{otherwise} \end{cases}$

Relational operators are used to define conditions for branching and constraint solution. They are analogous to the C language relational operators. Each of the two parametric function arguments must be of the same output dimension. The result is the logical conjunction of the relational operator applied to each coordinate of the two arguments. For example, if g and h are parametric functions of output dimension 2, then

```
g == h
```

is a parametric function that is 1 if the corresponding components of g and h are equal (i.e., if $g_1 = h_1$ and $g_2 = h_2$), and 0 otherwise.

A.3.9   Logical Operators

Function	Operator	GENMOD example	Explanation
and	&&	MAN F = f && g;	$F = \begin{cases} 1 & \text{if } f \neq 0 \text{ and } g \neq 0 \\ 0 & \text{otherwise} \end{cases}$
or	||	MAN F = f || g;	$F = \begin{cases} 1 & \text{if } f \neq 0 \text{ or } g \neq 0 \\ 0 & \text{otherwise} \end{cases}$
not	!	MAN F = !f;	$F = \begin{cases} 1 & \text{if } f = 0 \\ 0 & \text{otherwise} \end{cases}$

The logical operators are analogous to the C language logical operators. Each of the parametric function inputs must be of output dimension 1.

A.3.10   Conditional and Branching Operators

Three operators can be used for branching type functionality. The C language ? : ternary operator has been overloaded to do an if-then-else branch. For example, the parametric function

```
f < 0 ? -f : f
```

returns a function that is the absolute value of the function f.

A second type of branch returns a parametric function indexed by a number returned by another parametric function. Its functional prototype is

```
MAN m_index(MAN_ARRAY array,MAN index)
```

For example,

```
m_index(@[f0,f1,f2,f3],g);
```

returns the function f_i where i is computed by $i = \lfloor g \rfloor$. The parametric function g should therefore be of output dimension 1, with a value in the range $[0, 4)$.

A third type of branch takes an array of guard clauses and an array of an equal number of functions to evaluate. The result is the the value of the first function whose clause is true. Its functional prototype is

```
MAN m_case(MAN_ARRAY guards.MAN_ARRAY evals)
```

For example,

```
m_case(@[f < 0,1],@[-f,f])
```

returns a function that is the absolute value of the function f.

A.3.11 Substitution Operators

GENMOD supports two operators that compose already defined parametric functions. That is, the operators evaluate a parametric function on the output of another parametric function. The first operator, m_eval, takes a parametric function and substitutes another parametric function for one of its input coordinates. Its functional prototype is given by

```
MAN m_eval(MAN fun,int parameter,MAN at)
```

For example, let $g(x_0, x_1)$ and $h(x_2)$ be two parametric functions. The evaluation operator

```
m_eval(g,1,h)
```

then yields the parametric function $g(x_0, h)$.

A second form, m_eval_all, substitutes an output coordinate of a parametric function for each input coordinate of another parametric function. Its functional prototype is given by

```
MAN m_eval_all(MAN fun,INT_ARRAY inputs,MAN at)
```

In this case, the array inputs specifies which input coordinate of fun is replaced by each output of the parametric function at. For example, let $g(x_0, x_1, x_2)$ be a parametric function and $h(x_3, x_4)$ be a parametric function of output dimension 3. The operator

```
m_eval_all(g,@[0,1,2],h)
```

then yields the parametric function $g(h_1, h_2, h_3)$ where h_i denotes the i-th output coordinate of h.

A.3.12 Inverse Operator

The inverse operator computes the parameter where a given function matches another function. Its functional prototype is

```
MAN m_inverse(MAN invert,MAN match,int parameter)
```

Both the invert and match functions must be of output dimension 1. In addition, invert must be a monotonic function of the parametric coordinate indexed by parameter. The result of the operator is the value of the coordinate indexed by parameter where the value of invert equals the value of match. For example, if $f(x_0)$ and $g(x_1)$ are two scalar parametric functions,

```
m_inverse(f,g,0)
```

produces the value of x_0 where $f = g$. This result is therefore a function of x_1.

A.3.13   Constraint Solution and Constrained Minimization Operators

The constraint solution operator has the following functional prototype:

```
MAN m_solve(MAN_ARRAY constraints,char *continue_str,
            char *accept_str,INT_ARRAY parms, MAN domain,
            double acc)
```

The constraints argument is an array of parametric functions representing clauses in the constraint to be solved, and the solution acceptance set constraint (see Section 5.3), over a region specified by the domain argument. The continue_str and accept_str arguments represent the constraint to be solved and the solution acceptance set constraint, using a logical combination of the clauses in the constraints array. For example, let the constraints parameter be represented by an array containing the parametric functions e, f, g, and h (i.e., @[e,f,g,h]). Let the continue_str and accept_str arguments be defined by the following declarations

```
char *continue_str = "0 && 1";
char *accept_str = "2 || 3";
```

The constraint to be solved is then specified by the function e and f, while the solution acceptance set constraint is g or h. The constraint and solution acceptance functions are broken into clauses in this way for the sake of efficiency; as discussed in Section 5.3.7, once a clause becomes exactly true or false, there is no need to continually reevaluate it as part of a larger, indeterminate logical expression.

The parms argument specifies the indices of the parametric coordinates over which the constraint solution is to take place. The output dimension of domain should equal twice the number of elements in the parms array. Let the parametric function supplied as the domain argument be the parametric function D, of output dimension $2n$, and let the parms array contain the n indices $i_1, i_2, \ldots, i_n$. Then the constraint is computed over the domain where

$$x_{i_1} \in [D_1, D_2]$$
$$x_{i_2} \in [D_3, D_4]$$
$$\vdots$$
$$x_{i_n} \in [D_{2n-1}, D_{2n}].$$

Finally, the acc argument represents the tolerance in parameter space with which to compute the constraint solution. Indeterminate regions of width less than acc are accepted as solutions even if they do not satisfy the solution acceptance set constraint. A value of 0 disables this behavior and forces solution acceptance only when the solution acceptance set constraint is satisfied. In this case, an error is generated when subdivision reaches the floating point limit of the computer.

The resulting parametric function is of output dimension $2n$ and represents a solution point in the parameter space of the constraint problem. The evaluation returns a bad status if no solutions exist.

For example, let $f(x_0)$ and $g(x_1, x_2)$ be two parametric functions of output dimension 2. The function

```
h = m_solve(@[f == g,m_width(f) < eps,m_width(g) < eps],
            "0","1 && 2",@[0,1],@(MAN)(0,1,-1,1),0)
```

then returns a parametric function of output dimension 2 that is a function of x_2. This function is mathematically described as

$$h(x_2) = \begin{pmatrix} h_1(x_2) \\ h_2(x_2) \end{pmatrix} \ni f(h_1) = g(h_2, x_2),$$

where $h_1 \in [0, 1]$ and $h_2 \in [-1, 1]$. Solutions are accepted only when they satisfy

$$w(f(x_0)) < \epsilon \text{ and } w(g(x_1, x_2)) < \epsilon.$$

The constrained minimization operator is similar, but has an additional argument representing the objective function to be minimized. Its functional prototype is

```
MAN m_minimize(MAN objective,MAN_ARRAY constraints,
               char *continue_str,char *accept_str,
               INT_ARRAY parms, MAN domain,
               int return_min,double acc)
```

The `return_min` flag specifies whether the minimum value of the function, or a point in parameter space which minimizes the function, is returned. Of course, one can always reconstruct the minimum value of the objective function by evaluating it at the returned global minimizer. However, if only the minimum function value is required, a better bound on the minimum function value is possible than can be obtained by deriving it from a bound on the set of global minimizers. This is apparent, for example, for the case in which the objective function has more than one distinct minimizer.

In the case of both `m_solve` and `m_minimize`, a parametric function representing a single solution to the problem is returned. Alternate forms also exist that return **all** solutions, up to some maximum number. The technique of solution aggregation (described in Section 5.3.3) is used to compute a set of disjoint intervals bounding solutions. The midpoint of the interval is then used as the returned solution. Sections 5.3 and 5.4 discuss how these operators can be evaluated and bounded.

A.3.14   ODE Solution Operator

The ODE solution operator has the following functional prototype:

```
MAN m_ode(MAN f,INT_ARRAY y_parms,int t_parm,
         MAN t,MAN t0,MAN y0,
         double abserr,double relerr)
```

The operator returns the solution, $y(t)$, of the initial value ODE problem

$$y'(t) = f(y,t)$$

where

$$y(t_0) = y_0.$$

The argument f represents the function f in the ODE problem; the arrays y_parms and t_parm identify which parametric coordinates of f represent the y input coordinates, and which represent the t input coordinate (a -1 denotes no time-dependence; that is, $y'(t) = f(y)$). The arguments t0 and y0 indicate the initial conditions. Finally, the argument t is used to parameterize the solution $y(t)$.

For example, the code

```
MAN x = m_x(1);
MAN y = m_x(2);
MAN f = @(y + x@^2*m_sin(x*y),-x + y@^2*m_cos(x*y));
MAN t0 = 0;
MAN y0 = @(MAN)(0,m_x(3)*8);
MAN t = m_x(2)*2*pi;
MAN c = m_ode(f,@[1,2],-1,t,t0,y0,1e-6,1e-5);
```

produces a family of integral curves, $c(x_2, x_3)$, where the x_2 parameter increases along each integral curve, and the x_3 parameter specifies a different integral curve corresponding to the initial condition

$$c(0, x_3) = \begin{pmatrix} 0 \\ 8x_3 \end{pmatrix}.$$

The vector field for which c yields integral curves is given by

$$\begin{pmatrix} y + x^2 \sin(xy) \\ -x + y^2 \cos(xy) \end{pmatrix}.$$

This manifold was used to make the integral curves in Figure 2.12.

A.4   Language Extensibility: Building Higher-Level Operators

Given these primitive operators on parametric functions, the modeler can construct higher-level operators by defining C functions. These C functions take parametric functions as input and produce a new parametric function using nested composition of the primitive operators. This section presents three examples of how useful higher-level operators can be constructed.

A.4.1   Interpolation Operators

The m_interp function defines a linear interpolation operator on parametric functions:

```
MAN m_interp(MAN t,MAN a,MAN b)
{
    return a + (b - a)*t;
}
```

This function takes three parametric functions as input: a and b are the functions to be interpolated, and t specifies the interpolation variable. For example, the code sequence

```
MAN p1 = @(MAN)(0,0);
MAN p2 = @(MAN)(1,1);
MAN seg = m_interp(m_x(0),p1,p2);
```

produces the parametric function seg, which is a line segment in two dimensions parameterized by x_0 and continuing from the point $(0,0)$ to the point $(1,1)$. Note that the parametric functions a and b can be of any input or output dimension, as long as they have the same output dimension. This allows linear interpolation of curves, surfaces, or any other shape.

Similarly, the hermite interpolation operator, m_interp_hermite, is defined with the code (see page 72 for an explanation)

```
MAN m_interp_hermite(MAN t,MAN p0,MAN p1,MAN p0d,MAN p1d)
{
    MAN a = p1d + p0d + 2*(p0 - p1);
    MAN b = p1 - p0 - p0d - a;
    MAN c = p0d;
    MAN d = p0;

    return ((a*t + b)*t + c)*t + d;
}
```

A.4.2   Concatenation Operators

The m_concat function defines uniform concatenation of an array of shapes in a parametric coordinate (see page 37 for an explanation of uniform concatenation). Here we assume that all shapes are parameterized on the interval $[0, 1]$. A curve $c(x_0)$, for example, begins at $x_0 = 0$ and ends at $x_0 = 1$. The concatenation of several curves using this operator then yields a curve that also starts at $x_0 = 0$ and ends at $x_0 = 1$.

```
MAN m_concat(int parm, MAN in, MAN_ARRAY array)
{
    MAN a[MAXCONCAT];
    int n = array.n, i;
    MAN_ARRAY tmp;

    for (i = 0; i < n; i++) {
        a[i] = m_eval(array.ptr[i],parm,in*n - i);
    }

    tmp.ptr = a;
    tmp.n = n;

    return m_index(in*n,tmp);
}
```

For example, the code

```
MAN c1 = m_crv("crv1",m_x(0));
MAN c2 = m_crv("crv2",m_x(0));
MAN c3 = m_crv("crv3",m_x(0));
MAN c = m_concat(0,m_x(0),@[c1,c2,c3]);
```

creates a parametric function c that concatenates the three curves c1, c2, and c3.

The m_concat_with_density function defines nonuniform concatenation of an array of shapes, where an array of densities controls how much parameter space is devoted to each shape. This is in contrast to uniform concatenation, where each shape is parameterized by the constant amount $1/n$ in parameter space.

We are given n parametric shapes $m_i(u), i = 1, 2, \ldots, n$, and n corresponding density functions d_i. We first define the functions $s_i, i = 0, 1, \ldots, n$ via

$$s_0 = 0$$
$$s_i = \sum_{j=1}^{i} d_j \quad i = 1, 2, \ldots, n.$$

We then form a new function, $m(u)$, that concatenates the functions $m_i(u)$ in the u parameter. As the u parameter changes from s_{i-1} to s_i, $m(u)$ follows $m_i(u)$.

Mathematically, $m(u)$ is given by

$$m(u) = \begin{cases} m_1(\dfrac{us_n}{d_0}) & u \in [0, \dfrac{s_1}{s_n}] \\ \vdots \\ m_i(\dfrac{us_n - s_i}{d_i}) & u \in [\dfrac{s_{i-1}}{s_n}, \dfrac{s_i}{s_n}] \\ \vdots \\ m_n(\dfrac{us_n - s_n}{d_n}) & u \in [\dfrac{s_{n-1}}{s_n}, 1] \end{cases} .$$

The code for m_concat_with_density is

```
MAN m_concat_with_density(int parm, MAN in, MAN_ARRAY array,
                          MAN_ARRAY dens)
{
    if (array.n != dens.n) {
        printf("m_concat_with_density: number of manifolds \
does not equal number of densities\n");
        return m_null;
    }

    MAN *conds = malloc(sizeof(MAN)*array.n);
    MAN *mans = malloc(sizeof(MAN)*array.n);
    MAN *sum = malloc(sizeof(MAN)*(array.n+1));
    int i,n = array.n;
    MAN result;
    MAN_ARRAY conds_array = {conds,n};
    MAN_ARRAY mans_array = {mans,n};

    sum[0] = 0;
    for (i = 0; i < n; i++)
        sum[i+1] = sum[i] + dens.ptr[i];

    MAN q = in*sum[n];

    for (i = 0; i < n; i++) {
        MAN at = (q - sum[i])/dens.ptr[i];
        MAN next = m_eval(array.ptr[i],parm,at);
        mans[i] = next;
        if (i == n-1) conds[i] = 1;
        else          conds[i] = (q < sum[i+1]);
    }

    result = m_case(conds_array,mans_array);
    free(conds); free(mans); free(sum);
```

```
    return result;
}
```

A.4.3 Reparameterization Operator

The m_reparameterize_by_arclength operator reparameterizes its argument
by arclength. It assumes that its single argument is a curve (i.e., it has input dimension at least 1), and prints an error message otherwise. The parametric coordinate
reparameterized is assumed to be the input coordinate of curve with the lowest
index (stored in the local variable parm). This coordinate is assumed to vary from
0 (at the start of the curve) to 1 (at the end of the curve).

```
MAN m_reparameterize_by_arclength(MAN curve)
{
    if (curve->inputs < 1) {
        printf("m_resample_arclength: manifold is constant\n");
        return m_null;
    }
    int parm = curve->input_list[0];
    MAN tanlen = m_length(m_derivative(curve,parm));
    MAN curvelen = m_integrate(tanlen,0,m_x(parm),parm);
    MAN curvelen_total = m_eval(curvelen,parm,1);
    MAN curvelen_linear = m_interp(m_x(parm),0,curvelen_total);
    MAN newinput = m_inverse(curvelen,curvelen_linear,parm);

    return m_eval(curve,parm,newinput);
}
```

Note that the m_interp operator defined previously has been used in this new
definition. It is used to specify a linearly varying arclength from 0 to the total
arclength of the curve. For a more complete discussion of reparameterization by
arclength, see the section on the inversion operator beginning on page 39.

A.4.4 Closed Offset Operator

The concatenation operator can be used to form the closed offset of a planar curve.
The following code defines a closed offset operator, m_closed_offset, which is
used for the spoon example of Figure 3.17.

```
/*
** reverses a curve so that
** it starts at its old end
*/
```

```
MAN m_reverse(MAN m)
{
    int parm = m->input_list[0];
    return m_eval(m,parm,1-m_x(parm));
}


/*
** forms a semi-circle parameterized by
** in between the points p1 and p2.
** left_flag controls whether the semi-circle
** is to the right or left of the line
** from p1 to p2
*/
MAN m_semi(MAN p1,MAN p2,MAN in,int left_flag)
{
    MAN m = (p1 + p2)*0.5;
    MAN dhat = (p2-p1)*0.5;
    MAN nhat;

    if (left_flag) nhat = @(-dhat[1],dhat[0]);
    else           nhat = @(dhat[1],-dhat[0]);

    in = (in - 0.5)*pi;
    return m + nhat*m_cos(in) + dhat*m_sin(in);
}


/* forms the closed offset to a curve */
MAN m_closed_offset(MAN c,MAN r)
{
    int parm = c->input_list[0];
    MAN n = m_normal2d(c);

    MAN s1 = c - r/2*n;
    MAN s2 = m_reverse(c + r/2*n);

    MAN p0 = m_eval(s1,parm,1.0);
    MAN p1 = m_eval(s2,parm,0.0);
    MAN s3 = m_semi(p0,p1,m_x(parm),0);

    MAN p2 = m_eval(s2,parm,1.0);
    MAN p3 = m_eval(s1,parm,0.0);
    MAN s4 = m_semi(p2,p3,m_x(parm),0);

    return m_concat(parm,m_x(parm),@[s1,s3,s2,s4]);
}
```

A.5   Operator Libraries

While the primitive operators form a powerful basis for a shape representation, they do not always match the operations the designer wishes to perform. In these cases, the designer can employ non-primitive operators formed by composing the primitive operators. The GENMOD system includes operator libraries that predefine hundreds of such higher-level operators. The definitions of these operators are loaded from interpreted files when the program is first run, and can be dynamically modified and added to by the user.

A.5.1   Affine Transformation Library

The following library defines operators that form 4×4 matrices representing various affine transformations. As discussed in Section 3.2.1.4, such transformations can be composed using the matrix product operator, to build complicated transformations that can be applied to cross-section curves. Some of the operators defined in this library were used in the banana example (Figure 3.8) and turbine blade example (Figure 3.9).

Each operator is very simple: it forms a parametric function of output dimension 16 containing the components of the 4×4 matrix and then uses the `m_matrix` operator to create the matrix.

```
/* scale x axis */
MAN_MATRIX m_scalex(MAN scale)
{
    if (scale->outputs != 1)
        printf("m_scalex: input must be 1d out\n");
    return m_matrix(@(scale,0,0,0,
                      0,1,0,0,
                      0,0,1,0,
                      0,0,0,1),
                    4,4);
}

/* scale y axis */
MAN_MATRIX m_scaley(MAN scale)
{
    if (scale->outputs != 1)
        printf("m_scaley: input must be 1d out\n");
    return m_matrix(@(1,0,0,0,
                      0,scale,0,0,
                      0,0,1,0,
                      0,0,0,1),
                    4,4);
}

/* scale both x and y axes */
```

```
MAN_MATRIX m_scalexy(MAN scale)
{
    if (scale->outputs != 1)
        printf("m_scalexy: input must be 1d out\n");
    return m_matrix(@(scale,0,0,0,
                      0,scale,0,0,
                      0,0,1,0,
                      0,0,0,1),
                    4,4);
}

/* scale z axis */
MAN_MATRIX m_scalez(MAN scale)
{
    if (scale->outputs != 1)
        printf("m_scalez: input must be 1d out\n");
    return m_matrix(@(1,0,0,0,
                      0,1,0,0,
                      0,0,scale,0,
                      0,0,0,1),
                    4,4);
}

/* scale x, y and z using components of the
   input manifold */
MAN_MATRIX m_scale(MAN scale)
{
    if (scale->outputs != 3)
        printf("m_scale: input must be 3d out\n");
    return m_matrix(@(scale[0],0,0,0,
                      0,scale[1],0,0,
                      0,0,scale[2],0,
                      0,0,0,1),
                    4,4);
}

/* translate along x axis */
MAN_MATRIX m_transx(MAN trans)
{
    if (trans->outputs != 1)
        printf("m_transx: input must be 1d out\n");
    return m_matrix(@(1,0,0,trans,
                      0,1,0,0,
                      0,0,1,0,
                      0,0,0,1),
                    4,4);
}

/* translate along y axis */
MAN_MATRIX m_transy(MAN trans)
{
    if (trans->outputs != 1)
        printf("m_transy: input must be 1d out\n");
```

```
        return m_matrix(@(1,0,0,0,
                          0,1,0,trans,
                          0,0,1,0,
                          0,0,0,1),
                        4,4);
}

/* translate along z axis */
MAN_MATRIX m_transz(MAN trans)
{
    if (trans->outputs != 1)
        printf("m_transz: input must be 1d out\n");
    return m_matrix(@(1,0,0,0,
                      0,1,0,0,
                      0,0,1,trans,
                      0,0,0,1),
                    4,4);
}

/* rotate around x axis
     (rot argument in radians) */
MAN_MATRIX m_rotx(MAN rot)
{
    if (rot->outputs != 1)
        printf("rotx: input must be 1d out\n");

    MAN c = m_cos(rot);
    MAN s = m_sin(rot);
    return m_matrix(@(1,0,0,0,
                      0,c,-s,0,
                      0,s,c,0,
                      0,0,0,1),
                    4,4);
}

/* rotate around y axis
     (rot argument in radians) */
MAN_MATRIX m_roty(MAN rot)
{
    if (rot->outputs != 1)
        printf("m_roty: input must be 1d out\n");

    MAN c = m_cos(rot);
    MAN s = m_sin(rot);
    return m_matrix(@(c,0,s,0,
                      0,1,0,0,
                      -s,0,c,0,
                      0,0,0,1),
                    4,4);
}

/* rotate around z axis
     (rot argument in radians) */
```

```
MAN_MATRIX m_rotz(MAN rot)
{
    if (rot->outputs != 1)
        printf("m_rotz: input must be 1d out\n");

    MAN c = m_cos(rot);
    MAN s = m_sin(rot);
    return m_matrix(@(c,-s,0,0,
                      s,c,0,0,
                      0,0,1,0,
                      0,0,0,1),
                    4,4);
}
```

A.5.2   Line/Arc Library

GENMOD also predefines an extensive library of 2D operations on lines and arcs, including the definition of the m_arc_2pt_height operator used in the spoon example of Figure 3.17. The following is an excerpt from that library which defines the m_arc_2pt_height operator.

```
/*
** forms an arc with origin org, radius rad,
** parameterized by polar angle (argument in)
** from theta1 (in=0) to theta2 (in=1)
*/
MAN m_arc(MAN org,MAN rad,MAN theta1,MAN theta2,MAN in)
{
    return org + rad*m_circle(m_interp(in,theta1,theta2));
}


/*
** forms a directed arc with origin org, radius rad,
** parameterized by polar angle (argument in)
** from theta1 to theta2.  The clockwise
** argument is 1 for a clockwise arc, 0 for a
** counterclockwise arc
*/
MAN m_arc_directed(MAN org,MAN rad,MAN theta1,MAN theta2,
                   MAN in,MAN clockwise)
{
    theta2 = (clockwise) ? /* theta should decrease */
        ((theta2 > theta1) ? theta2 - 2*pi : theta2)
                     : /* theta should increase */
        ((theta2 < theta1) ? theta2 + 2*pi : theta2);

    return m_arc(org,rad,theta1,theta2,in);
}
```

```
/*
** computes the angle of the 2D vector p
** to vector along the positive x direction
*/
MAN m_angle(MAN p)
{
    return (p[0] == 0 && p[1] == 0) ? 0 : m_atan2(p[1],p[0]);
}


/*
** forms a directed arc with origin org,
** radius rad, which goes between the angles
** determined by two points, p1 and p2
*/
MAN m_arc2(MAN org,MAN rad,MAN p1,MAN p2,MAN in,MAN clockwise)
{
    MAN theta1 = m_angle(p1-org);
    MAN theta2 = m_angle(p2-org);

    return m_arc_directed(org,rad,theta1,theta2,in,clockwise);
}


/*
** forms an arc with endpoints at two points, p1 and p2,
** with a specified height above their line of connection
*/
MAN m_arc_2pt_height(MAN p1,MAN p2,MAN h,MAN in)
{
    MAN m = (p1+p2)*0.5;
    MAN q = p2-p1;
    MAN dsq = m_dot(q,q);
    MAN dhalfsq = dsq*0.25;
    MAN d = m_sqrt(dsq);
    MAN a = (dhalfsq - h@^2)/(2*h);
    MAN r = m_fabs(a + h);
    MAN nhat = @(q[1],-q[0])/d;
    MAN o = m + a*nhat;

    return (h == 0) ? m_interp(in,p1,p2)
                    : m_arc2(o,r,p1,p2,in,h > 0);
}
```

A.5.3   Physical Properties of Rigid Bodies Library

The rigid body library computes physical properties (volume, surface area, center of mass, and moments of inertia) of solids bounded by an array of generative
surfaces. The code supplied here assumes a constant unit density for all solids. It
supports computation of physical properties of both solids and thin shells bounding
the solids. Before presenting the code, some explanation is in order.

Let V be a solid in $\mathbf{R}^3$ bounded by a closed, orientable surface S with unit outward pointing normal $\hat{n}$. Let $g(x_1, x_2, x_3)$ be a continuously differentiable function. Then Gauss's Theorem (also called the Divergence Theorem) states that, for any $i = 1, 2, 3$,

$$\iiint_V \frac{\partial g}{\partial x_i} \, dx_1 \, dx_2 \, dx_3 = \iint_S g \, \hat{n}_i \, dS$$

where S is the surface boundary of V. Let S be represented as a parametric surface $S(u, v)$ with domain $(u, v) \in D_{uv}$, whose normal

$$n(u, v) = \frac{\partial S}{\partial u} \times \frac{\partial S}{\partial v}$$

is outward pointing. Note that $n(u, v)$ is not necessarily a unit vector. Then the surface integral in Gauss's Theorem can be replaced by an interated integral via

$$\iint_S g \, \hat{n}_i \, dS = \iint_{D_{uv}} g(S_1(u, v), S_2(u, v), S_3(u, v)) \, n_i(u, v) \, du \, dv.$$

Let $\rho(x_1, x_2, x_3)$ be the density of the solid V. The volume, Γ, of this solid is given by

$$\Gamma = \iiint_V dx_1 \, dx_2 \, dx_3.$$

Using Gauss's Theorem, we have

$$\Gamma = \iint_{D_{uv}} S_i(u, v) \, n_i(u, v) \, du \, dv \tag{A.1}$$

where we are free to choose $i \in \{1, 2, 3\}$. The mass of the solid, m, is given by

$$m = \iiint_V \rho(x_1, x_2, x_3) \, dx_1 \, dx_2 \, dx_3.$$

This library assumes a constant unit density for all shapes; i.e.,

$$\rho(x_1, x_2, x_3) = 1.$$

Thus $m = \Gamma$ and can be computed using Equation A.1.

The center of mass, O, of the solid V is given by

$$O = \frac{1}{m} \int \int \int_V \rho(x_1, x_2, x_3)\, x$$

where

$$x = \begin{pmatrix} x_1 \\ x_2 \\ x_3 \end{pmatrix}.$$

Again assuming unit density, and applying Gauss's Theorem,

$$O_i = \frac{1}{m} \int \int_{D_{uv}} \frac{1}{2} S_i^2(u, v)\, n_i(u, v)\, du\, dv,$$

since

$$g(x_1, x_2, x_3) = \frac{x_i^2}{2} \quad \Rightarrow \quad \frac{\partial g}{\partial x_i} = x_i.$$

Finally, to compute the moments of inertia, I, of the solid V, we change coordinates to $(\tilde{x}_1, \tilde{x}_2, \tilde{x}_3)$ by translating so that the center of mass is at the origin; i.e.,

$$\tilde{x} = x - O.$$

The moments of inertia matrix is given by

$$I = \int \int \int_V \rho(\tilde{x}_1, \tilde{x}_2, \tilde{x}_3)\, M(\tilde{x}_1, \tilde{x}_2, \tilde{x}_3)\, d\tilde{x}_1\, d\tilde{x}_2\, d\tilde{x}_3$$

where the matrix M is given by

$$M(x_1, x_2, x_3) = \begin{bmatrix} x_2^2 + x_3^2 & -x_1 x_2 & -x_1 x_3 \\ -x_1 x_2 & x_1^2 + x_3^2 & -x_2 x_3 \\ -x_1 x_3 & -x_2 x_3 & x_1^2 + x_2^2 \end{bmatrix}.$$

Assuming $\rho(\tilde{x}_1, \tilde{x}_2, \tilde{x}_3) = 1$ and applying Gauss's Theorem to one component of I yields, for example,

$$I_{11} = \int \int_{D_{uv}} (\tilde{S}_2^2(u, v) + \tilde{S}_3^2(u, v))\, \tilde{S}_1(u, v)\, n_1(u, v)\, du\, dv$$

where

$$\tilde{S}(u, v) = S(u, v) - O.$$

Writing out all the components of I, we get

$$I_{11} = \iint_{D_{uv}} (\tilde{S}_2^2(u,v) + \tilde{S}_3^2(u,v))\,\tilde{S}_1(u,v)\,n_1(u,v)\,du\,dv$$

$$I_{12} = I_{21} = \iint_{D_{uv}} -\tilde{S}_1(u,v)\tilde{S}_2(u,v))\,\tilde{S}_3(u,v)\,n_3(u,v)\,du\,dv$$

$$I_{13} = I_{31} = \iint_{D_{uv}} -\tilde{S}_1(u,v)\tilde{S}_2(u,v))\,\tilde{S}_3(u,v)\,n_2(u,v)\,du\,dv$$

$$I_{22} = \iint_{D_{uv}} (\tilde{S}_1^2(u,v) + \tilde{S}_3^2(u,v))\,\tilde{S}_2(u,v)\,n_2(u,v)\,du\,dv$$

$$I_{23} = I_{32} = \iint_{D_{uv}} -\tilde{S}_1(u,v)\tilde{S}_2(u,v))\,\tilde{S}_3(u,v)\,n_1(u,v)\,du\,dv$$

$$I_{33} = \iint_{D_{uv}} (\tilde{S}_1^2(u,v) + \tilde{S}_2^2(u,v))\,\tilde{S}_3(u,v)\,n_3(u,v)\,du\,dv.$$

If the solid V is bounded by a set of N surfaces $S^j(u,v)$, each with outward pointing normal, then the physical properties of V can be calculated by summing the integrals over j. For example, the volume of V is given by

$$\Gamma = \sum_{j=1}^{N} \Gamma^j$$

where Γ^j is the volume result for an individual surface S^j using Equation A.1.

Physical properties can also be obtained considering the shape as a thin shell rather than a solid. The surface area, A, of the solid V is given by

$$A = \iint_S dS = \iint_{D_{uv}} \|n(u,v)\|\,du\,dv.$$

The center of mass of a thin shell bounding V is given by

$$O = \frac{1}{A} \iint_S x\,dS = \iint_{D_{uv}} S(u,v)\|n(u,v)\|\,du\,dv.$$

The moments of inertia of the thin shell is given by

$$
\begin{aligned}
I &= \iint\limits_{S} M(x_1, x_2, x_3)\, dS \\
  &= \iint\limits_{D_{uv}} M(S_1(u,v), S_2(u,v), S_3(u,v))\, \|n(u,v)\|\, du\, dv.
\end{aligned}
$$

The following GENMOD library creates parametric functions representing these physical properties, given an array of parametric surfaces bounding V. The function m_rigid_solid takes an array of surfaces and returns three manifolds representing the volume, center of mass, and moments of inertia of the solid enclosed by these surfaces. The function m_rigid_shell takes an array of surfaces and returns the surface area, center of mass, and moments of interia of a thin shell represented by the surfaces.

```
double m_rigid_abserr = 1e-6;
double m_rigid_relerr = 1e-6;

/*
** compute the double integral of f(u,v)
** for u,v in [0,1]
*/
MAN m_double_integ(MAN f)
{
    return m_integrate_multi(f,@(MAN)(0,0),@(MAN)(1,1),
                             @[f->input_list[0],f->input_list[1]],
                             m_rigid_abserr,m_rigid_relerr);
}

/*
** compute the volume of the solid
** bounded by an array of surfaces
*/
MAN m_volume(MAN_ARRAY surfaces)
{
    int i;
    MAN result;

    for (i = 0; i < surfaces.n; i++) {
        MAN s = surfaces.ptr[i];
        MAN n = m_normal(s);
        MAN V = m_double_integ(s[0]*n[0]);
        if (i == 0) result = V; else result = result + V;
    }
    return result;
}
```

```
/*
** compute the surface area of the solid
** bounded by an array of surfaces
*/
MAN m_surface_area(MAN_ARRAY surfaces)
{
    int i;
    MAN result;

    for (i = 0; i < surfaces.n; i++) {
        MAN s = surfaces.ptr[i];
        MAN n = m_normal(s);
        MAN dS = m_length(n);
        MAN A = m_double_integ(dS);
        if (i == 0) result = A; else result = result + A;
    }
    return result;
}

/*
** compute the center of mass of a solid
** of constant density
** bounded by an array of surfaces
*/
MAN m_com_solid(MAN_ARRAY surfaces,MAN volume)
{
    int i;
    MAN result;

    for (i = 0; i < surfaces.n; i++) {
        MAN s = surfaces.ptr[i];
        MAN n = m_normal(s);
        MAN x = (s[0]@^2*n[0]);
        MAN y = (s[1]@^2*n[1]);
        MAN z = (s[2]@^2*n[2]);
        MAN c = m_double_integ(@(x,y,z));
        if (i == 0) result = c; else result = result + c;
    }
    return result/(2*volume);
}

/*
** compute the center of mass of a thin
** shell formed by an array of surfaces
*/
MAN m_com_shell(MAN_ARRAY surfaces,MAN area)
{
    int i;
    MAN result;

    for (i = 0; i < surfaces.n; i++) {
        MAN s = surfaces.ptr[i];
```

```
    MAN n = m_normal(s);
    MAN dS = m_length(n);
    MAN x = (s[0]*dS);
    MAN y = (s[1]*dS);
    MAN z = (s[2]*dS);
    MAN c = m_double_integ(@(x,y,z));

    if (i == 0) result = c; else result = result + c;
}
return result/area;
}

/*
** compute the moments of inertia of a solid
** of constant density
** bounded by an array of surfaces
*/
MAN m_moi_solid(MAN_ARRAY surfaces,MAN volume,MAN com)
{
    int i;
    MAN result;

    for (i = 0; i < surfaces.n; i++) {
        MAN s = surfaces.ptr[i];
        MAN n = m_normal(s);
        MAN r = s - com;

        MAN A = (r[0]*(r[1]@^2 + r[2]@^2)*n[0]);
        MAN B = (r[1]*(r[0]@^2 + r[2]@^2)*n[1]);
        MAN C = (r[2]*(r[0]@^2 + r[1]@^2)*n[2]);
        MAN P = -(r[0]*r[1]*r[2]*n[0]);
        MAN Q = -(r[0]*r[1]*r[2]*n[1]);
        MAN R = -(r[0]*r[1]*r[2]*n[2]);
        MAN I = m_double_integ(@(A,R,Q,  R,B,P,  Q,P,C));

        if (i == 0) result = I; else result = result + I;
    }
    return result;
}

/*
** compute the moments of inertia of a thin
** shell formed by an array of surfaces
*/
MAN m_moi_shell(MAN_ARRAY surfaces,MAN area,MAN com)
{
    int i;
    MAN result;

    for (i = 0; i < surfaces.n; i++) {
        MAN s = surfaces.ptr[i];
        MAN n = m_normal(s);
        MAN dS = m_length(n);
```

```
        MAN r = s - com;

        MAN A = ((r[1]@^2 + r[2]@^2)*dS);
        MAN B = ((r[0]@^2 + r[2]@^2)*dS);
        MAN C = ((r[0]@^2 + r[1]@^2)*dS);
        MAN P = -(r[1]*r[2]*dS);
        MAN Q = -(r[0]*r[2]*dS);
        MAN R = -(r[0]*r[1]*dS);
        MAN I = m_double_integ(@(A,R,Q,  R,B,P,  Q,P,C));

        if (i == 0) result = I; else result = result + I;
    }
    return result;
}

/*
** return all physical properties of a
** solid bounded by an array of surfaces
*/
void m_rigid_solid(MAN_ARRAY s,MAN *vol,MAN *com,MAN *moi)
{
    *vol = m_volume(s);
    *com = m_com_solid(s,*vol);
    *moi = m_moi_solid(s,*vol,*com);
}

/*
** return all physical properties of a
** thin shell formed by an array of surfaces
*/
void m_rigid_shell(MAN_ARRAY s,MAN *area,MAN *com,MAN *moi)
{
    *area = m_surface_area(s);
    *com = m_com_shell(s,*area);
    *moi = m_moi_shell(s,*area,*com);
}
```

Appendix B

GENMOD Code Examples

This appendix gives the GENMOD code for the more complicated examples of Chapter 3: the sphere/cylinder fillet example of Section 3.2.2, the screwdriver tip examples of Section 3.2.3, the bottle example of Section 3.2.4, and the teddy bear example of Section 3.3.3.

B.1 Sphere/Cylinder Fillet Example

The following GENMOD code defines a surface `fillet`, which is a smooth filleting surface between a cylinder and a sphere. The code is an example of the idea of hermite interpolation for filleting discussed on page 72. Note that similar code to produce a fillet between arbitrary surfaces could be accomplished using the global minimization operator, rather than implementing the analytic ray/sphere and ray/cylinder intersection formulae.

```
/* solves || u + v t ||^2 == r^2 */
static MAN m_solve_len(MAN u,MAN v,MAN r)
{
    MAN a = m_dot(v,v);
    MAN b = 2*m_dot(u,v);
    MAN c = m_dot(u,u) - r@^2;
    return (-b - m_sqrt(b@^2 - 4*a*c)) / (2*a);
}

/* returns nearest intersection with sphere */
MAN m_ray_sph(MAN a,MAN b,MAN o,MAN r)
{
    MAN t = m_solve_len(a-o,b,r);
    return a + b*t;
```

```
}

/* returns nearest intersection with cylinder */
MAN m_ray_cyl(MAN a,MAN b,MAN o,MAN d,MAN r)
{
    MAN t = m_solve_len(o-a+d*m_dot(a-o,d),d*m_dot(b,d)-b,r);
    return a + b*t;
}

/* returns normal to sphere centered at o, at point p */
MAN m_sph_nor(MAN o,MAN p)
{
    return m_normalize(p-o);
}

/* returns normal to cylinder of origin o, direction d,
   at point p */
MAN m_cyl_nor(MAN o,MAN d,MAN p)
{
    MAN q = o + d*m_dot(p-o,d);
    return m_normalize(p-q);
}

MAN u = m_x(0);
MAN v = m_x(1);
MAN w = m_x(2);

/* cylinder origin, direction, and radius */
MAN cyl_o = @(MAN)(0,0,0);
MAN cyl_d = @(MAN)(1,0,0);
MAN cyl_r = 0.6;

/* sphere origin and radius */
MAN sph_o = @(MAN)(0,-0.1,1.5);
MAN sph_r = 0.6;

/* sphere and cylinder surfaces */
MAN cyl = @(m_interp(v,-1,1),m_circle(2*pi*u)*cyl_r);
MAN sph = m_sphere(u*2*pi,v*pi)*sph_r + sph_o;

/* ray origin (a) and direction (b) for a collection
   of rays, arranged in circle in the xy plane */
MAN a = @(m_circle(m_x(0)*2*pi)*0.4,0.5);
MAN b = @(MAN)(0,0,1);

/* intersection of rays with cylinder */
```

```
MAN c1 = m_ray_cyl(a,-b,cyl_o,cyl_d,cyl_r);
MAN c1tan = m_normalize(m_derivative(c1,0));
MAN c1nor = m_cyl_nor(cyl_o,cyl_d,c1);
MAN c1d = m_cross(c1nor,c1tan);

/* intersection of rays with sphere */
MAN c2 = m_ray_sph(a,b,sph_o,sph_r);
MAN c2tan = m_normalize(m_derivative(c2,0));
MAN c2nor = m_sph_nor(sph_o,c2);
MAN c2d = m_cross(c2nor,c2tan);

MAN z = m_interp(w,0.01,1.0);
MAN fillet = m_interp_hermite(v,c1,c2,c1d*z,c2d*z);
```

B.2 Screwdriver Tip Examples

The following GENMOD code defines two surfaces representing the tip of a regular and a Phillips screwdriver. The code is an example of the idea of CPG discussed in Section 3.2.3. The code is dependent on a module that builds curves with a PostScript-like interface. The following are descriptions of the relevant functions:

- `newpath(int coord)`
  specifies the start of a new curve that will be based on parametric coordinate `coord`.

- `closepath()`
  closes a curve begun with `newpath`.

- `getpath(MAN input)`
  returns a parametric function (of type `MAN`) representing the last curve built, parameterized by parametric function `input`.

- `moveto(MAN p)`
  moves to the 2D point `p`.

- `lineto(MAN p)`
  adds a line segment to the curve from the last point to the point `p`.

- `lineto_arc(MAN p,MAN o,MAN r,int min,int cc,MAN fillet)`
  adds a line segment to the curve from the last point in the direction of point `p`. The segment is ended when it hits a circle centered at `o` of radius `r`. `min` is a flag specifying whether the first or second intersection of the line segment from the last point to `p` is to be used. `cc` is a flag specifying whether the arc

is traversed counterclockwise. fillet is a parametric function specifying the radius of a fillet placed between the line segment and the arc. Using the special function m_null for this argument removes the fillet.

- arcto_line(MAN o,MAN r,MAN p1,MAN p2,int min,int cc,MAN fillet)
  adds an arc to the curve. The arc is a piece of a circle centered at o of radius r. The first arc endpoint is determined from the projection of the last point onto the circle. The second arc endpoint is the intersection of the line segment from p1 to p2 with the circle. The min, cc, and fillet arguments are as in lineto_arc.

We first present the GENMOD code for the regular screwdriver tip. The parametric surface regular is the final result.

```
MAN u = m_x(0);
MAN v = m_x(1);

MAN o = @(MAN)(0,0);
MAN r = 0.5;
MAN fillet = m_null; /* 0 radius fillet */
MAN w = m_interp(v,0.015,0.75);
MAN p0 = @(w/2,-1.0);
MAN p1 = @(w/2,1.0);
MAN p2 = @(-w/2,1.0);
MAN p3 = @(-w/2,-1.0);

newpath(0);
moveto(p0);
lineto_arc(p1,o,r,0,1,fillet);
arcto_line(o,r,p2,p3,1,1,fillet);
lineto_arc(p3,o,r,0,1,fillet);
arcto_line(o,r,p0,p1,1,1,fillet);
closepath();

MAN regular = @(getpath(u),m_interp(v,0,1.0));
```

The Phillips screwdriver tip is based on two curves, shown in Figure B.1. The GENMOD code for the Phillips screwdriver follows. The parametric surface phillips is the appropriate final result.

```
MAN u = m_x(0);
MAN v = m_x(1);

MAN o = @(MAN)(0,0);
```

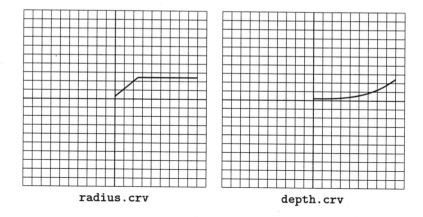

radius.crv   depth.crv

Figure B.1: Curves used in the Phillips screwdriver example. □

```
MAN r = m_crv("radius.crv",v)[1];
MAN depth = m_crv("depth.crv",v);
MAN p = @(depth[1],0);
MAN p1 = @(0,p[0]);
MAN p2 = @(0,-p[0]);

MAN fillet = m_null;

MAN theta = pi/2;
MAN d1 = @(m_cos(theta/2),m_sin(theta/2));
MAN d2 = @(d1[0],-d1[1]);
MAN d0 = @(d1[1],d1[0]);
MAN d3 = @(d1[1],-d1[0]);

newpath(0);
moveto(p2);
lineto_arc(p2+d3,o,r,0,1,fillet);
arcto_line(o,r,p+d2,p,1,1,fillet);
lineto(p);
lineto_arc(p+d1,o,r,0,1,fillet);
arcto_line(o,r,p1+d0,p1,1,1,fillet);
lineto(p1);

MAN c = m_mirrorx(getpath(u));
MAN phillips = @(c,depth[0]);
```

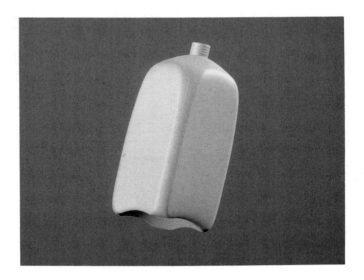

Figure B.2: Bottle surface. Plate 4 contains a color image of the bottle surface. □

B.3   Bottle Example

The following GENMOD code yields the bottle surface of Section 3.2.4, shown in Figure B.2. The code is dependent on four curves, shown in Figure B.3. The parametric surface bottle is the final result of the code.

```
/* offset m by radius r */
MAN m_offset(MAN m,MAN r)
{
    MAN n = m_normalize(m_normal2d(m));
    return m + r*n;
}

/* warp m by making its z coordinate
   by a function of its length.  That
   function is given by w              */
MAN m_warp(MAN m,MAN w)
{
    int parm = w->input_list[0];

    MAN d = m_length(m);
```

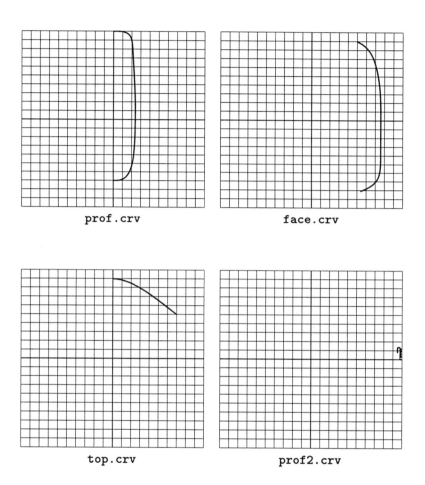

Figure B.3: Curves used in the bottle example. The curve prof.crv relates the amount the cross section of the bottle is to be offset (x axis) with the amount of translation in z (y axis). The curve face.crv specifies how much the cross section is to be rounded out at the three corner points as it is swept. The curve top.crv specifies the shape of the bottle near the top; specifically, how much the cross section is warped upward in z as a function of its distance from the z axis. The curve prof2.crv controls the shape of the bottle at the nozzle. □

```
    MAN new = m_inverse(w[0],d,parm);
    MAN z = m_eval(w[1],parm,new);

    return @(m,z);
}

/* concatenate a sequence of hermite curves */
MAN m_herm(MAN_ARRAY p,MAN_ARRAY t,int parm,MAN in)
{
    MAN array[20];
    int i;

    for (i = 0; i < p.n-1; i++) {
        MAN p1 = p.ptr[i];
        MAN p2 = p.ptr[i+1];
        MAN t1 = t.ptr[i];
        MAN t2 = t.ptr[i+1];
        array[i] = m_interp_hermite(m_x(parm),p1,p2,t1,t2);
    }
    return m_concat(parm,in,m_array(array,p.n-1));
}

/* reparameterize curve by matching y value
   to that of another curve                 */
MAN m_resample_y_by_curve(MAN c1,MAN c2,int parm)
{
    MAN newparm = m_inverse(c1[1],c2[1],parm);
    return m_eval(c1,parm,newparm);
}

/* construct a bottle surface */
MAN m_bottle(MAN prof, MAN _face,MAN top,MAN prof2)
{
    MAN face = m_resample_y_by_curve(_face,prof,1);

    MAN in = m_interp(m_x(0),0.1,0.9);

    MAN q1 = -face[0];
    MAN q2 = face[0];
    MAN q3 = -face[0];
    MAN q4 = face[0];

    MAN p2 = m_interp(0.5*(q1+1),@(MAN)(-1,0),@(MAN)(0,1));
    MAN p3 = m_interp(0.5*(q2+1),@(MAN)(-1,0),@(MAN)(0,1));
    MAN p4 = m_interp(0.5*(q3+1),@(MAN)(0,1),@(MAN)(1,0));
    MAN p5 = m_interp(0.5*(q4+1),@(MAN)(0,1),@(MAN)(1,0));
```

```
        MAN p1 = @(p2[0],-p2[1]);
        MAN p6 = @(p5[0],-p5[1]);

        MAN t2 = m_normalize(p3-p2)*0.2;
        MAN t3 = t2;
        MAN t4 = m_normalize(p5-p4)*0.2;
        MAN t5 = t4;
        MAN t1 = @(-t2[0],t2[1]);
        MAN t6 = @(-t5[0],t5[1]);

        MAN c = 0.5*m_herm(@[p1,p2,p3,p4,p5,p6],
                            @[t1,t2,t3,t4,t5,t6],0,in);
        MAN c_ = c*(1+prof[0]);

        /* main body of bottle */
        MAN s = m_warp(c_,top) + @(0,0,prof[1]-1);

        /* "shoulders" of bottle */
        MAN c0 = m_eval(c,1,0.0);
        MAN ctop = m_normalize(c0)*0.1;
        MAN reg = m_interp(m_x(1),ctop,c0);
        MAN s0 = m_warp(reg,top);

        /* nozzle of bottle */
        MAN c2 = m_warp(ctop,top);
        MAN s2 = @( @(c2[0],c2[1])*prof2[0], c2[2] + prof2[1]);

        /* bottom of bottle */
        MAN c1 = (1-m_x(1))*m_eval(c,1,1.0);
        MAN s1 = m_warp(c1,top) + @(0,0,m_eval(prof[1],1,1.0));

        /* concatenate all the pieces */
        return m_concat(1,m_x(1),@[s2,s0,s,s1]);
}

MAN u = m_x(0);
MAN v = m_x(1);
MAN face = m_crv("face.crv",v);
MAN prof = m_crv("prof.crv",v);
MAN top = m_crv("top.crv",v);
MAN prof2 = m_crv("prof2.crv",v);

MAN bottle = m_bottle(prof,face,top,prof2);
```

Figure B.4: Teddy bear surface. Plate 2 contains a color image of the bear surface, and the final image of the bear with fur. □

B.4   Teddy Bear Example

The following GENMOD code yields the teddy bear surface of Section 3.3.3. The teddy bear consists of 9 separate surfaces: two identical arms, two identical legs, a head, a body, two identical ears, and a nose, and is shown in Figure B.4. Each is defined using an affine transformation as discussed in Section 3.2.1.4.

The routine define_bear creates an object called bear in the graphics library with all of the bear's parts (arms, legs, nose, etc.) positioned correctly. The routine m_surface, the surface visualization method, causes the manifold representing one of the bear's parts to be sampled and a polygonal mesh for it generated within the graphics library. Note that graphics library calls, such as dbf_translate (which translates the following geometry) and dbf_set_surface (which sets the diffuse and specular colors and the specular exponent of the following polygons) are used between the open_object and close_object calls, to specify properties of the object defined. The routines dbf_push and dbf_pop cause the stack containing the graphics state, including transformations and surface and line colors, to be pushed or popped.

Figures B.5 through B.10 show the curves used in the definition of the bear surface.

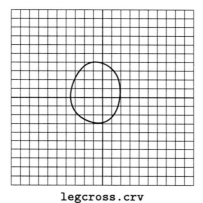

`legcross.crv`

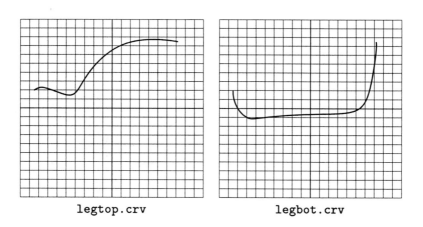

`legtop.crv`   `legbot.crv`

Figure B.5: Curves used in the bear leg. The leg cross section, `legcross.crv`, is transformed so that its x extent is transformed to lie between the two curves `legtop.crv` and `legbot.crv`. The transformation is similar to the rail product of Section 3.2.1.3. □

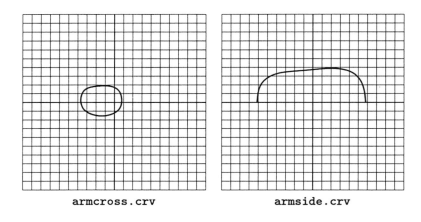

armcross.crv   armside.crv

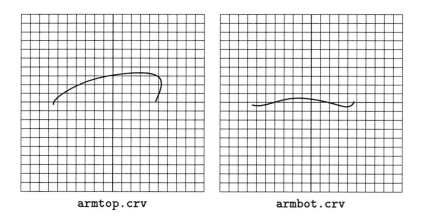

armtop.crv   armbot.crv

Figure B.6: Curves used in the bear arm. The arm cross section, armcross.crv, is scaled in x according to the y coordinate of armside.ps. It is also transformed so that its y extent lies between the two curves armtop.crv and armbot.crv. □

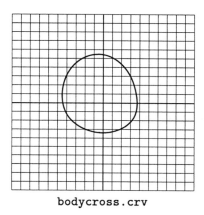

bodycross.crv

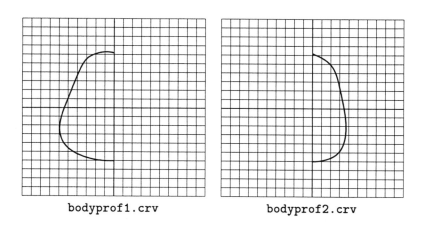

bodyprof1.crv   bodyprof2.crv

Figure B.7: Curves used in the bear body. The body cross section, bodycross.crv, is transformed so that its x extent is mapped between the two curves bodyprof1.crv and bodyprof2.crv. □

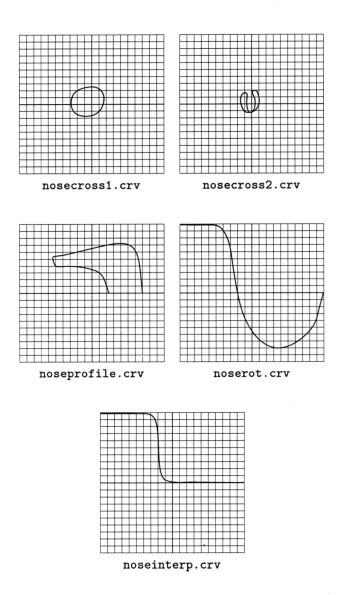

nosecross1.crv   nosecross2.crv

noseprofile.crv   noserot.crv

noseinterp.crv

Figure B.8: Curves used in the bear nose. The bear nose cross section is formed by the linear interpolation of two curves, nosecross1.crv and nosecross2.crv. The curve noseprofile.crv specifies how the resulting interpolation is scaled in x and y and translated in z. The cross section is also rotated around x according to the curve noserot.crv to cause the backward tilt of the nose. □

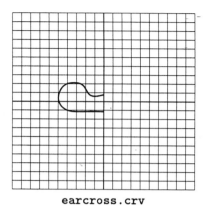

earcross.crv

Figure B.9: Curves used in the bear ear. The ear cross section, earcross.crv, is scaled in x and y, and rotated around y. □

```
/* computes scale that transforms 1d range [xmin0,xmin1]
   to [xmin1,xmax1] */
MAN m_inter_scale(MAN xmin0,MAN xmax0,MAN xmin1,MAN xmax1)
{
    return (xmax1-xmin1)/(xmax0-xmin0);
}

/* computes translation that transforms 1d range [xmin0,xmin1]
   to [xmin1,xmax1] */
MAN m_inter_trans(MAN xmin0,MAN xmax0,MAN xmin1,MAN xmax1)
{
    return xmin1 - xmin0*(xmax1-xmin1)/(xmax0-xmin0);
}

/* reparameterizes a curve by its x parameter */
MAN m_resample_x(MAN curve)
{
    if (curve->inputs < 1) {
        printf("m_resample_x: manifold is not a curve\n");
        return 0;
    }
    int parm = curve->input_list[0];
    MAN curvex = curve[0];
    MAN newinput = m_inverse(
        curvex,
        m_interp(m_x(parm),
                 m_eval(curvex,parm,0),
                 m_eval(curvex,parm,1)),
        parm);
```

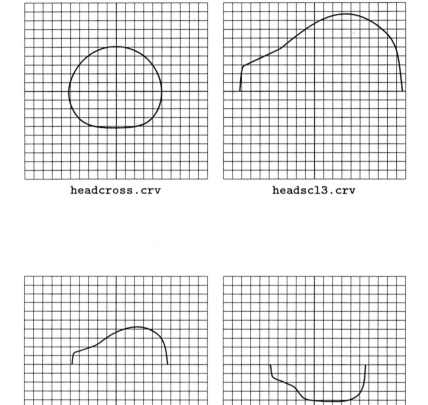

headcross.crv   headscl3.crv

headscl1.crv   headscl2.crv

Figure B.10: Curves used in the bear head. The head cross section, headcross.crv, is translated in z, scaled in x according to the curve headscl3.crv, and transformed so that its y extent is mapped between the two curves headscl2.crv and headscl1.crv. □

```
        return m_eval(curve,parm,newinput);
}

/* reparameterizes a curve by its y parameter */
MAN m_resample_y(MAN curve)
{
    if (curve->inputs < 1) {
        printf("m_resample_y: manifold is not a curve\n");
        return 0;
    }
    int parm = curve->input_list[0];
    MAN curvey = curve[1];
    MAN newinput = m_inverse(
        curvey,
        m_interp(m_x(parm),
                 m_eval(curvey,parm,0),
                 m_eval(curvey,parm,1)),
        parm);

    return m_eval(curve,parm,newinput);
}

/* finds an xy bounding box for a curve */
void curve_extent(MAN curve,MAN *xmin,MAN *xmax,MAN *ymin,MAN *ymax)
{
    *xmin = m_minimize(curve[0],@(MAN)[1],"T","F",
                       @[1],@(MAN)(0,1),1,1e-5);
    *xmax = -m_minimize(-curve[0],@(MAN)[1],"T","F",
                        @[1],@(MAN)(0,1),1,1e-5);
    *ymin = m_minimize(curve[1],@(MAN)[1],"T","F",
                       @[1],@(MAN)(0,1),1,1e-5);
    *ymax = -m_minimize(-curve[1],@(MAN)[1],"T","F",
                        @[1],@(MAN)(0,1),1,1e-5);
}

MAN bear_leg()
{
    MAN u = m_x(0);
    MAN v = m_x(1);

    MAN p1 = m_crv("legtop.crv",u);
    MAN p2 = m_crv("legbot.crv",u);

    MAN prof1 = m_resample_x(p1);
    MAN prof2 = m_resample_x(p2);

    MAN cross = m_crv("legcross.crv",v);
    MAN xmin,xmax,ymin,ymax;
    curve_extent(cross,&xmin,&xmax,&ymin.&ymax);

    MAN mat = @(m_inter_scale(xmin,xmax,prof1[1],prof2[1]),
               0,0,m_inter_trans(xmin,xmax,prof1[1],prof2[1]),
```

```
                    0,m_inter_scale(ymin,ymax,prof2[1],prof1[1]),0,0,
                    0,0,1,prof1[0],
                    0,0,0,1);

    MAN leg = m_transform3d(cross,m_matrix(mat,4,4));
    return leg;
}


MAN bear_arm()
{
    MAN u = m_x(0);
    MAN v = m_x(1);

    MAN p1 = m_crv("armtop.crv",v);
    MAN p2 = m_crv("armbot.crv",v);
    MAN p3 = m_crv("armside.crv",v);

    MAN prof1 = m_resample_x(p1);
    MAN prof2 = m_resample_x(p2);
    MAN prof3 = m_resample_x(p3);

    MAN cross = m_crv("armcross.crv",u);
    MAN xmin,xmax,ymin,ymax;
    curve_extent(cross,&xmin,&xmax,&ymin.&ymax);

    MAN mat = @(prof3[1]*3.0,0,0,0,
                0,m_inter_scale(ymin,ymax,prof2[1],prof1[1])*1.3,
                0,m_inter_trans(ymin,ymax,prof2[1],prof1[1]),
                0,0,1,prof1[0]*1.2,
                0,0,0,1);

    MAN arm = m_transform3d(cross,m_matrix(mat,4,4));
    return arm;
}

MAN bear_body()
{
    MAN u = m_x(0);
    MAN v = m_x(1);

    MAN p1 = m_crv("bodyprof1.crv",u);
    MAN p2 = m_crv("bodyprof2.crv",u);

    MAN prof1 = m_resample_y(p1);
    MAN prof2 = m_resample_y(p2);

    MAN cross = m_crv("bodycross.crv",v);
    MAN xmin,xmax,ymin,ymax;
    curve_extent(cross,&xmin,&xmax,&ymin.&ymax);

    MAN mat = @(m_inter_scale(xmin,xmax,prof1[0],prof2[0]),0,0,
```

```
                    m_inter_trans(xmin,xmax,prof1[0],prof2[0]),
                    0,m_inter_scale(ymin,ymax,prof1[0],prof2[0]),0,0,
                    0,0,1,prof1[1],
                    0,0,0,1);

    MAN body = m_transform3d(cross,m_matrix(mat,4,4));
    return body;
}

MAN bear_nose()
{
    MAN u = m_x(0);
    MAN v = m_x(1);

    MAN noseinterp = m_crv("noseinterp.crv",u);
    MAN nosecros1 = m_crv("nosecross1.crv",v)*0.7;
    MAN nosecros2 = m_crv("nosecross2.crv",v);
    MAN noseprof = m_crv("noseprofile.crv",u);
    MAN noserot = m_crv("noserot.crv",u);

    MAN cross = m_interp(noseinterp[1],nosecros2,nosecros1);
    MAN nose = m_transform3d(cross,
                   m_scalex(noseprof[1])*
                   m_scaley(noseprof[1])*
                   m_rotx(noserot[1]*-0.1*pi)*
                   m_transz(noseprof[0]*0.15)
               );
    return nose;
}

MAN bear_ear()
{
    MAN u = m_x(0);
    MAN v = m_x(1);

    MAN cross = m_crv("earcross.crv",u);
    MAN ear = m_transform3d(cross,
                   m_scalex(m_interp(v,1.5,1.0))*
                   m_scaley(m_interp(v,0.6,1.0))*
                   m_roty(v*1.2*pi)
               );
    return ear;
}

MAN bear_head()
{
    MAN u = m_x(0);
    MAN v = m_x(1);

    MAN cross = m_crv("headcross.crv",u);

    MAN headscl1 = m_crv("headscl1.crv",v);
    MAN headscl2 = m_crv("headscl2.crv",v);
```

```
        MAN headscl3 = m_crv("headscl3.crv",v);

        MAN head = 1.015*m_transform3d(cross,
                             m_transy(-0.05)*
                             m_intery(-0.47,0.47,headscl2[1],headscl1[1])*
                             m_scalex(headscl3[1])*
                             m_transz(m_interp(v,0.56,-0.48))
                      );
        return head;
}

#define DEG *M_PI/180.0


int precision[] = {40,40};

void define_bear()
{
    open_object("sphere");
    sphere(40,20);
    close_object();

    MAN leg = bear_leg();
    open_object("leg");
    m_surface(leg,0,canonical_parm_space,precision);
    close_object();

    MAN arm = bear_arm();
    open_object("arm");
    m_surface(arm,0,canonical_parm_space,precision);
    close_object();

    MAN body = bear_body();
    open_object("body");
    m_surface(body,0,canonical_parm_space,precision);
    close_object();

    MAN nose = bear_nose();
    open_object("nose");
    m_surface(nose,0,canonical_parm_space,precision);
    close_object();

    MAN ear = bear_ear();
    open_object("ear");
    m_surface(ear,0,canonical_parm_space,precision);
    close_object();

    MAN head = bear_head();
    open_object("head");
    m_surface(head,0,canonical_parm_space,precision);
    close_object();

    open_object("bear");
```

```
dbf_push();

/* head */
dbf_push();
    dbf_translate(0.0,0.03,0.0);
    dbf_scale(1.03,1.03,1.03);
    dbf_translate(0.0,0.07634,0.0);
    dbf_draw_object("head",0);

    dbf_push();
        dbf_translate(-0.29,0.23,0.2);
        dbf_scale(0.4,0.4,0.4);
        dbf_rotate(64 DEG,3);
        dbf_rotate(-90 DEG,1);
        dbf_draw_object("ear",0);
    dbf_pop();

    dbf_push();
        dbf_translate(0.29,0.23,0.2);
        dbf_scale(-0.4,-0.4,-0.4);
        dbf_rotate(-64 DEG,3);
        dbf_rotate(90 DEG,1);
        dbf_draw_object("ear",0);
    dbf_pop();
dbf_pop();

/* left eye */
dbf_push();
    dbf_translate(0.0,0.0,-0.01); // new
    dbf_translate(-0.229,0.2036,-0.1654);
    dbf_scale(0.0458,0.0458,0.0458);
    dbf_draw_object("sphere",0);
dbf_pop();

/* right eye */
dbf_push();
    dbf_translate(0.0,0.0,-0.01);
    dbf_translate(0.229,0.2036,-0.1654);
    dbf_scale(0.0458,0.0458,0.0458);

    dbf_draw_object("sphere",0);
dbf_pop();

/* nose */
dbf_push();
    dbf_translate(0.0,-0.05,-0.02); // new
    dbf_translate(0.019,0.0827,-0.4389);
    dbf_scale(0.9313,0.9313,0.9313);
    dbf_rotate(-10.53 DEG, 3);
    dbf_rotate(5.038 DEG,2);
    dbf_draw_object("nose",0);
dbf_pop();
```

```
        /* body */
        dbf_push();
            dbf_translate(0.1145,-1.031,0.0891);
            dbf_scale(1.293,1.293,1.293);
            dbf_rotate(3.206 DEG,3);
            dbf_rotate(-6.412 DEG,2);
            dbf_rotate(-74.06 DEG,1);
            dbf_draw_object("body",0);
        dbf_pop();

        /* left arm */
        dbf_push();
            dbf_translate(-0.388,-0.7188,-0.369);
            dbf_scale(0.8982,0.8982,0.8982);
            dbf_rotate(9.16 DEG,3);
            dbf_rotate(18.78 DEG,2);
            dbf_rotate(-13.28 DEG,1);
            dbf_draw_object("arm",0);
        dbf_pop();

        /* right arm */
        dbf_push();
            dbf_translate(0.2354,-0.5852,-0.458);
            dbf_scale(-0.8982,-0.8982,-0.8982);
            dbf_rotate(-211.6 DEG,3);
            dbf_rotate(-172.7 DEG,2);
            dbf_draw_object("arm",0);
        dbf_pop();

        /* left leg */
        dbf_push();
            dbf_translate(-0.5216,-1.45,-0.8397);
            dbf_scale(0.944,0.944,0.944);
            dbf_rotate(109 DEG,3);
            dbf_rotate(-28.55 DEG,2);
            dbf_rotate(5 DEG,1);
            dbf_draw_object("leg",0);
        dbf_pop();

        /* right leg */
        dbf_push();
            dbf_translate(0.4135,-1.52,-0.9097);
            dbf_scale(-0.9567,-0.9567,-0.9567);
            dbf_rotate(74.66 DEG,3);
            dbf_rotate(161.7 DEG,2);
            dbf_draw_object("leg",0);
        dbf_pop();

        dbf_pop();
    close_object();
}
```

Appendix C

Theorems in Interval Analysis

This Appendix proves the interval analysis theorems used in Chapters 5 and 6.

C.1 Second Order Convergence of the Mean Value Form

We begin with a proof of the second order convergence of the mean value form, starting with two lemmas.

Lemma C.1 Let $A, B \subset I$ with $0 \in B$. Then

$$w(A *_\square B) \leq w(B)(\max(|\text{ lb } A|, |\text{ ub } A|) + w(A)).$$

Proof. Let $A = [a, b]$ and $B = [c, d]$. Let P be the hypothesized upper bound on the width of the product, i.e.,

$$P = w(B)(\max(|\text{ lb } A|, |\text{ ub } A|) + w(A)).$$

We have that $c \leq 0$ and $d \geq 0$ because $0 \in B$. There are three cases to consider: $a \geq 0$, $b \leq 0$, and $0 \in [a, b]$.

If $a \geq 0$, then $\max(|a|, |b|) = b$, and

$$[a, b] *_\square [c, d] = [bc, bd].$$

Hence,

$$w(A *_\square B) = bd - bc = b(d - c) = w(B)b \leq P.$$

If $b \leq 0$, then $\max(|a|, |b|) = |a| = -a$, and

$$[a, b] *_\square [c, d] = [ad, ac].$$

Hence,

$$w(A *_\square B) = ac - ad = -a(d - c) = w(B)|a| \leq P.$$

Finally, if $0 \in [a, b]$, we first assume $|d| \geq |c|$. But, for arbitrary intervals X, Y, and Z, where Y and Z are not disjoint,

$$X *_\square (Y \bigcup Z) = (X *_\square Y) \bigcup (X *_\square Z)$$

and hence

$$w(X *_\square (Y \bigcup Z)) \leq w(X *_\square Y) + w(X *_\square Z).$$

Thus, since $[c, d] = [c, -c] \bigcup [-c, d]$,

$$
\begin{aligned}
w(A *_\square B) &\leq w([a, b] *_\square [c, -c]) + w([a, b] *_\square [-c, d]) \\
&\leq |c| \max(|a|, |b|) + dw(A) \\
&\leq w(B) \max(|a|, |b|) + w(A) \max(|c|, |d|) \\
&\leq w(B)(\max(|a|, |b|) + w(A))
\end{aligned}
$$

since $\max(|c|, |d|) \leq w(B)$ if $0 \in B$. The case where $|c| < |d|$ can be treated similarly. ∎

Lemma C.2 Let f be a differentiable function, $f : \mathbf{R}^n \to \mathbf{R}$, over an interval domain, $X \in \mathbf{I}^n$, with coordinates $x_1, \ldots, x_n$. Let inclusion functions for $\dfrac{\partial f}{\partial x_i}$ exist, $\square \dfrac{\partial f}{\partial x_i}$, and let $Q_i = \square \dfrac{\partial f}{\partial x_i}(X)$. Then

$$w(\overset{\text{idl}}{\square} f(X)) \geq \sum_{i=1}^{n} w(X_i)|q_i|$$

for some choice of $q_i \in Q_i$, $i = 1, \ldots, n$.

Proof. Form the points $\alpha, \beta \in X$, as follows:

$$
\alpha_i = \begin{cases} \text{lb } X_i, & \text{if lb } Q_i > 0 \\ \text{ub } X_i, & \text{if ub } Q_i < 0 \\ \text{lb } X_i, & \text{if } 0 \in Q_i \end{cases}
$$

$$
\beta_i = \begin{cases} \text{ub } X_i, & \text{if lb } Q_i > 0 \\ \text{lb } X_i, & \text{if ub } Q_i < 0 \\ \text{lb } X_i, & \text{if } 0 \in Q_i. \end{cases}
$$

Note that lb $Q_i > 0$ implies that f is an increasing function of the coordinate x_i throughout the region X. Similarly, ub $Q_i < 0$ implies that f is a decreasing function of the coordinate x_i throughout X. Hence,

$$w(\overset{\text{idl}}{\square} f(X)) \geq |f(\beta) - f(\alpha)| = f(\beta) - f(\alpha).$$

But, by the Mean Value Theorem, and since X is convex,

$$f(\beta) - f(\alpha) = \sum_{i=1}^{n} \frac{\partial f}{\partial x_i}(\xi)(\beta_i - \alpha_i) \quad \text{for some } \xi \in X.$$

We now show that, for each i,

$$\frac{\partial f}{\partial x_i}(\xi)(\beta_i - \alpha_i) \geq w(X_i)|q_i| \quad \text{for some } q_i \in Q_i.$$

If lb $Q_i > 0$, then $\beta_i - \alpha_i = w(X_i)$ by our definition of α and β. Also, $\frac{\partial f}{\partial x_i}(\xi) > 0$ for all $\xi \in X$. If $q_i = \frac{\partial f}{\partial x_i}(\xi)$, then

$$\frac{\partial f}{\partial x_i}(\xi)(\beta_i - \alpha_i) = w(X_i)|q_i|.$$

Similarly, if ub $Q_i < 0$, then $\beta_i - \alpha_i = -w(X_i)$ and $\frac{\partial f}{\partial x_i}(\xi) < 0$ for all $\xi \in X$. If $q_i = \frac{\partial f}{\partial x_i}(\xi)$, then

$$\frac{\partial f}{\partial x_i}(\xi)(\beta_i - \alpha_i) = -w(X_i)q_i = w(X_i)|q_i|.$$

Finally, if $0 \in Q_i$, then $\alpha_i - \beta_i = 0$, and letting $q_i = 0$,

$$\frac{\partial f}{\partial x_i}(\xi)(\beta_i - \alpha_i) = 0 = w(X_i)|q_i|.$$

Therefore, since $w(X_i)|q_i| \geq 0$, we have

$$w(\overset{\text{idl}}{\square} f(X)) \geq f(\beta) - f(\alpha) \geq \sum_{i=1}^{n} w(X_i)|q_i|. \quad \blacksquare$$

Theorem C.1 (Krawczyk–Nickel (1982)) Let $f: \mathbf{R}^n \to \mathbf{R}^m$ be differentiable in region X. Let $\Box f$ be the mean value form for f, i.e.,

$$\Box f(Y) = f(c) + \Box f'(Y)(Y - c) \text{ for } c \in Y, \ Y \subset X.$$

If f' is Lipschitz, i.e.,

$$w(\Box f'(Y)) < Kw(Y) \quad \text{for all } Y \in \mathbf{I}(X),$$

then the mean value form has convergence order 2.

Proof. Without loss of generality, we can assume that f is a scalar function (i.e., $m = 1$), since if each component of f, f_i, has convergence order 2, we have

$$w(f(c) + \Box f'_i(Y)(Y - c)) - w(\overset{\text{idl}}{\Box} f_i(Y)) \le c_i w(Y)^2.$$

Hence, $w(f(c) + \Box f'(Y)(Y - c)) - w(\overset{\text{idl}}{\Box} f(Y))$

$$
\begin{aligned}
&= \max_{i=1,\ldots,n} w(f(c) + \Box f'_i(Y)(Y - c)) - \max_{i=1,\ldots,n} w(\overset{\text{idl}}{\Box} f_i(Y)) \\
&\le \max_{i=1,\ldots,n} (w(f(c) + \Box f'_i(Y)(Y - c)) - w(\overset{\text{idl}}{\Box} f_i(Y))) \\
&\le \max_{i=1,\ldots,n} c_i w(Y)^2 \\
&\le Kw(Y)^2 \text{ where } K = \max_{i=1,\ldots,n} c_i.
\end{aligned}
$$

Thus let f be a scalar function parameterized by $x_1, \ldots, x_n$, and let $\Box \dfrac{\partial f}{\partial x_i}(Y) = Q_i$. Because $\Box f'$ is Lipschitz, $Q_i \le Kw(Y)$. Let the excess width of the mean value form on the interval Y be named χ, given by

$$\chi(Y) = w(\sum_{i=1}^{n} \Box \frac{\partial f}{\partial x_i}(Y)(Y_i - c_i)) - w(\overset{\text{idl}}{\Box} f(Y)).$$

Note that since $c \in Y$, $0 \in Y_i - c_i$. By Lemma C.1, we have

$$\chi(Y) \le \sum_{i=1}^{n} w(Y_i)(\max(|\operatorname{lb} Q_i|, |\operatorname{ub} Q_i|) + w(Q_i)) - w(\overset{\text{idl}}{\Box} f(Y)).$$

Minimizing the second term, by Lemma C.2,

$$\chi(Y) \le \sum_{i=1}^{n} w(Y_i)(\max(|\operatorname{lb} Q_i|, |\operatorname{ub} Q_i|) + w(Q_i)) - \sum_{i=1}^{n} w(Y_i)|q_i|$$

for some choice of $q_i \in Q_i$. Therefore,

$$
\begin{aligned}
\chi(Y) &\leq \sum_{i=1}^{n} w(Y_i)w(Q_i) + \sum_{i=1}^{n} w(Y_i)(\max(|\operatorname{lb} Q_i|, |\operatorname{ub} Q_i|) - |q_i|) \\
&\leq \sum_{i=1}^{n} w(Y_i)c_i w(Y) + \sum_{i=1}^{n} w(Y_i)w(Q_i) \\
&\leq 2\sum_{i=1}^{n} w(Y_i)Kw(Y) \\
&\leq 2nKw(Y)w(Y) \\
&\leq K'w(Y)^2
\end{aligned}
$$

where $K' = 2nK$. ∎

C.2   Convergence of the Constraint Solution Algorithm

We first assume that Algorithm 5.1 is allowed to iterate forever. That is, no indeterminate or feasible solutions are accepted and removed from the list (i.e., $\square A(Y) \neq [1, 1]$ for any Y). Let S be the set of solutions to the constraint problem, given an initial region X. Let the constraint system, $F(x)$, be given by the simultaneous satisfaction of

$$
\begin{aligned}
g_i(x) &= 0 & i &= 1, \ldots, r \\
h_j(x) &\leq 0 & j &= 1, \ldots, s.
\end{aligned}
$$

The functions g_i and h_j are called the *constraint functionals*.

We also assume that regions are added to the list L so that all regions present at a given iteration are eventually subdivided or discarded. For example, this can be achieved simply by inserting newly subdivided regions at the end of the list and obtaining the "next" region Y from the top of the list (i.e., the list is a LIFO). We further assume that subdivision occurs so that all dimensions of a region are eventually subdivided (see Section 5.3.2). The combination of these two assumptions implies

$$
w(U_n^i) \to 0 \text{ as } n \to \infty \quad \text{for } i = 1, 2, \ldots, s_n,
$$

where U_n^i denotes the i-th region on the list after iteration n, and s_n denotes the total number of such regions. The set of intervals $\{U_n^i\}$ for any n are called the *candidate intervals* of the algorithm. Let U_n be the union of all the candidate intervals after n iterations, i.e.,

$$U_n = \bigcup_{i=1}^{s_n} U_n^i.$$

Theorem C.2 Let the inclusion functions for the constraint functionals be convergent, i.e.,

$$w(\Box g_i(Y)) \to 0 \quad \text{as} \quad w(Y) \to 0$$
$$w(\Box h_j(Y)) \to 0 \quad \text{as} \quad w(Y) \to 0$$

for $Y \in I(X)$. Then the set of solutions generated by Algorithm 5.1 converges to S, i.e.,

$$S = \bigcap_{n=1}^{\infty} U_n.$$

Proof. Clearly, $S \subset \bigcap_{n=1}^{\infty} U_n$ because no solution is discarded by the algorithm. We show that $x \in U_n$ for all n implies $x \in S$.

Assume $x \notin S$. Then $g_k(x) \neq 0$ for some $k \in \{1, \ldots, r\}$ or $h_l(x) > 0$ for some $l \in \{1, \ldots, s\}$. Consider first that $g_k(x) = q \neq 0$. Because $w(\Box g_k(Y)) \to 0$ as $w(Y) \to 0$, there exists an interval $V_x \subset X$ whose interior contains x such that $0 \notin \Box g_k(V_x)$. Furthermore, for any subset $W \subset V_x$, $0 \notin \Box g_k(W)$. But because $w(U_n^i) \to 0$ as $n \to \infty$, there exists $U_p^{i_p} \subset V_x$ such that $x \in U_p^{i_p}$ for some p and i_p. Hence, $0 \notin \Box g_k(U_p^{i_p})$, so a region containing x is eventually discarded. This violates the condition that $x \in U_n$ for all n. The proof for the case of violation of an inequality constraint, $h_l(x) \leq 0$, is similar. ∎

C.3 Convergence of the Minimization Algorithm

We now turn to an analysis of the convergence of Algorithm 5.2. As in the analysis of Algorithm 5.1, we first assume that Algorithm 5.2 is allowed to iterate forever. That is, no solutions are accepted and removed from the list. To perform the theoretical analysis, we also modify Algorithm 5.2 slightly. Instead of using a priority queue for the list L, we use a LIFO, as in Algorithm 5.1. We assume that each dimension of each interval on the candidate list is eventually subdivided, so that the width of all candidate intervals goes to zero, i.e.,

$$w(U_n^i) \to 0 \text{ as } n \to \infty.$$

This assumption does not hold if a priority queue is used, since some regions in the queue may never be subdivided if they never rise to the top of the queue. In practice, Algorithm 5.2 does not iterate forever, and regions of small width are eventually removed from the queue, so that all regions are eventually considered. Therefore, use of a priority queue is reasonable for the actual implementation.

Let S be the set of solutions to the constraint system $F(x)$, for $x \in X$, given by simultaneous satisfaction of

$$
\begin{aligned}
g_i(x) &= 0 \quad i = 1, \ldots, r \\
h_j(x) &\leq 0 \quad j = 1, \ldots, s.
\end{aligned}
$$

We first prove a lemma.

Lemma C.3 Let the inclusion functions for the constraint system be convergent, i.e.,

$$
\begin{aligned}
w(\square g_i(Y)) &\to 0 \quad \text{as} \quad w(Y) \to 0 \\
w(\square h_j(Y)) &\to 0 \quad \text{as} \quad w(Y) \to 0
\end{aligned}
$$

for $Y \in I(X)$. The modified Algorithm 5.2 will reject any infeasible interval after a finite number of iterations.

Proof. Let Y be an infeasible interval. Clearly Y could be rejected by the algorithm because of objective function bounds checking, thus verifying the hypothesis. We assume it is not rejected. Define $q(x)$ for $x \in X$ by

$$
q(x) = \sum_{i=1}^{r} |g_i(x)| + \sum_{i=1}^{s} \max(0, h_i(x)).
$$

The function $q(x)$ is continuous because $g_i(x)$ and $h_j(x)$ are continuous, since their inclusion functions are convergent. We note that $q(x) \geq 0$ and $q(x) = 0$ if and only if x is a feasible point. Since Y is an interval, q attains its minimum on Y, q^*. But because Y is infeasible, $q^* > 0$. Since $\square g_i$ and $\square h_j$ are convergent, and $w(U_n^i) \to 0$ as $n \to \infty$, the algorithm, after a finite number of iterations, is able to subdivide Y into a finite collection of regions $\{V_k\}$ satisfying

$$
\begin{aligned}
w(\square g_i(V_k)) &< \epsilon \quad i \in [1, \ldots, r] \\
w(\square h_j(V_k)) &< \epsilon \quad j \in [1, \ldots, s]
\end{aligned}
$$

where

$$
\epsilon = \frac{q^*}{2(r+s)}.
$$

Consider a specific element of this collection, V_k. Let $x \in V_k$. We have that $q(x) \geq q^*$. Hence, at least one of the following holds:

$$|g_i(x)| \geq \frac{q^*}{r+s} \qquad \text{for some } i \in [1, \dots, r]$$

$$h_i(x) \geq \frac{q^*}{r+s} \qquad \text{for some } i \in [1, \dots, s].$$

Therefore, at least one of the following holds:

$$|\Box g_i(V_k)| \geq \frac{q^*}{r+s} - \frac{q^*}{2(r+s)} > 0 \quad \text{for some } i \in [1, \dots, r]$$

$$\text{lb } \Box h_i(V_k) \geq \frac{q^*}{r+s} - \frac{q^*}{2(r+s)} > 0 \quad \text{for some } i \in [1, \dots, s].$$

where the notation $|A| \geq a$ for $A \in \mathbf{I}$ means that $x \geq a$ for any $x \in A$. Therefore, V_k would be rejected by the algorithm's infeasibility test. ∎

Lemma C.3 shows that if $\Box g_i$ and $\Box h_j$ are convergent and no feasible points exist in X (i.e., $S = \emptyset$), then a modified Algorithm 5.2 will eventually discard all candidate regions. Let f^* be the minimum value of f over the feasible region S. If $S \neq \emptyset$, then f^* exists. Let the region $\tilde{U}_n$ be the region on the candidate list after iteration n that has the smallest lb $\Box f(U_n^i)$.[1] Let l_n be this minimum lower bound, i.e.,

$$l_n \equiv \text{lb } \Box f(\tilde{U}_n).$$

The following theorem proves the convergence of the algorithm in the case that S is nonempty.

Theorem C.3 Let the inclusion functions for the constraint system and objective function be convergent, i.e.,

$$w(\Box f(Y)) \to 0 \quad \text{as} \quad w(Y) \to 0$$

$$w(\Box g_i(Y)) \to 0 \quad \text{as} \quad w(Y) \to 0$$

$$w(\Box h_j(Y)) \to 0 \quad \text{as} \quad w(Y) \to 0$$

for all $Y \in \mathbf{I}(X)$. If $S \neq \emptyset$ then $l_n \to f^*$ as $n \to \infty$.

Proof. Clearly, if $S \neq \emptyset$, then $\{l_n\}$ is a well-defined infinite sequence. For any n, $l_n \leq f^*$. Let an arbitrary $\epsilon > 0$ be given. Assume that an iteration level has been reached, given by m, such that

$$U \subset U_m^i \Rightarrow w(\Box f(U)) < \epsilon \qquad \text{(C.1)}$$

---

[1]Recall that for this analysis we are no longer assuming a priority queue in the minimization algorithm, so U_n^1 does not necessarily contain the smallest lower bound for f.

for all candidate intervals U_m^i. This is possible because $w(U_m^i) \to 0$ as $m \to \infty$, and because $\Box f$ is convergent.

Consider further the intervals in the collection $\{U_m^i\}$ that contain no feasible points. Since there is a finite number of them, by Lemma C.3, they will be rejected after a finite number of further iterations of the algorithm. Not all will be rejected, since S is nonempty. Assume that this iteration level has been reached, given by n. We have, for any candidate interval of this iteration level, U_n^i,

$$U_n^i \subset U_m^j \text{ for some } j \qquad (C.2)$$

since $n > m$. Let U_n^k be an interval having l_n as its lower bound for $\Box f$. We have that $f^* \in \Box f(U_n^k)$ because U_n^k contains at least one feasible point, and $l_n \leq f^*$. We also have that $w(\Box f(U_n^k)) < \epsilon$ by Equations (C.1) and (C.2). Therefore, $f^* \leq l_n + \epsilon$ or $l_n \to f^*$ as $n \to \infty$. ∎

The proof of this theorem not only shows that $l_n \to f^*$ from below, but also that f^* can be bounded from both sides in an interval whose width shrinks to 0 as $n \to \infty$. This is because

$$f^* \in \Box f(U_n^k) \Rightarrow \text{lb } \Box f(U_n^k) \leq f^* \leq \text{ub } \Box f(U_n^k)$$

C.4   Existence of Zeroes

This section presents conditions, computable with interval techniques, that guarantee the existence of a unique solution of $f(x) = 0$, for a differentiable function $f: \mathbf{R}^n \to \mathbf{R}^n$. We now turn to a formal statement and proof of the result, beginning with a lemma.

Lemma C.4 Let $\Box M$ be an $n \times n$ interval matrix, i.e.,

$$\Box M = \{M \mid M_{ij} \in \Box M_{ij}, \ \Box M_{ij} \in \mathbf{I}, \ i,j \in \{1..n\}\}.$$

If, for a vector b, the set of solutions

$$S = \{x \mid \exists M \in \Box M \ni Mx = b\}$$

is bounded and nonempty, then $\det M \neq 0$ for any $M \in \Box M$.

Proof. If a matrix $M \in \Box M$ exists such that $\det M = 0$, then the equation $Mx = b$ either has no solutions or an infinite, unbounded collection of solutions. Hence, because S is nonempty and bounded, there exists an $A \in \Box M$ such that $\det A \neq 0$.

Assume that another matrix $B \in \square M$ exists such that $\det B = 0$. We will prove that this yields a contradiction.

Consider changing the matrix A to the matrix B one matrix element at a time. Let C_i be a sequence of $n^2 + 1$ matrices defined by

$$
\begin{aligned}
C_0 &= (A_{11}, A_{12}, A_{13}, \ldots, A_{nn}) = A \\
C_1 &= (B_{11}, A_{12}, A_{13}, \ldots, A_{nn}) \\
C_2 &= (B_{11}, B_{12}, A_{13}, \ldots, A_{nn})
\end{aligned}
$$

$$\vdots$$

$$
C_{n^2} = (B_{11}, B_{12}, B_{13}, \ldots, B_{nn}) = B.
$$

Since A and B are members of $\square M$, so is each C_i. Since $\det C_0 \neq 0$ and $\det C_{n^2} = 0$, there is some transition, C_i to C_{i+1}, such that $\det C_i \neq 0$ and $\det C_{i+1} = 0$. Hence, without loss of generality, let our matrices A and B be chosen so that $\det A \neq 0$, $\det B = 0$, and A and B differ in a single coordinate, i.e., $A_{pq} \neq B_{pq}$.

Let the matrix $C(t)$ be defined by

$$C(t) = A + (B - A)\, t.$$

Note that $C(t) \in \square M$ for $t \in [0, 1]$. Let η be the solution to the equation $Ax = b$; i.e., $\eta = A^{-1} b$. Consider the solutions to the equation

$$C(t)\, x = b.$$

Since A is nonsingular, this equation can be rewritten

$$
\begin{aligned}
A^{-1} C(t) x &= A^{-1} b \\
A^{-1} (A + (B - A)\, t) x &= \eta \\
(I + A^{-1} (B - A)\, t) x &= \eta
\end{aligned}
$$

where I represents the identity matrix.

Let $Q(t) = I + A^{-1}(B - A)\, t$. Note that $B - A$ is a matrix of all zero elements except for the pq component, with value $B_{pq} - A_{pq} = s \neq 0$. That is,

$$(B - A)_{ij} = \delta_{ip} \delta_{jq} s.$$

where δ_{ij} is the Kronecker delta, the ij-th element of the identity matrix. Then,

$$
\begin{aligned}
Q_{ij}(t) &= \delta_{ij} + \sum_{k=1}^{n} A_{ik}^{-1} (B - A)_{kj}\, t \\
&= \delta_{ij} + \sum_{k=1}^{n} A_{ik}^{-1} \delta_{kp} \delta_{jq} s\, t \\
&= \delta_{ij} + A_{ip}^{-1} \delta_{jq} s\, t.
\end{aligned}
$$

Hence $Q(t)$ is a matrix like the identity matrix except for its q-th column. Because of its simple structure, we can readily compute its determinant:

$$\det Q(t) = 1 + A_{qp}^{-1} st.$$

We now solve the equation $Qx = \eta$, or in component notation

$$\sum_{j=1}^{n} Q_{ij} x_j = \eta_i.$$

Letting $i = q$ yields

$$x_q + A_{qp}^{-1} x_q st = \eta_q,$$

which implies

$$x_q \det Q = \eta_q.$$

Letting $i \neq q$ yields

$$x_i + A_{ip}^{-1} x_q st = \eta_i,$$

which implies

$$x_i = \eta_i - A_{ip}^{-1} x_q st.$$

Thus the equation $Qx = \eta$ can be solved if x_q exists.

There are two possibilities, $\eta_q = 0$ and $\eta_q \neq 0$. If $\eta_q = 0$, then $Q(1)x = \eta$ has an infinite, unbounded collection of solutions since $\det Q(1) = \det B = 0$. Therefore, any x_q solves the equation. If $\eta_q \neq 0$, then the solution diverges as $t \to 1$ since $\det Q(t) \to 0$ as $t \to 1$, and since $\det Q(t)$ is a continuous function of t. Hence, the solution set is unbounded. Therefore, there is no matrix $B \in \square M$ such that $\det B = 0$. ∎

Theorem C.4 (Bao–Rokne (1987)) Let $f \colon \mathbf{R}^n \to \mathbf{R}^n$ be continuously differentiable in an interval domain X, and let $c \in X$. Let $\square J$ be the interval Jacobian matrix of f over X, i.e.,

$$\square J = \left\{ J \mid J_{ij} \in \square \frac{\partial f_i}{\partial x_j}(X) \right\}.$$

Let Q be the solution set of the linear interval equation

$$f(c) + \square J(x - c) = 0.$$

That is,

$$Q = \{ x \mid \exists J \in \square J \ni f(c) + J(x - c) = 0 \}.$$

If $Q \neq \emptyset$ and $Q \subset X$, then f has a unique zero in X.

Proof. Assume the existence of a matrix function $J(x) \in \Box J$, a continuous function of x, such that

$$f(x) = f(c) + J(x)(x - c)$$

for any $x \in X$. We will later show how such a function may be defined.

By Lemma C.4, for each $J \in \Box J$, we have that $\det J \neq 0$. Hence the inverse, J^{-1}, exists for each $J \in \Box J$. Thus the solution set Q may be written

$$Q = \{c - J^{-1}f(c) \mid J \in \Box J\}.$$

Since $Q \subset X$, we have that $c - J^{-1}f(c) \in X$ for any $J \in \Box J$. Consider the function

$$S(x) = c - J^{-1}(x)f(c).$$

This is a continuous function of x since $J(x)$ is continuous. But since $S(x) \in X$ if $x \in X$, and since X is a convex set, $S(x)$ has a fixed point x^*. We have

$$\begin{aligned}
x^* &= c - J^{-1}(x^*)f(c) \\
J(x^*)x^* &= J(x^*)c - f(c) \\
J(x^*)(x^* - c) + f(c) &= 0 = f(x^*).
\end{aligned}$$

Therefore, x^* is a zero of f in X.

To see that this zero is unique, assume the contrary. Let x_1 and x_2 be zeroes of f such that $x_1 \neq x_2$. We have by the Mean Value Theorem,

$$0 = f_i(x_2) - f_i(x_1) = \nabla f_i(\xi_i) \cdot (x_2 - x_1)$$

for each component f_i of f. Combining these results for all components of f,

$$0 = f(x_2) - f(x_1) = J(x_2 - x_1) \quad \text{for some } J \in \Box J.$$

But since $x_2 - x_1$ is not the zero vector, this implies that the matrix J is singular. But, $\det J \neq 0$ for any $J \in \Box J$. Hence, the zero is unique.

We now show how $J(x)$ may be defined. Let $x \in X$ be given. We define a sequence of points in X as follows

$$\begin{aligned}
y_0 &= (c_1, c_2, c_3, \ldots, c_n) = c \\
y_1 &= (x_1, c_2, c_3, \ldots, c_n) \\
y_2 &= (x_1, x_2, c_3, \ldots, c_n) \\
&\vdots \\
y_n &= (x_1, x_2, x_3, \ldots x_n) = x.
\end{aligned}$$

Each of the points y_j is in X. By the Mean Value Theorem, there exists a point p_{ij} on the line from y_j to y_{j-1} such that, for each component function f_i of f,

$$f_i(y_j) = f_i(y_{j-1}) + \frac{\partial f_i}{\partial x_j}(p_{ij})(x_j - c_j) \quad \text{for } j = 1, \ldots, n.$$

Further, the required $\frac{\partial f_i}{\partial x_j}(p_{ij})$ is a well-defined, continuous function of x since

$$\frac{\partial f_i}{\partial x_j}(p_{ij}) = \frac{f_i(y_j) - f_i(y_{j-1})}{x_j - c_j} \quad \text{if} \quad x_j \neq c_j$$

$$\frac{\partial f_i}{\partial x_j}(p_{ij}) = \frac{\partial f_i}{\partial x_j}(y_j) \quad \text{if} \quad x_j = c_j$$

and because the f_i are continuously differentiable. But we have that

$$\begin{aligned} f_i(x) &= f_i(y_n) - f_i(y_{n-1}) + \cdots + f_i(y_1) - f_i(c) + f_i(c) \\ &= \frac{\partial f_i}{\partial x_n}(p_{in})(x_n - c_n) + \cdots + \frac{\partial f_i}{\partial x_1}(p_{i1})(x_1 - c_1) + f_i(c), \end{aligned}$$

where each $\frac{\partial f_i}{\partial x_j}(p_{ij}) \in \square \frac{\partial f_i}{\partial x_j}(X)$. Combining these results for all the components of f,

$$f(x) = f(c) + \begin{pmatrix} \sum\limits_{j=1}^{n} \frac{\partial f_1}{\partial x_j}(p_{1j})(x_j - c_j) \\ \sum\limits_{j=1}^{n} \frac{\partial f_2}{\partial x_j}(p_{2j})(x_j - c_j) \\ \vdots \\ \sum\limits_{j=1}^{n} \frac{\partial f_n}{\partial x_j}(p_{nj})(x_j - c_j) \end{pmatrix}$$

$$= f(c) + J(x)(x - c),$$

where $J(x)$ is a continuous function of x, and $J(x) \in \square J$. $\blacksquare$

We note this test for existence and uniqueness is only applicable when the determinant of the Jacobian of f is not zero in the neighborhood of each solution, as Lemma C.4 shows.

What happens if we have a bound for $f(c)$ (i.e., $\square f([c, c])$), rather than an exact value? This question is important because finite precision arithmetic does not allow exact computation of $f(c)$. Fortunately, a simple corollary to Theorem C.4 exists that allows us to robustly compute conditions when exactly one zero exists to a system of equations, even when $f(c)$ can only be bounded.

Corollary C.1 Let $f: \mathbf{R}^n \rightarrow \mathbf{R}^n$ be continuously differentiable in an interval domain X, and let $c \in X$. Let $\square J$ be the interval Jacobian matrix of f over X. Let Q be the solution set

$$Q = \{x \mid \exists J \in \square J, b \in \square f([c,c]) \ni b + J(x - c) = 0\}.$$

If $Q \neq \emptyset$ and $Q \subset X$, then f has a unique zero in X.

Proof. The set Q is a larger set containing the old Q from Theorem C.4. Hence the hypothesis of the corollary is actually more restrictive than that of the theorem, so the conclusion holds. ∎

C.5   Interval Implicit Function Theorem

Consider an r-dimensional manifold defined as the solution to a system of $n - r$ equations in n parameters ($r = 0, 1, \ldots, n - 1$):

$$\begin{aligned}
f_1(x_1, x_2, \ldots, x_n) &= 0 \\
f_2(x_1, x_2, \ldots, x_n) &= 0 \\
&\vdots \\
f_{n-r}(x_1, x_2, \ldots, x_n) &= 0.
\end{aligned}$$

Given a set of r parameter indices, $A = \{k_1, k_2, \ldots, k_r\}$, and an interval $X \in \mathbf{I}^n$, we define a *subinterval* of X over A as a set depending on r parameters $(y_1, y_2, \ldots, y_r)$, $y_i \in X_{k_i}$, defined by

$$\text{subinterval}(y_1, y_2, \ldots, y_r; X) \equiv \left\{ x \in X \mid \begin{array}{ll} x_i = y_j & \text{if } i = k_j \in A \\ x_i \in X_i & \text{otherwise} \end{array} \right\}.$$

Thus, a subinterval is an interval subset of X, r of whose coordinates are a specified constant, and the rest of whose coordinates are the same as in X.

The solution to a system of $n - r$ equations in n parameters is called *globally parameterizable* in the r parameters indexed by A over an interval X if there is at most one solution to the system in any subinterval of X over A. Put more simply, the system of equations is globally parameterizable if r parameters can be found such that there is at most one solution to the system for any particular value of the r parameters in the interval.

We define $\Box J_{\{k_1,k_2,\ldots,k_r\}}(X)$, called the *interval Jacobian submatrix*, as an $(n-r) \times (n-r)$ interval matrix given by

$$\Box J_{\{k_1,k_2,\ldots,k_r\}}(X) \equiv \left[\Box\frac{\partial f_i}{\partial x_j}(X)\right]_{j \notin \{k_1,k_2,\ldots,k_r\}}.$$

For an $n \times n$ interval matrix $\Box M$, we write

$$\det \Box M \neq 0$$

if there exists no matrix $M \in \Box M$ such that $\det M = 0$. We now prove a theorem guaranteeing the global parameterizability of the solution in an interval X. This theorem, which might be called the Interval Implicit Function Theorem, is analogous to the Implicit Function Theorem from multidimensional calculus, except that it deals with the global parameterizability of the solution manifold rather than its local parameterizability.

Theorem C.5 (Interval Implicit Function Theorem) Let the constraint functions, $f_i(x)$, $i = 1, 2, \ldots, n - r$, be continuously differentiable. Let a region $X \in \mathbf{I}^n$ exist such that

$$\det \Box J_{\{k_1,k_2,\ldots,k_r\}}(X) \neq 0.$$

Then the solution to the system of equations $f_i(x) = 0$ is globally parameterizable in the r parameters indexed by $\{k_1, k_2, \ldots, k_r\}$ over X.

Proof. Assume the contrary. Then there exists two points $p, q \in X$ such that

1. $p \neq q$

2. p and q are in the same subinterval with respect to the index set $A = \{k_1, k_2, \ldots, k_r\}$

3. $f_i(p) = f_i(q) = 0$ for $i = 1, 2, \ldots, n - r$

But by the Mean Value Theorem, and since any coordinate of p indexed by the set A is equal to the corresponding coordinate of q, we have

$$f_i(p) - f_i(q) = \sum_{j \notin A} \frac{\partial f_i}{\partial x_j}(\xi_i)(p_j - q_j)$$

for $n - r$ points $\xi_i \in X$. But then

$$f_i(p) - f_i(q) = 0 = J(p - q),$$

where $J \in \Box J_A(X)$ and $p - q \neq 0$. Therefore J is singular. But this is impossible since $\det \Box J_A(X) \neq 0$. ∎

Bibliography

[ADOB85]   Adobe Systems Incorporated, *PostScript Language Reference Manual,* Addison-Wesley, Reading, MA, 1985.

[BAJA88]   Bajaj, C., C. Hoffman, J. Hopcroft, and R. Lynch, "Tracing Surface Intersections," *Computer Aided Geometric Design,* 5, 1988, pp. 285–307.

[BARN85]   Barnhill, R. E., "Surfaces in CAGD: A Survey of New Results," Computer Aided Geometric Design, 2(1), September 1985, pp. 1–18.

[BARR81]   Barr, A. H., "Superquadrics and Angle Preserving Transformations," *Computer Graphics,* 15(3), August 1981, pp 11–23.

[BARR84]   Barr, A. H., "Global and Local Deformations of Solid Primitives," *Computer Graphics,* 18(3), July 1984, pp. 21–30.

[BARR86]   Barr, A. H., "Ray Tracing Deformed Surfaces," *Computer Graphics,* 20(4), August 1986, pp. 287–296.

[BARS88]   Barsky, B., *Computer Graphics and Geometric Modeling Using Beta-splines,* Springer–Verlag, New York, 1988.

[BART87]   Bartels, R., J. Beatty, and B. Barsky, *An Introduction to Splines for Use in Computer Graphics and Geometric Modeling,* Morgan Kaufmann, Los Altos, CA, 1987.

[BART89]   Bartels, R., and R. T. Hardock, "Curve-to-Curve Associations in Spline-Based Inbetweening and Sweeping," *Computer Graphics,* 23(3), July 1989, pp. 167–174.

[BAUM72]   Baumgart, B. G., *Winged Edge Polyhedron Representation,* Technical Report STAN-CS-320, Computer Science Department, Stanford University, Palo Alto, CA, 1972.

[BAUM74]   Baumgart, B. G., *Geometric Modeling for Computer Vision,* Ph.D. Thesis, Report AIM-249, STAN-CS-74-463, Computer Science Department, Stanford University, Palo Alto, CA, October 1974.

[BAUM87]   Baumann, E., "Optimal Centered Forms," *Freiburger IntervallBerichte 87/3*, Institut fur Angewandte Mathematik, Universitat Freiburg, 1987, pp. 5–21.

[BEZI74]   Bezier, P., "Mathematical and Practical Possibilities of UNISURF," in Barnhill, R. E., and R. F. Riesenfeld, eds. *Computer Aided Geometric Design*, Academic Press, New York, 1974.

[BINF71]   Binford, T., in *Visual Perception by Computer, Proceedings of the IEEE Conference on Systems and Control*, Miami, FL, December 1971.

[BLIN78]   Blinn, J. F., *Computer Display of Curved Surfaces*, Ph.D. Thesis, Department of Computer Science, University of Utah, Salt Lake City, UT, December 1978.

[BLIN82]   Blinn, J. F., "A Generalization of Algebraic Surface Drawing," *ACM Transactions on Graphics*, 1(3), July 1982, pp. 235–256.

[BLOO88]   Bloomenthal, J., "Polygonisation of Implicit Surfaces," *Computer Aided Geometric Design*, 5(4), November 1988, pp. 341–355.

[BOHM84]   Bohm, W., G. Farin, and J. Kahmann, "A Survey of Curve and Surface Methods in CAGD," *Computer Aided Geometric Design*, 1(1), July 1984, pp. 1–60.

[BORN81]   Borning, A., "The Programming Language Aspects of Thinglab, a Constraint-Oriented Simulation Laboratory," *ACM Transactions on Programming Languages and Systems*, 3(4), October 1981, pp. 353–387.

[BOYS79]   Boyse, J. W., "Interference Detection Among Solids and Surfaces," *Communications of the ACM*, 22(1), January 1979, pp. 3–9.

[BOYS82]   Boyse, J. W., and J. E. Gilchrist, "GMSolid: Interactive Modeling for Design and Analysis of Solids," *IEEE Computer Graphics and Applications*, 2(2), March 1982, pp. 27–40.

[BRON85]   Bronsvoort, W. F., and F. Klok, "Ray Tracing Generalized Cylinders," *ACM Transactions on Graphics*, 4(4), October 1985, pp. 291–303.

[BROW82]   Brown, C. M., "PADL-2: A Technical Summary," *IEEE Computer Graphics and Applications*, 2(2), March 1982, pp. 69–84.

[CARL82a]   Carlson, W. E., "An Algorithm and Data Structure for 3D Object Synthesis using Surface Patch Intersections," *Computer Graphics*, 16(3), July 1982, pp. 255–263.

[CARL82b]   Carlson, W. E., *Techniques for Generation of Three Dimensional Data for Use in Complex Image Synthesis*, Ph.D. Thesis, Ohio State University, September 1982.

[CHIY83]   Chiyakura, H., and F. Kimura, "Design of Solids with Free-Form Surfaces," *Computer Graphics*, 17(3), July 1983, pp. 289–298.

[COHE80]   Cohen, E., T. Lyche, and R. Riesenfeld, "Discrete B-Splines and Subdivision Techniques in Computer-Aided Geometric Design and Computer Graphics," *Computer Graphics and Image Processing*, 14(2), October 1980, pp. 87–111.

[COHE83]   Cohen, E., "Some Mathematical Tools for a Modeler's Workbench," *IEEE Computer Graphics and Applications*, 5(2), 1983, pp. 63–66.

[COHE85]   Cohen, M. F., and D. P. Greenberg, "The Hemi-Cube: A Radiosity Solution for Complex Environments," *Computer Graphics*, 19(3), July 1985, pp. 31–40.

[COOK84]   Cook, R. L., "Shade Trees," *Computer Graphics*, 18(3), July 1984, pp. 223–232.

[COON67]   Coons, S. A., "Surfaces for Computer Aided Design of Space Forms," MIT Project MAC, MAC-TR-41, Massachusetts Institute of Technology, Cambridge, MA, June 1967.

[COQU87]   Coquillart, S. "A Control Point Based Sweeping Technique," *IEEE Computer Graphics and Applications*, 7(11), November 1987, pp. 36–45.

[COQU90]   Coquillart, S., "Extended Free-Form Deformation: A Sculpturing Tool for 3D Geometric Modeling," *Computer Graphics*, 24(4), August 1990, pp. 187–196.

[CROC87]   Crocker, G. A., and W. F. Reinke, "Boundary Evaluation of Non-Convex Primitives to Produce Parametric Trimmed Surfaces," *Computer Graphics*, 21(4), July 1987, pp. 129–136.

[DEBO72]   deBoor, C., "On Calculating with B-splines," *Journal of Approximation Theory*, 6, 1972, pp. 50–62.

[DEBO78]   deBoor, C., *A Practical Guide to Splines*, Applied Mathematical Sciences, Volume 27, Springer-Verlag, New York, 1978.

[DONA85]   Donahue, B., *Modeling Complex Objects with Generalized Sweeps*, M.S. Thesis, University of Utah, 1985.

[FARO85]   Farouki, R. T., "Exact Offset Procedures for Simple Solids," *Computer Aided Geometric Design*, 2(4), December 1985, pp. 257–280.

[FARO86]   Farouki, R. T., "The Approximation of Non-Degenerate Offset Surfaces," *Computer Aided Geometric Design*, 3(1), 1986, pp. 15–44.

[FAUX79]   Faux, I. D., and M. J. Pratt, *Computational Geometry for Design and Manufacture*, Halsted, Chichester, England, 1980.

[FOLE90]   Foley, J. D., A. van Dam, S. K. Feiner, and J. F. Hughes, *Computer Graphics Principles and Practice*, Second Edition, Addison-Wesley Publishing Company, Reading, MA, 1990.

[FRAN81]   Franklin, W. F. and A. H. Barr, "Faster Calculation of Superquadrics," *IEEE Computer Graphics and Applications*, 1(3), 1981, pp. 41–47.

[GABR85]   Gabriel, S. A., and J. T. Kajiya, "Spline Interpolation in Curved Manifolds," *SIGGRAPH '85 Course Notes, State of the Art*, 1985.

[GOLD83]   Goldman, R. N., "Quadrics of Revolution," *IEEE Computer Graphics and Applications*, 3(2), 1983, pp. 68–76.

[GOLD84]   Goldman, R. N., T. W. Sederberg, and D. C. Anderson, "Vector Elimination: A Technique for the Implicitization, Inversion, and Intersection of Planar Parametric Rational Polynomial Curves," *Computer Aided Geometric Design*, 1(4), December 1984, pp. 327–356.

[GORA85]   Goral, C. M., K. E. Torrance, D. P. Greenberg, and B. Battaile, "Modeling the Interaction of Light between Diffuse Surfaces," *Computer Graphics*, 18(3), July 1984, pp. 213–222.

[GORD74]   Gordon, W., and R. E. Riesenfeld, "B-Spline Curves and Surfaces," in *Computer Aided Geometric Design*, Barnhill, R. E. and R. F. Riesenfeld, eds., Academic Press, New York, 1974.

[HANR83]   Hanrahan, P., "Ray Tracing Algebraic Surfaces," *Computer Graphics*, 17(3), July 1983, pp. 83–90.

[HANR89]   Hanrahan, P., "A Survey of Ray-Surface Intersection Algorithms," in Glassner, A. S., ed., *An Introduction to Ray Tracing*, Academic Press, London, 1989, pp. 79–119.

[HILD76]   Hildebrand, F. B., *Advanced Calculus for Applications*, Prentice Hall Inc., Englewood Cliffs, NJ, 1976, pp. 269–341.

[HOFF85]   Hoffman, C. M., and J. Hopcroft, *Automatic Surface Generation in Computer Aided Design*, TR-85-661, Department of Computer Science, Cornell University, January 1985.

[HOFF88]   Hoffman, C. M., *A Dimensionality Paradigm for Surface Interrogations*, Technical Report CSD-TR-837, Computer Sciences Department, Purdue University, West Lafayette, IN, December 1988.

[IMME86]   Immel, D. S., M. F. Cohen, and D. P. Greenberg, "A Radiosity Method for Non-Diffuse Environments," *Computer Graphics*, 20(4), August 1986, pp. 133–142.

[JENS66]   Jenson, J. E., ed., *Forging Industry Handbook*, Forging Industry Association, Ann Arbor Press, Cleveland, OH, 1966.

[JOY86]   Joy, K. I., and M. N. Bhetanabhotla, "Ray Tracing Parameteric Patches Utilizing Numerical Techniques and Ray Coherence," *Computer Graphics,* 20(4), August 1986, pp. 279–285.

[KAJI82]   Kajiya, J. T., "Ray Tracing Parametric Patches," *Computer Graphics,* 16(3), July 1982, pp. 245–254.

[KAJI83]   Kajiya, J. T., "Ray Tracing Procedurally Defined Objects," *Computer Graphics,* 17(3), July 1983, pp. 91–102.

[KAJI86]   Kajiya, J. T., "The Rendering Equation," *Computer Graphics,* 20(4), August 1986, pp. 143–150.

[KAJI89]   Kajiya, J. T., and Timothy L. Kay, "Rendering Fur with Three Dimensional Textures," *Computer Graphics,* 23(3), July 1989, pp. 271–280.

[KALR89]   Kalra, D., and A. H. Barr, "Guaranteed Ray Intersections with Implicit Surfaces," *Computer Graphics,* 23(3), July 1989, pp. 297–304.

[KERN88]   Kernigan, B. W., and D. M. Ritchie, *The C Programming Language,* Second Edition, Prentice Hall, Englewood Cliffs, NJ, 1988.

[KOCH84]   Kochanek, D., and R. Bartels, "Interpolating Splines with Local Tension, Continuity, and Bias Control," *Computer Graphics,* 18(3), July 1984, pp. 33-41.

[LAID86]   Laidlaw, D. H., W. B. Trumbore, and J. F. Hughes, "Constructive Solid Geometry for Polyhedral Objects," *Computer Graphics,* 20(4), August 1986, pp. 161–170.

[LANE80]   Lane, J., L. Carpenter, T. Whitted, and J. Blinn, "Scan Line Methods for Displaying Parametrically Defined Surfaces," *IEEE Transactions on Pattern Analysis and Machine Intelligence,* PAMI-2(1), January 1980, pp. 35–46.

[LEE80]   Lee, Y. T., and A. A. G. Requicha, *Algorithms for Computing the Volume and other Integral Properties of Solid Objects,* Technical Memo No. 35, Production Automation Project, University of Rochester, Rochester, NY, 1980.

[LEE82a]   Lee, Y. T., and A. A. G. Requicha, "Algorithms for Computing the Volume and Other Integral Properties of Solids. Part 1, Known Methods and Open Issues," *Communications of the ACM,* 25(9), September 1982, pp. 635–641.

[LEE82b]   Lee, Y. T., and A. A. G. Requicha, "Algorithms for Computing the Volume and Other Integral Properties of Solids. Part 2, A Family of Algorithms Based on Representation Conversion and Cellular Approximation," *Communications of the ACM,* 25(9), September 1982, pp. 642–650.

[LIEN84]   Lien, S. and J. T. Kajiya, "A Symbolic Method for Calculating Integral Properties of Arbitary Nonconvex Polyhedra," *IEEE Computer Graphics and Applications,* 4(10), 1984, pp. 35–41.

[LOSS74]   Lossing, D. L., and A. L. Eshleman, "Planning a Common Data Base for Engineering and Manufacturing," *SHARE XLIII,* Chicago, IL, August 1974.

[MIDD85]   Middleditch, A. E., and K. H. Sears, "Blend Surfaces for Set Theoretic Volume Modelling Systems," *Computer Graphics,* 19(3), July 1985, pp. 161–170.

[MILL87]   Miller, J. R., "Geometric Approaches to Nonplanar Quadric Surface Intersection Curves," *ACM Transactions on Graphics,* 6(4), October 1987, pp. 274–307.

[MITC90]   Mitchell, D., "Robust Ray Intersections with Interval Arithmetic," Proceedings Graphics Interface '90, May 1990, pp. 68–74.

[MITC91]   Mitchell, D., "Three Applications of Interval Analysis in Computer Graphics," Course Notes for Frontiers in Rendering, Siggraph '91.

[MOOR66]   Moore, R. E., *Interval Analysis,* Prentice Hall, Englewood Cliffs, NJ, 1966.

[MOOR79]   Moore, R. E., *Methods and Applications of Interval Analysis,* SIAM, Philadelphia, 1979.

[MORT85]   Mortenson, M. E., *Geometric Modeling,* John Wiley and Sons, New York, 1985.

[MUDU84]   Mudur, S. P., and P. A. Koparkar, "Interval Methods for Processing Geometric Objects," *IEEE Computer Graphics and Applications,* 4(2), Febuary 1984, pp. 7–17.

[NAYL90]   Naylor, B., J. Amanatides, and W. Thibault, "Merging BSP Trees Yields Polyhedral Set Operations," *Computer Graphics,* 24(4), August 1990, pp. 115–124.

[NELS85]   Nelson, G., "Juno, a Constraint-based Graphics System," *Computer Graphics,* 19(3), July 1985, pp. 235–243.

[NEWM73]   Newman, W. M., and R. F. Sproull, *Principles of Interactive Comuter Graphics,* McGraw-Hill Book Company, New York, 1973.

[NISH83]   Nishita, H., H. Ohno, T. Kawata, I. Shirakawa, and K. Omura, "LINKS-1: A Parallel Pipelined Multicomputer System for Image Creation," *Proceedings of the Tenth International Symposium on Computer Architecture, ACM SIGARCH Newsletter,* 11(3), 1983, pp. 387–394.

[OKIN73]   Okino, N., and H. Kubo, "Technical Information System for Computer-Aided Design, Drawing, and Manufacturing," *Proceedings of the Second PROLAMAT 73*, 1973.

[PERL85]   Perlin, K., "An Image Synthesizer," *Computer Graphics,* 19(3), July 1985, pp. 287–296.

[PREP85]   Preparata, F. P., and M. I. Shamos, *Computational Geometry: An Introduction,* Springer-Verlag, New York, 1985.

[PRES86]   Press, W. H., B. P. Flannery, S. A. Teukolsky, and W. T. Vetterling, *Numerical Recipes,* Cambridge University Press, Cambridge, England, 1986.

[PUTN86]   Putnam, L. K., and P. A. Subrahmanyam, "Boolean Operations on N-Dimensional Objects," *IEEE Computer Graphics and Applications,* 6(6), June 1986, pp. 43–51.

[RATS84]   Ratschek, H., and J. Rokne, *Computer Methods for the Range of Functions,* Ellis Horwood Limited, Chichester, England, 1984.

[RATS88]   Ratschek, H., and J. Rokne, *New Computer Methods for Global Optimization,* Ellis Horwood Limited, Chichester, England, 1988.

[REQU74]   Requicha, A. A. G., N. Samueal, and H. Voelcker, *Part and Assembly Description Languages — Part 2,* Technical Memo 20b, Production Automation Project, University of Rochester, Rochester, NY, 1974.

[REQU77a]   Requicha, A. A. G., *Mathematical Models of Rigid Solids,* Technical Memo 28, Production Automation Project, University of Rochester, Rochester, NY, 1977.

[REQU77b]   Requicha, A. A. G., *Part and Assembly Description Languages — Part 1, Dimensioning and Tolerancing,* Technical Memo No. 19, Production Automation Project, University of Rochester, Rochester, NY, 1977.

[REQU77c]   Requicha, A. A. G., and H. B. Voelcker, *Constructive Solid Geometry,* Technical Memo No. 25, Production Automation Project, University of Rochester, Rochester, NY, 1977.

[REQU78]   Requicha, A. A. G., and R. B. Tilove, *Mathematical Foundations of Constructive Solid Geometry: General Topology of Regular Closed Sets,* Technical Memo No. 27, Production Automation Project, University of Rochester, Rochester, NY, 1978.

[REQU80]   Requicha, A. A. G., "Representations for Rigid Solids: Theory, Methods, and Systems," *ACM Computing Surveys,* 12(4), December 1980, pp. 437–464.

[REQU85]   Requicha, A. A. G., and H. B. Voelcker, "Boolean Operations in Solid Mod-
            eling: Boundary Evaluation and Merging Algorithms," *Proceedings of the
            IEEE*, 73(1), January 1985, pp. 30–44.

[RIES73]   Riesenfeld, R. F., *Applications of B-Spline Approximation to Geometric
            Problems of Computer Aided Design*, Ph.D. Thesis, Syracuse University,
            1973.

[ROCK86]   Rockwood, A. P., and J. Owen, "Blending Surfaces in Solid Modeling," in
            Geometric Modeling, Farin, G., ed., SIAM, 1986.

[ROSS84]   Rossignac, J. R., and A. A. G. Requicha, "Constant Radius Blending in
            Solid Modeling," *Comp. Mech. Engr.*, 3, 1984, pp. 65–73.

[ROSS86a]   Rossignac, J. R., and A. A. G. Requicha, "Offsetting Operations in Solid
            Modeling," *Computer Aided Geometric Design*, 3(2), August 1986, pp.
            129–148.

[ROSS86b]   Rossignac, J. R., and A. A. G. Requicha, "Depth-Buffering Display Tech-
            niques for Constructive Solid Geometry," *IEEE Computer Graphics and
            Applications*, 6(9), September 1986, pp. 29–39.

[ROSS88]   Rossignac, J. R., P. Borrel, and L. R. Nackman, "Interactive Design with
            Sequences of Parameterized Transformations," IBM Research Report RC
            13740 (#61565), Yorktown Heights, NY, June 1988.

[SARR83]   Sarraga, R. F., "Algebraic Methods for Intersections of Quadric Surfaces in
            GMSOLID," *Computer Graphics and Image Processing*, 22(2), May 1983,
            pp. 222–238.

[SCHW82]   Schweitzer, D., and E. Cobb, "Scanline Rendering of Parametric Surfaces,"
            Computer Graphics, 16(3), July 1982, pp. 265–271.

[SEDE83]   Sederberg, T. W., *Implicit and Parametric Curves and Surfaces for Com-
            puter Aided Geometric Design*, Ph.D. Thesis, Mechanical Engineering,
            Purdue University, 1983.

[SEDE84]   Sederberg, T. W., and D. C. Anderson, "Ray Tracing Steiner Patches,"
            Computer Graphics, 18(3), July 1984, pp. 159–164.

[SEDE85]   Sederberg, T. W., "Piecewise Algebraic Surface Patches," *Computer Aided
            Geometric Design*, 2(1), September 1985, pp. 53–59.

[SEDE86]   Sederberg, T. W., and S. R. Parry, "Free-Form Deformation of Solid Geo-
            metric Models," *Computer Graphics*, 20(4), August 1986, pp. 151–160.

[SEDE89]   Sederberg, T. W., and A. K. Zundel, "Scan Line Display of Algebraic Sur-
            faces," *Computer Graphics*, 23(3), July 1989, pp. 147–156.

[SEGA90]   Segal, M., "Using Tolerances to Guarantee Valid Polyhedral Modeling Results," *Computer Graphics,* 24(4), August 1990, pp. 105–114.

[SHAN87]   Shantz, M., and S. Lien, "Shading Bicubic Patches," *Computer Graphics,* 21(4), July 1987, pp. 189–196.

[SHAN89]   Shantz, M., and S. Chang, "Rendering Trimmed NURBS with Adaptive Forward Differencing," *Computer Graphics,* 23(3), July 1989, pp. 189–198.

[SHIG80]   Shigley, J. E., and J. J. Uicker, Jr., *Theory of Machines and Mechanisms,* McGraw-Hill Book Company, New York, 1980.

[SNYD87]   Snyder, J. M., and A. H. Barr, "Ray Tracing Complex Models Containing Surface Tessellations," *Computer Graphics,* 21(4), July 1987, pp. 119–128.

[SNYD91]   Snyder, J., *Generative Modeling: An Approach to High Level Shape Design for Computer Graphics and CAD,* Ph.D. Thesis, California Institute of Technology, 1991.

[SUFF90]   Suffern, K. G., and E. Fackerell, "Interval Methods in Computer Graphics," Proceedings of Ausgraph '90, Melbourne, Australia, 1990, pp. 35–44.

[SUTH63]   Sutherland, I., "Sketchpad, a Man-Machine Graphical Communication System," Ph.D. Thesis, MIT, January 1963.

[TAMM84]   Tamminen, M., and H. Samet, "Efficient Octree Conversion by Connectivity Labeling," *Computer Graphics,* 18(3), July 1984, pp. 43–51.

[THOM84]   Thomas, S. W., *Modeling Volumes Bounded by B-Spline Surfaces,* Ph.D. Thesis, Technical Report UUCS-84-009, Department of Computer Science, University of Utah, Salt Lake City, UT, June 1984.

[THOM85]   Thompson, J. F., Z. U. A. Warsi, and C. W. Mastin, *Numerical Grid Generation,* North-Holland, New York, 1985.

[TILL83]   Tiller, W., "Rational B-Splines for Curve and Surface Representation," *IEEE Computer Graphics and Applications,* 3(6), September 1983, pp. 61–69.

[TILL84]   Tiller, W., and E. G. Hanson, "Offsets of 2-Dimensional Profiles," *IEEE Computer Graphics and Applications,* 4(9), 1984, pp. 36–46.

[TILO77]   Tilove, R. B., *A Study of Set-Membership Classification,* Technical Memo No. 30, Production Automation Project, University of Rochester, Rochester, NY, November 1977.

[TILO80]   Tilove, R. B., "Set-Membership Classification: A Unified Approach to Geometric Intersection Problems," *IEEE Transactions on Computers,* C-29(10), 1980, pp. 847–883.

[TIMM77]   Timmer, H. G., *Analytic Background for Computation of Surface Intersections*, Douglas Aircraft Company Technical Memorandum CI-250-CAT-77-036, April 1977.

[TIMM80]   Timmer, H. G., and J. M. Stern, "Computation of Global Geometric Properties of Solid Objects," *Computer Aided Design*, 12(6), November 1980.

[TOTH85]   Toth, D. L., "On Ray Tracing Parametric Surfaces," *Computer Graphics*, 19(3), July 1985, pp. 171–179.

[TURN84]   Turner, J. A., *A Set-Operation Algorithm for Two- and Three-Dimensional Geometric Objects*, Architecture and Planning Research Laboratory, College of Architecture, University of Michigan, Ann Arbor, MI, August 1984.

[VANW84a]   van Wijk "Ray Tracing Objects Defined by Sweeping Planar Cubic Splines," *ACM Transactions on Graphics*, 3(3), 1984, pp. 223–237.

[VANW84b]   van Wijk "Ray Tracing Objects Defined by Sweeping a Sphere," *Proceedings of Eurographics 1984*, 1984, pp. 73–82.

[VONH85]   Von Herzen, B. P.,"Sampling Deformed, Intersecting Surfaces with Quadtrees," Caltech CS Technical Report 5179:TR:85, 1985, pp. 1-40.

[VONH87]   Von Herzen, B. P. and A. H. Barr,"Accurate Sampling of Deformed, Intersecting Surfaces with Quadtrees," *Computer Graphics*, 21(4), July 1987, pp. 103–110.

[VONH89]   Von Herzen, B. P., *Applications of Surface Networks to Sampling Problems in Computer Graphics*, Ph.D. Thesis, California Institute of Technology, 1989.

[VONH90]   Von Herzen, B. P., A. H. Barr, and H. R. Zatz, "Geometric Collisions for Time-Dependent Parametric Surfaces," *Computer Graphics*, 24(4), August 1990, pp. 39–48.

[WEIL85]   Weiler, K., "Edge-Based Data Structures for Solid Modeling in Curved-Surface Environments," *IEEE Computer Graphics and Applications*, 5(1), January 1985, pp. 21–40.

[WANG86]   Wang, W. P. and K. K. Wang, "Geometric Modelling for Swept Volume of Moving Solids," *IEEE Computer Graphics and Applications*, 6(12), 1986, pp. 8–17.

[WEIS66]   Weiss, R., "BE VISION, a Package of IBM 7090 Programs to Draw Orthographic Views of Combinations of Planes and Quadric Surfaces," *Journal of the ACM*, 13(2), 1966, pp. 194–204.

[WOLF91]   Wolfram, S., *Mathematica: A System for Doing Mathematics by Computer*, *Second Edition*, Addison-Wesley, Redwood City, CA, 1991.

[WOON71]   Woon, P. Y., and H. Freeman, "A Computer Procedure for Generating Visi-
             ble Line Drawings of Solids Bounded by Quadric Surfaces," in *IFIP 1971*,
             v.2, North Holland, Amsterdam, 1971, pp. 1120–1125.

[WYVI86]   Wyvill, G., C. McPheeters, and B. Wyvill, "Data Structures for Soft Ob-
             jects," *The Visual Computer*, 2(4), April 1986, pp. 227–234.

Index

I

J

K